Philip Bowcock served in the Sudan Political Service and the Colonial Administrative Service in Northern Rhodesia.

Last Guardians

Crown Service in Sudan, Northern Rhodesia and Britain

To Joan and Richard

Peter Bowcock

Philip Bowcock

The Radcliffe Press
LONDON • NEW YORK

An imprint of I.B.Tauris

First published in 2016 by
The Radcliffe Press
An imprint of I.B.Tauris & Co Ltd
London • New York
www.ibtauris.com

ISBN: 978 1 78453 438 7
eISBN: 978 0 85773 937 7

A full CIP record for this book is available from the British Library
A full CIP record is available from the Library of Congress

Library of Congress Catalog Card Number: available

Typeset by Saxon Graphics Ltd, Derby
Printed and bound by CPI Group (UK) Ltd, Croydon, CR0 4YY

Those of us who had a part in winding up the British Empire owe a tremendous debt to our predecessors, who by their devotion to the interests of the people they ruled, their acceptance of hardship and their fairness and courtesy won the friendship of the population and broad consent to British authority. This greatly aided us as we handed over power in a spirit of amity and good will.

To them this book is dedicated.

CONTENTS

CONTENTS

MAPS

ILLUSTRATIONS

ILLUSTRATIONS

ILLUSTRATIONS

All photos © Philip Bowcock.

INTRODUCTION

My main purpose in writing these memoirs was to leave with my children, grandchildren and further generations an account of the fascinating and fortunate life which my wife, Brenda, and I experienced and which could never be repeated. The most obvious reason for this uniqueness is that I was a confirmed member of four great services under the Crown, in succession: the 15/19 King's Royal Hussars, the Sudan Political Service, the Colonial Administrative Service (later Her Majesty's Overseas Civil Service) and the Administrative Class of the Home Civil Service. Although a few men started that sequence of service in the Indian or the Malayan Civil Services, I was the only one who began in the Sudan. My old regiment is now, after merger, part of the Light Dragoons; the Sudan Political Service was wound up after independence for the Sudan in 1956; HM Overseas Civil Service came to an end with the handover of Hong Kong in 1997; the Administrative Class of the Home Civil Service has been reorganised; and the civil service department where I served, the Ministry of Technology, only lasted for about five years. So I am a kind of political fossil, the result of the three wars of the last century – the Great War of 1914–18, World War II of 1939–45, and the Cold War 1945–91, which ended after the fall of the Berlin Wall.

My father and I were both fortunate in the dates of our births. Father was just short of 18 and had received his call-up papers when the Armistice was signed on 11 November

1918. By 1939 he was 39 and in a reserved occupation as a farmer, although he was very active as the local commander of the Home Guard the following year. I was already at Oxford when I reached 18 in April 1945 and was allowed to continue with my degree course, starting National Service after graduation in 1947 at the age of a little over 20.

These vast political changes have been accompanied, as might be expected, by social upheaval. One of the most significant aspects of this is the feminist movement. As I grew up it was taken for granted that the male was and ought to be dominant. Father's view was that women had no concept of organisation and logical thought; they softened and weakened men, he maintained. With three sons and the workers on an isolated farm the atmosphere was very masculine. Later experience taught me that this prejudice was misconceived. My own mother, wife and daughter have all been vital influences, so in recognition of this, I reverse the usual order of things and place an account of Mother's family first.

The title *Last Guardians* is a reference to the second volume of Philip Woodruff's *The Men Who Ruled India* published in 1954. The reforms resulting from the Northcote-Trevelyan report in the 1850s brought about a fundamental change in attitude to public service. Appointment was henceforth to be by open public examination, impartially assessed. Material reward would be limited to a fixed salary and defined allowances. It is not surprising that the men who had passed an intellectual examination, often in classics, charged with administering an alien people far from home, saw themselves as the class of guardian proposed by Plato in *The Republic*. They also inherited from English common law the concept of the trust, which led to the conclusion that power was held in trust for the people they ruled and especially the weakest.

Plato saw the ideal state as containing three classes: the guardians who governed, the soldiers who defended and the people who carried on their various callings. The guardians received special training which placed emphasis on wisdom and duty. They received only the pay and allowances necessary for life and their true reward was satisfaction in their work.

In British African territories the influence of classical studies was less than in India before World War I but there was still a residue of these ideas and it is not presumptuous to describe British officials as last guardians. In spite of the rush to withdraw from Africa they somehow managed to leave the new states with a constitution, a functioning civil service, a full treasury and a properly elected government.

In the appendices are some official reports. They may be rather detailed and technical but it is hoped that they will help students of British Africa to appreciate the wide range of preoccupations of a rural District Commissioner, as well as to obtain a flavour of daily life.

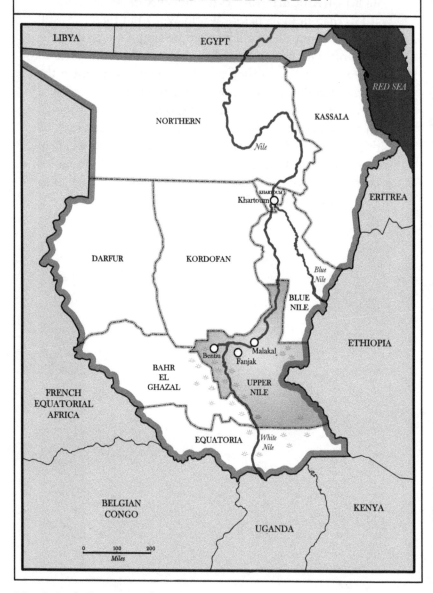

Map 1 *Anglo-Egyptian Sudan, 1951.*

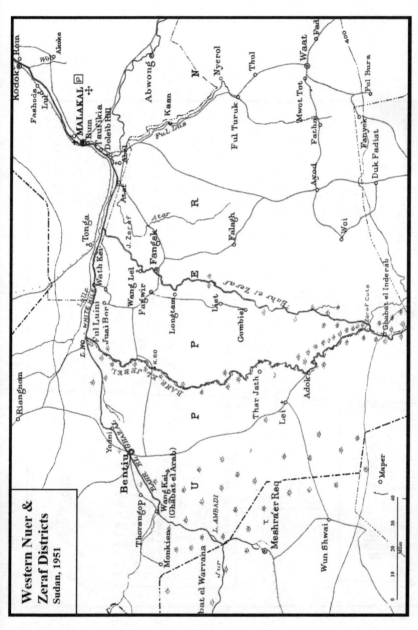

Map 2 Western Nuer and Zeraf Districts, Sudan, 1951. © The British Library Board, 66800 (4).

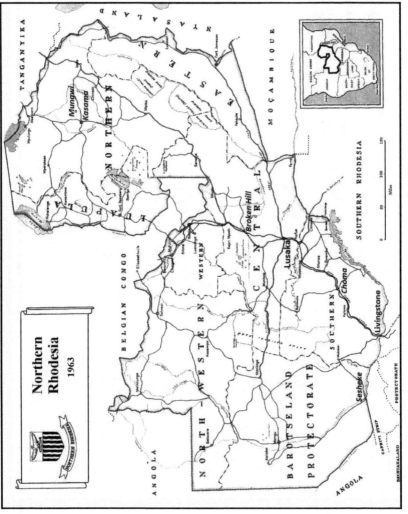

Map 3 Northern Rhodesia 1962, from the Colonial Office Report on Northern Rhodesia, 1962.

1

THE GENETIC INHERITANCE

Both sides of my mother's family came from the south-west of England. Her father, John James Parnell, was from a poor dairy farm at Chaldon in Dorset and her mother, Emma Lavinia (Veen) Pullen, was from Bath. Her father had a tailoring business specialising in servants' livery, for which there was probably a good demand in that area. I still have a black marble or jet mantel clock in the style of a Greek temple which is inscribed "*Presented to Miss Lavinia Pullen on her marriage by the Congregation and Sunday School ... [illegible] ... Bath 10 August 1892*". The name of the church has been worn off by polishing but was probably Walcott, St Swithin.

Granny's parents were George Pullen and Anne Hole, who married in December 1861 in Taunton and died in Bath. The family tree takes us back even further to Thomas Hole, who married Elizabeth Ridler in 1832 and died in 1889. They lived at Colly Hill, Luxborough, near Washford, Somerset and there is a charming photograph of him, his face fringed with white whiskers, making a basket outside his cottage, with the cat sitting quietly looking the other way. It could illustrate a Hardy novel.

While all the Pullens seem to have stayed in England, at least four of the eight Parnells of my grandfather's generation emigrated to New Zealand to found farming families in the

Figure 1 Thomas Hole (d. 1889) in his garden in Somerset.

North Island. Grandpa Parnell's parents were Henry Charles Parnell and Elizabeth Anne Palmer, who were small dairy farmers in Chaldon, Dorset, near Wool Heath in Hardy country.

Grandpa (John James Parnell) trained as a teacher, and a certificate from the Diocese of Salisbury showed that he spent five years as a pupil teacher at Winfrith School. He joined a corps of instructors in the army. There is a photograph of him in uniform with colleagues, all wearing pillbox hats. With this experience and perhaps some savings or gratuity he was able to marry and become head of the elementary school in far-away Cheddleton, three miles from Leek in North Staffordshire. He and Granny became closely involved in village life for over 30 years. On moving to work in Leek in 1968, I used to meet people who remembered them with evident affection and respect. Granny was so active in the church that she was known as the assistant curate. They lived in a semi-detached house near the church and opposite the old school, bearing the uninspired name of Sunnyside. There Kathleen was born on

23 August 1896 and May Louise (my mother) on 24 May 1899. In those days 24 May was significant: it was Queen Victoria's birthday and was a public holiday known as Empire Day up to my time at elementary school. It is still celebrated as Victoria Day in Canada. Both Kathleen and May went to a women's college at Derby and trained as primary teachers.

Some time in the 1930s the Parnells retired to Much Wenlock in Shropshire, where I used to stay with them as a child. They had an old stone house and a big garden. By coincidence we stopped in Much Wenlock for a meal in 1968 when looking for a school for our son, and found that we were eating in the Parnells' former house. Grandpa seemed to me as a child to be a quiet, uncomplaining man, submitting stoically to an injection for diabetes administered by Granny after each meal. His chief pleasure seemed to be reading accounts of adventure, which he could never himself experience, in a magazine called "The Wide World". He had a very rickety old car, a Jowett I think, which was so underpowered that on one hill Granny always walked behind with a wooden chock to put under the rear wheel to stop it running backwards when there was a change of gear. I enjoyed my visits to Much Wenlock, but as the Parnells lived further away with a more modest way of life they did not take such a big part in my childhood as my father's family.

Much more prosperity and consequence attached to the Bowcocks. This was principally due to the ambition and enterprise of grandfather Solomon, who was born in 1870. At one time he talked of researching a family tree, but his subsequent silence suggested that some discoveries were unwelcome. My son Matthew undertook some research into the family and with help from a distant relative in Australia traced them back to 1712, when a Peleg Bowcock married Elizabeth Dale, who was born in Leek in 1689. It seems that for generations the Bowcocks were mainly mill workers in the silk industry in Leek, appearing variously as dyers, weavers, spinners and occasionally clog makers, until my great grandfather Henry, Solomon's father.

Henry was born in 1839 and died in 1887, and is described in one census as a confectioner and in another as a baker. He had a shop at the top of Leek Market Place, and judging from the three I met he must have provided satisfactorily for his eight children, of whom Solomon was number five. One of them, Elijah, became headmaster of Wem Grammar School, North Shropshire. When cycling in the area at the age of about 15 (a boy could do that then) I called on him without warning on a hot summer afternoon and found him seated at his dining table reading Virgil in the Latin.

Grandad had a sister Mary Selina (born in 1872, called Lena) for whom I acted years later when practising law in Leek. She married John Lockett, who farmed his own land at Rushton Spencer and was described in legal documents as "John Lockett, Gentleman". I believe Solomon also had a brother called Bodgie who liked the bottle, but I never met him – perhaps because he did not quite suit the family's growing respectability.

Grandma also had to earn status and respectability. She was born Emma Simpson and I believe that she came from a textile working family, like so many in Leek. She was a handsome and rather forbidding woman, protective of her unexpectedly elevated position. I remember a gentle figure called Uncle Ned who lived in one of the brick terraced streets, and who I think was Grandma's brother. He had not risen in the world.

Grandad's success came from ability, hard work and enterprise. He started as a clerk in the Westminster Bank, and in 1917 was invited to join the then Leek United and Midlands Building Society as Secretary, later becoming General Manager. It was a small organisation in those days, to be far outstripped by the Leek and Moorlands Building Society, which later became the Britannia Building Society. The Leek and Moorlands expanded by taking over other building societies, while the Leek United stuck to its policy of growing organically, and, as a result, is one of the few building societies that, by sticking to traditional business principles, has survived the financial turbulence since 2008 largely unscathed. Father remembered much debate at home as to whether Grandad should give up the security and pension earned at the bank. He made the brave decision and was well rewarded. On his own account he later undertook a number of residential developments in and around Leek, part of the policy of providing homes fit for heroes after World War I. Recently it was found that he still owned a strip of land in Cheddleton, which provided some pocket money for his descendants.

Solomon and Emma moved up the housing ladder to a house called Square Croft in Fynney Street on the edge of Leek. It had a certain bourgeois opulence. As a boy I often used to stay there and was particularly impressed by the purple marble bathroom fittings, which are still there.

Solomon and Emma had three children – my father Henry, born 22 November 1900, Elaine born two years later and Philip Thornley in March 1905. Father went to Leek High School, the local grammar school, and then began to train as an agricultural valuer, but at the age of about 18 he decided that he wanted to farm himself rather than inspect and value farms. He became a pupil with a fine farmer, George Parrot of Great Bridgeford Farm near Stafford, who later became my godfather. He was always kind to me and was an example of a sound farmer and citizen.

After five years of pupillage Father obtained the tenancy of Riverside Farm, Chebsey, about 220 acres some five miles west of Stafford and two miles from Eccleshall, which he rented from the Earl of Lichfield. There was a spacious farmhouse, a tennis court, and a range of buildings and Dutch barns. The shallow River Sow, a tributary of the Trent, was only 100 yards away. The ducks lived there during the day, returning to their sleeping quarters in procession each evening. We boys played in the water. About half a mile away, still on the farm, the river was deep enough to swim. When I revisited Riverside Farm recently it had been greatly gentrified and landscaped. The church where I was baptised stands opposite, and the records of the Mothers Union show my mother as a founder member in 1929.

Our parents were married in 1925, but I did not arrive as soon as the grandparents expected. Grandma is said to have asserted, "I'm sure it is not our Henry's fault". The attitude that their eldest son could never be less than perfect undoubtedly influenced my father's character. I was born at home on 28 April 1927, the same day as a heifer calf we called Spot, who was my twin for some 13 years. My brother, David Henry, arrived on 31 January 1929, and John Michael, known as Michael or Mick, on 31 May 1932.

When I was five I went to the elementary school at the other end of Chebsey village. I remember being in one fight with another boy, but overall it was a happy childhood. We had a young maid who helped with my reading, and a stout lady called Mrs Tilsley who came in to help with Monday's washing day, mostly by turning the mangle handle. However, Father was having a hard time. He had stocked the farm when prices were still high in the years after the war. Then came a severe depression, while three babies arrived. I was more aware of life's improvements, though. We still had an outside lavatory reached by a path in the garden. It had three holes in the bench seat, two large and one small. The buckets were emptied daily by one of the two or three men who worked on the farm. However, both electricity and telephone arrived during our tenancy of Riverside, tremendous benefits which were probably installed in 1931–2.

In 1933 life changed dramatically. Grandad and his brother, always known as Uncle Phil, who by then was a successful young solicitor with his own practice in Leek, jointly bought a farm called Willoughbridge Lodge, 13 miles to the north-west of Chebsey. This was very different from a working tenanted farm such as Riverside. It was a gentleman's country estate, with 335 acres of good but somewhat difficult land. It had six workers' cottages and a superior house for a bailiff. Our predecessor, Colonel Cross, had employed 12 staff, but Father managed with three men and a boy; the school leaving age was then 14. There were extensive farm buildings, horse loose boxes, kennels and workshops, many

Figure 2 Parents' wedding in Cheddleton, Staffordshire, 1925.

of stone. The house stands on a hill with wide views and is approached by a half-mile drive. At the bottom of the hill a pump and ram provided the water supply, and there was a private electricity generator with ranks of glass storage batteries. The house had central heating provided by an enormous boiler in the below-ground stokehold. Both electricity and central heating collapsed about eight years later, during the war. After two years of discomfort and inefficiency mains electricity arrived; this diversion of resources was justified by the need for food for the population during the Battle of the Atlantic.

I remember vividly the day of the move to Willoughbridge in 1933 – I was just over six. The cows were milked at Riverside Farm in the morning, driven the 13 miles along the roads, and had their evening milking at Willoughbridge. (It was another five years before machine milking arrived.) We passed the cowman and the herd on the way. The new house seemed enormous, which it was. There were upstairs and downstairs water flush lavatories. I remember baby Michael sat on the parquet floor in the huge entrance hall crying with fatigue.

One night in about 1950, Father and some friends heard extensive banging in the nurseries. They could not understand why David, whose room was above, was moving so much furniture for so long. Then David appeared, having been out with friends. Some time later Father had a visit from a Mr Layard who had lived in Willoughbridge Lodge when the extension was built. He said that as the foundations were excavated a skeleton was found. Brothers David and Michael both spoke of noises they could not account for, occurring after I went to Africa in 1948 with the army. I was never aware of any such phenomena.

2

SCHOOL EDUCATION

Willoughbridge is quite isolated, being about two miles from each of three villages – Mucklestone, Aston and Knighton. Each had a village elementary school. David and I were sent to Knighton, which meant a walk of two miles, nearly all across fields, trying to avoid a flock of fierce geese on the way. The school consisted of two large rooms which contained all the classes from ages five up to fourteen. There was a teacher for each room who had to teach several school years at the same time, though there were not many children in each class. Outside there were two blue brick playgrounds for infants and older children. Play breaks could be wild. The infant teacher was Miss Monk who was rather daring, using lipstick and eyebrow pencil. She soon left to be married.

Being an early reader I made good progress, and when I was about seven and a half years old I jumped a form. This meant that I was always at least a year younger than the average age of the class throughout my school and university career, and that I missed out the year when I should have moved from single letters to joined up writing; as a result I have always inflicted poor handwriting on my correspondents and secretaries.

By the time I was nine in 1936 my parents decided, probably rightly, that I was becoming "rough" and should be moved.

In that summer I was sent as a weekly boarder to the principal school in the area, the High School at Newcastle-under-Lyme, about ten miles away. It had a substantial number of boys on local authority scholarships. The remainder were paying pupils at about £5 per term, of whom I was one. It was strictly for boys only. There was a sister school for girls, the Orme Girl's School only 200 yards away, with the same Governors on the same foundation, the Newcastle-under-Lyme Endowed Schools. In spite of this the two schools never met, not even for music or drama. In later life I was to have a part in changing this. The Headmaster, the enormous and terrifying Tom Stinton, was a member of the Headmasters' Conference, which gave the school the somewhat exaggerated status of a public school – though Father always described it, quite accurately I think, as a glorified grammar school.

The school had been founded in 1874, using charitable funds from the seventeenth-century and later. The first headmaster, Kitchener, had been at Rugby and put that stamp on the new school: thus we had praepostors, not prefects, and we played rugby, then commonly called rugger. There were about 350 boys, and I joined the prep department. The form roll read "... Bailey, Bourne, Bowcock ...", and I met these other two again later in life: Bailey became Sir Richard, Chairman of Royal Doulton China, while Paul Bourne was, like me, to become a District Officer in the Colonial Service in Northern Rhodesia.

The local authority scholars meant that the school maintained a reasonable academic standard, getting one or two Oxbridge scholarships each year. The staff were mostly well qualified, as the economic depression of the thirties had made the security of even a poorly paid job like teaching more attractive than it is now. John Wain, the writer, who was a contemporary though slightly older than me, was later very critical of the school, which he called Do-The-Boys-Hall. This was unfair and is to be attributed to a rather unpleasing tendency of intellectuals to disparage their education, and so by implication to praise themselves for overcoming difficulties.

It is true that the standard of music was dreadful, and this I have always regretted. Fortunately my wife, children and grandchildren have partly remedied this lack. Other cultural activities were necessarily cut back during the war, which began when I was 12, three years after I went to the school. Many of the best staff went into the forces and were replaced by some competent women teachers. The men that remained had to undertake fire watching, Home Guard or Air Raid Precaution duties.

I began school as a weekly boarder at the age of just nine. There were games on Wednesday and Saturday afternoons, so it was a weary journey home by bus and on foot on Saturday evenings. The practice of collecting school children from the bus or train was then almost unknown. In any case there was not enough petrol.

The housemaster in the school boarding house was a young bachelor English master, A.K. Barton, known as Jake. Amazingly he remained active and mentally alert, living in his own house until he died at the age of 90 when he was almost blind. He remained devoted to the school and boys he knew. Years later he coached my son Matthew in A-level English and refused to accept a fee.

The boarders were on the whole a happy group. Perhaps being able to go home at weekends provided relief from the stresses of close proximity. It may be significant that today there is much more contact between school and home and weekly boarding is common. There was a good library of boys' books. Each boy had a sleeping cubicle, partitioned in wood. Although there were several feet open above the partitions, previous generations had carved small holes so that boys could talk privately to their neighbours. At the end of the central corridor there was a stout bar of adjustable height and a mattress, where we had about 20 minutes in pyjamas before bed to practise gymnastics.

By 1938 the boarding house had dwindled to about 20 boys aged 9 to 18, and it closed after I had been there for seven terms when I was about 11 and a half. Two masters living nearby then took boys who still needed to board. My brother David, Eric Aspin, a dentist's son from Stafford, and I went to Mr Edmund Dudley, the senior French master.

The Dudley household lived in a Victorian semi-detached house overlooking the school playing field, the Upper Close, and living there was an education in itself. Mr Dudley was a devout Anglo-Catholic, on saints' days walking frequently to mass before school in a church about one and a half miles away. He had a strong sense of duty and was a worthy product of Keble College, Oxford. He lacked a sense of humour, perhaps, and this made the visits of his brother, a jolly Jesuit, all the more welcome. Mrs Dudley had been brought up in France and was kind, with anti-capitalist views, but I think she was subdued by her husband and bright daughters. There were five remarkable girls ranging from about 21 to close to my own age. All went in their time to the sister school, the Orme Girls' School. The eldest, Marjorie, was finishing at London University and I did not see much of her. The next, Denise, was a great friend though she was seven years older than I. She won a scholarship to St Hilda's, Oxford to read English, and her conversation was always lively and intelligent. She once sat me down with a map of Oxford and discussed what college I would try for about five years later.

The third daughter was Christine, who won a scholarship to Newnham, Cambridge. She also read English and there were good conversations about books and plays. The fourth was Ruth, a sporty girl who got a physical education qualification at Homerton College, Cambridge. Finally there was my contemporary Elizabeth, who was not surprisingly rather retiring, with so much talent and ebullience ahead of her. We got on well and she made up a four for games of monopoly and cards. There was a wind-up gramophone, and our favourite was Paul Robeson singing "Old Man River". Elizabeth went on to Westfield College, London University to read English and then to teach.

It was a remarkable achievement by Mr and Mrs Dudley to bring up such a lively family of five on a schoolmaster's salary in the thirties. We ate adequately and the boarding fee was £17½ a term. I learnt what was meant by the phrase 'plain living and high thinking'. Above all I acquired sisters, which I had not experienced before.

I was 12 and a half when the war started in September 1939, of an age to follow it with great interest. A year later bombs began to fall on Newcastle and the Pottery towns. The raids were probably nothing more than bombs being unloaded by German planes which had missed their Manchester target, but they were frightening enough. David and I suggested that it would be safer if we became day boys, which would mean we could also help more on the farm. I was then 13 and we often had a farm boy; our most recent one had just left school, so the suggestion was not a wild one. It was not easy to keep staff at Willoughbridge Lodge, which was over two miles from a shop and six miles from the nearest small town, Market Drayton. Farm workers never had cars then, and in any case petrol was strictly rationed, so a tied cottage at Willoughbridge was not a farm worker's wife's first choice. Added to this, Father, although fair, was a demanding employer who could not resist a cutting remark. So David and I travelled to and from school each day, about three miles by bicycle and then seven miles on the bus. Sometimes we went by train instead – a shorter cycle ride but a less convenient timetable. The line from Market Drayton to Stoke-on-Trent has long since closed.

In the summer we often cycled the whole ten miles and saved the fare. Transport was very overcrowded during the war, and for some time there was no queuing system. We were brought up well enough not to push, particularly when in school uniform, and so we often found ourselves behind others who had arrived later at the bus stop. We then had to wait an hour for the next bus. I always had a book or homework for these occasions. Later, queuing was enforced and the British sense of order and fairness was restored – still observable when different nationalities meet.

School was not too difficult. After my first full year I skipped a year again, which meant I was usually two years

Figure 3 Philip, with brother David and Michael and Bill, the Jack Russell terrier, a gift from the North Staffordshire Hunt, about 1939.

younger than the average age of my form. I did not find it a particular problem, perhaps because I was well grown and quite competent at games so I could not be written off as a swot. A school Scout troop had been formed and I joined as soon as I was 11, enjoying the camping particularly. After about four years I was a Queen's Scout and Troop Leader. When the Scoutmaster Alan Horne (naturally known as Trader after a popular book and film) went into the Forces, he and the Headmaster asked me to carry the troop on. It was quite successful and there was a waiting list of boys wanting to join. We had two summer camps on farms I knew, one near Oakamoor in East Staffordshire and the other near Shawbury, Shropshire, on the farm of our former help Connie Baker, who had now married. Connie had been Mother's help for several years after training in making cheese and butter at an agricultural college. She was a great friend to us all and represented the popular taste, insisting on having the Sunday Pictorial, part of the Mirror Group, to balance Father's Observer.

To return to the Scouts, it now seems amazing that a boy of 15 was able to take thirty slightly younger boys away camping for a fortnight in the middle of the war, but no one thought it odd or foolhardy at the time. Anyway, nothing terrible happened. I was helped enormously by the troop leader Donald Bullough. He later took over the troop from me and passed it to Jeremy Davies, and so in good order back to Trader Horne on his return from the Forces. When I became a governor of the school forty years later, it was pleasing to find that the Scout troop was still going strong having enjoyed continuous existence since its foundation in 1938.

Maths and the sciences did not appeal; I was definitely aligned with the arts side of the school. In the lower fourth there was the opportunity to start Greek and I gave up art and physics to make time for it – a choice which would probably not be permitted today. In 1941 aged just over 14 I took the School Certificate, which preceded O levels, which in turn gave way to GCSEs. The result was two distinctions (Latin and French, I think) and seven credits, which included maths and chemistry. There was thus the opportunity for three years in the sixth form before going into the Forces, a prospect which dominated a boy's life then. Old boys came back in uniform and occasionally there was an announcement that one would not be returning. In the Canterbury Quad cloister at St John's College, Oxford two Newcastle boys who won awards there, John Philip Barlow and Tony Roscoe, are remembered. Barlow had come top in the Civil Service open examination after graduation and was killed while he was a sub-lieutenant on active service in the Navy. Roscoe was killed in the defence of Calais, protecting the Dunkirk evacuation in 1940. Another hero of the junior school was "Sammy" Broadhurst, a young giant with curly blonde hair, who broke the record for putting the shot. He was shot down as an RAF pilot.

The sixth form master was an historian, Eric Warne, a rather aloof and cold man but very able. For the Higher School Certificate one took two main and two subsidiary subjects. He virtually directed me that I would choose history as one of my main subjects. I later realised that he would select at least one boy a year to coach for an Oxbridge scholarship. I owe a debt to Eric Warne, because through him I began to understand about scholarship and the evaluation of sources.

Warne and the author John Wain, then about 17, sparred constantly. It was very entertaining and I was surprised when Wain drew a most unkind picture of Warne as "the Bloater" in one of his novels The Contenders. I was sorry to learn years later that Warne was very hurt, asking, "Why did Wain hate me so much? I thought we were friends."

Life in the sixth form was very busy. I was running the Scout group, which consisted of six patrols of six boys each, and an Air Scout troop of about eight boys. School met on Saturdays, with lessons in the morning and compulsory games in the afternoon as well as on Wednesday afternoons. Few enjoyed a five-day week then. Although 16 was supposed to be the minimum age for a praepostor (school prefect), I was appointed while still 15. I played in the first team at rugby, cricket and hockey, and captained school house. All this was while helping on the farm as much as possible.

After two years, in June 1943 came Higher School Certificate where I achieved distinctions in French and History. I also had received good teaching in both French grammar and French. It was assumed that I would need to collect some scholarships to raise the funds to go to Oxford, so I spent a third year in the sixth form. The main subjects remained the same but I saw no point in repeating the subsidiaries, so I started German and Italian from scratch. A charming refugee woman took me for German and I learnt Italian by myself, with the help of some Italian prisoners of war who were working on the farm, of whom more later. Studying largely on my own was sometimes difficult because most of the sixth form were just killing time until they went into the Forces and were not very interested in academic pursuits. However, they were learning to appreciate music – mostly classical, but some jazz.

In December 1943, aged sixteen and eight months, I travelled to Oxford for the scholarship examination at St

John's College. Another historian from the previous year at Newcastle High School, Ian Taylor, was already there on a Forces Short Course, though he had an exhibition at Queen's College, Cambridge to be taken up after the war. (He later became the manager of Wedgwood Pottery in Australia and settled there, I believe.) Ian took me under his wing and I could scarcely believe that such a magnificent place was a possibility for me, a boy from a remote farm in the Midlands.

The scholarship papers gave a list of questions, without any requirement to answer a given number. I could write fully on the Welsh Wars of Edward I and spent two and a half out of three hours on that topic. At the final interview with a number of dons the senior history tutor Austin Lane Poole introduced me: "This is Mr Bowcock, another of Mr Warne's pupils from Newcastle High School." Shortly after my return home a telegram told me that I had an open scholarship for three years worth £100 a year.

At that time Oxbridge cost about £350 a year, including board and lodging, so I needed more funding. A number of state scholarships worth £100 per year were awarded on the Higher School Certificate performances, and I got one the following June. The same exam resulted in a Staffordshire County Major Scholarship worth I think £40 annually, and a school leaving exhibition for £35. Father made up the balance and Grandfather Solomon gave me £10 per term pocket money, so I was all set to go up to Oxford the following October at the age of 17 and a half. As my birthday was in April I planned to fit in an academic year before joining the Forces, assuming that I could get a two-month deferment after my eighteenth birthday.

I was and am grateful to my school, making allowances for all the problems of the war. With publicised fortnightly test results it was very competitive, which suited me as I was usually first or second in the form. My wife, Brenda, like John Wain, was less sympathetic to such a competitive culture.

I tried to repay the school many years later when I became a Governor and later Vice Chairman of Governors for some twenty years, helping to take the school out of its then mediocre maintained Voluntary Aided status into highly successful independence. In combination with the Orme Girls School, it became Newcastle-under-Lyme School.

3

FARMING IN THE NINETEEN THIRTIES AND FORTIES

The farm was the background, and sometimes the foreground, to life until I went into the army at the age of 20. Returning from school or university I was immediately plunged into a different and rather isolated life. Sometimes for days on end one saw only a corn merchant or Mr Cushing, travelling from Market Drayton to take the weekly grocery order. The newspapers were left at the bottom of the drive half a mile away. All the employees lived on the estate.

Until I was 11 the only powered vehicle was the family car, a Vauxhall with two chrome ribs on the bonnet. It had a trailer which could take one cow or several sheep to market. Small calves were put in a bag tied round the neck and carried between the front and back seats. The only traction on the farm consisted of the four shire horses, Boxer, Captain, Dinah and Jolly, two geldings and two mares, under the care of Jim the Wagoner. I spent much time leading a horse or riding it to work in the fields. Jolly was a menace: she was a very slow chestnut who threw her front feet out sideways as she walked, and I often had to dance out of the way when leading her. Captain, a big grey, was as fast and willing as Jolly was slow and reluctant. I suppose I was usually left with Jolly because Jim had taken the other horses for the hard work.

In 1938 the first tractor arrived, an American Allis-Chalmers, looking like an orange spider. It could only pull a single furrow plough on our heavy soil, but even so, ploughing productivity went up from one and a quarter acres to six acres per day. Then it could quickly get through the harrowing, rolling and drilling, making sowing much more timely. Of course, six acres per day now seems absurd compared to what a modern tractor can plough. David and I soon learned to drive the tractor, though probably only aged 12 or less. There were no roll bars and the machine was rather unstable, especially on slopes, of which there were plenty, so I suppose we were lucky to escape accident.

The engine was started on petrol but as soon as it was warm it was switched over to a kind of paraffin, tractor vaporising oil or TVO, which was much cheaper, being free of excise duty. It was quite a tricky operation and much time was spent drying out spark plugs. As the war went on more and more land was ploughed up for cereals, wheat and barley for sale and oats for consumption by the stock. Oat and barley straw was a useful winter feed for cattle. The horses ate some of the wheat straw and the rest of it was used for bedding. It eventually found its way to the manure heap, called the midden, and then, as time allowed, to the fields by horse and cart. About the mid-thirties inflatable rubber tyres for carts arrived, a great advance on iron-rimmed wooden wheels. Quite apart from the difficulty of pulling them over soft rutted ground, iron-rimmed wheels became loose in dry weather and had to be drawn into the farm pond when not in use to make the wood swell so that the iron rims became tight again. Manure taken out to the fields was deposited in piles, being dragged off the tipped cart. The horse knew just how far to go to stop for the next pile. Later one would spread the piles with a muck fork so that the whole field was covered, without large lumps which would kill the grass beneath. This system did not change during my time and it was not until after the war that the combined manure container and spreader arrived.

We had between ninety and one hundred milking cows at Willoughbridge in three large cowsheds, or shippons as we called them, two facing each other with a large feed area or bing in between. Three men and sometimes a boy or woman would milk twice a day. Each cow would go to her stall without trouble and her corn ration was chalked on a blackboard, the amount depending on the state of lactation. The milk was collected in buckets, which were carried across a yard to the dairy. There it was tipped into a large container at a height of about seven feet where it dribbled down a ribbed surface cooled by water running internally, and from there into a churn. Some churns were a reasonable size of ten gallons, i.e. 100lbs, but others were 17 gallons which was too much, for me anyway. (Until I was 15 or so I had the same problem with grain sacks: one hundred weight, 112lbs, was all right but one and a half hundred weight was a haul.) After breakfast the churns from that morning's and the previous evening's milking were loaded on to the four-wheeled milk float drawn by Dinah and taken about a mile to Arthur Simpson's milk factory near the infant River Tern. The driver was a rather lugubrious man called Lafford who had a drip at the end of his nose. Sitting beside him I tried to calculate when it would fall.

There was a big change in the milking when the first machine, an Alfa Laval, arrived in about 1938. Then two men could do the job easily, but still the buckets had to be carried across the yard and the churns delivered. Bulk storage and collections were still some years away – surprising when one considers how well a liquid can be handled with pipes and containers. Mucking out the shippons was also made easier by a bucket suspended from an overhead rail, though often it broke down and one had to revert to the wheelbarrow.

Fieldwork at this time still largely used the technology developed in the American prairies in the nineteenth-century, above all the binder that had superseded the sickle and scythe. By the mid-forties there was talk of the combine harvester, but most thought our island was far too damp for it to be

Figure 4 Willoughbridge Lodge, Market Drayton, Shropshire, but geographically in Staffordshire.

suitable. In the event this objection was met by drying techniques, which took much of the uncertainty out of cereal growing. Before then the weather was a constant worry and one dreaded the harvest dragging on until late October or even November, when it was hardly worth gathering as the ears were sprouting a new crop.

The sheaves of corn thrown out by the binder were immediately collected and set up in stooks or mows (to rhyme with cows), the job being known as mowing up. When dry the sheaves were loaded with pikles (pitchforks) onto a wagon drawn often by two horses, with special attachments fore and aft to hold a high load and boys on top as it swayed towards the hay barn. Later in the year the threshing machine would arrive, drawn and driven by a steam engine. On one occasion when I was 14 I was pressed into feeding the machine with sheaves, as one of the travelling crew had not arrived. At the end of the day I was offered the job of travelling with the outfit. Boys left school to work at 14 then, so the proposal was not quite as outlandish as it might appear. It seemed exciting, but I had enough sense to stick to my books. On another occasion I was responsible for the bags which were attached to the hoppers at the back of the machine to receive the separated grain. After tying up each one I then carried the 234lb (1½ cwt) bags of wheat for about eighty yards and upstairs to a granary for the whole of the eight-hour day. I still remember how tired I was, but I have not shirked weights since. Fortunately my back still holds up, as sadly my brother Michael's has not.

There was always excitement when the cutting of a field of corn was reaching its end. As the binder reduced the area of corn rabbits and hares began to run out, jumping through the lying sheaves with dogs, men and sometimes guns after them. This was before myxomatosis struck the rabbit population, and rabbits were popular eating. In winter an old stack of corn would harbour hordes of rats, and Bill, my brother David's Jack Russell terrier, was in his element as the rats rushed out as the last sheaves were threshed, once up one of the men's trousers.

Hay was gathered between late May and early July. It was cut with a cutter bar machine, drawn by a horse and later the tractor. The blade was placed in a vice and sharpened with a file before work each morning. The grass lay in swaths, and after some drying the swath turner exposed the underside to the sun and air. If rain came the damp grass would be picked up by a tedder. When ready it would be raked into long lines and then put into mounds, called quiles. It was desirable to have hay with a touch of green colour as this was more palatable and nutritious, but if it was too green it would spontaneously combust in the stack, or if it was damp it could go mouldy and be inedible, as well as causing a serious chest complaint called farmer's lung.

So haymaking was a tricky business, and silage was very welcome when promoted by the Ministry of Agriculture in about 1942. It really cut out the hazard of the weather, and the farmer could be confident of being able to feed his stock with nutritious fodder the following winter.

Fresh food for the animals in winter was provided by mangolds (a type of turnip) kept in clumps covered with straw and soil, and by kale. This grew on a thick stem about five feet in height with a canopy of leaves, and it withstood most weather. It had to be cut by bending down under the leaves and slashing the stem with a kale knife, a sort of small machete. This was most disagreeable in wet weather with icy water pouring onto one's neck and down the back. The plants had then to be loaded on to a cart by hand and taken either to the cows inside the shippon or to young stock in yards. Kale was very labour intensive and handling it was probably the most disagreeable job on the farm, but it was good fresh food for the cattle.

The first three years of the war were very difficult for labour. We were greatly helped by a pupil farmer called John Nicholls, about three years older than I, who lived with us for some three years. His parents were schoolteachers in Leek and there really was no apparent reason why he should have conceived the ambition to be a farmer. But he was keen and indefatigable. In due course he moved on, for more experience or perhaps because Father had been exceptionally sharp with him. He married a Land Girl as tough and devoted to the land as he was, acquired a small farm near Ashbourne and showed how to climb the farming ladder with little capital.

After the Battle of El Alamein in October 1942 things looked up, not only in the war but on the labour front. Italian prisoners of war were held at Hawkstone Park west of Market Drayton (where the fine monuments have been restored by a gift from the Barclay brothers). The prisoners were sent out to work on farms, and we had three. They lived in one of the cottages but took their lunch, always of pasta, in our kitchen. They made no bones about their happiness at being out of the war and the fields rang with Italian opera. They had brown uniforms with yellow patches, but otherwise they were quite free and did not abuse their liberty. Leone Rossi was a short squat working man from Turin, very strong and resilient and a great practical joker. Giulio Barello was a gentle law student from Milan and he mostly did the domestic jobs. Natale Maturin from the south was the least positive of the three, but he formed an attachment to Jean who helped with the laundry, though she was not at all ornamental. She seized her chance, and after the war Natale returned with her to work on the farm for some years. The most senior was Nicolo from Bergano, a more serious northerner. We were all very fond of the POWs as they were called, especially Mother whom they flattered and teased to get cakes, either given or filched. After Italy came over to our side and Mussolini was killed the prisoners were repatriated. For some time afterwards we received affectionate letters and inscribed photographs from them. My pleasure in Italy, its language and culture, dates from getting to know these men.

There was a happy postscript to this wartime relationship. In 2006 a letter from Italy arrived at Willoughbridge Lodge addressed to the Bowcock family. The present owners, Mr and Mrs Randall Mcdowell, found my brother Michael's address in Devon and sent the letter on to him. It runs in English:

Dear Bowcock family.

My name is Mario Barello and I am Mr Giulo Barello's son. He was made prisoner in 1941 during the war and until 1947, he stayed in England with your family. I have just become aware of a small box containing my father's souvenirs, and among them there are many records of his correspondence with your family. The most recent one is dated 3 February 1948, that is just a few days before my birth. I have tried to translate some sentences and found that he had a very strong link with your family, and in particular with a lady called Eva whom it seems, he loved very much. That is why I have thought to try and contact you. I remember that when I was a child, my father used to put me on his knees and try to teach English to me since England was always on his mind. Unluckily, he did so with very poor results! My father died in 1972, followed a few years later by my mother. I look forward to hearing from you since I would like to know more on the subject.

We corresponded, and Mario and his glamorous wife Ilva came to stay with me in Otford in Kent, where I now live. The following year I visited them in Savigliano, about 30 miles south of Turin and a day's drive over the Alps from Mario's to our own house in Provence. They were exceedingly kind and hospitable. They had retired from what appeared to have been a successful clothing shop for which Ilva had obviously provided the fashion input. Since then they have taken up travelling, and we exchange cards from unexpected places.

My brother Michael and I have searched our memories for Giulo's correspondent called Eva, but nobody comes to mind, unless she was Mrs Harris who helped with the washing and would not have been a romantic attachment. In any case, Mr Harris would have been dangerous as a wronged husband.

The Italians were replaced by two Germans who were utterly different. They were deeply resentful at being prisoners and were surly and probably still Nazis in secret – especially one of them, Hermann. But they did their jobs because they were disciplined, and they knew that if they did not they would have to go back to the Prisoner of War camp. German Prisoners of War were kept in Britain for some time after the war to repair the damage their bombing had caused, and it should be recorded that after I had gone abroad the farm had a splendid POW called Albrecht, the son of a small farmer in Germany, who became Father's right-hand man.

Life was hard and uncomfortable through much of the war. The private electricity system failed in the first year, so in the winter milking was done with hurricane lamps and we used oil lamps and candles to read in the evening. Mains electricity was connected in about 1943, since it was considered desirable to increase food production. It made an enormous difference, although the motor pumping the private water supply from the bottom of the hill often failed. We had enough timber from the farm for domestic heating but it involved considerable work to collect, saw and carry indoors, and the house was very large and draughty. Mother managed to get an Aga cooker, in the middle of the war, which burnt anthracite and made a big difference to her morale, our diet and the comfort of the big kitchen.

Food was a constant preoccupation. We were able to supplement our diet in several ways, which made me realise how hard town dwellers would have found it. But few actually went hungry, as bread was never rationed during the war. It took a Labour Government after the end of the war to manage that. We produced enough milk to be able to take off some cream without falling below the butterfat formula required by the Milk Marketing Board. Having mostly Friesians which naturally produce low butterfat we were conscious of this, and when buying a bull we would study how his progeny or his sire's progeny had performed in this respect. Occasionally butter was made by long hand-churning. To make jam one could get extra sugar and use the raspberries, plums etc., which were plentiful. Every six months a licence could be obtained to kill a house pig, which grew fat in a nearby loose box, convenient for all scraps. Tom Mountford of the Chetwode Arms, a skilled butcher, came to slaughter and cut up the animal in the wash house, which had a large copper bowl over a fire, normally used on Monday which was washing day. Mother then spent several days making use of every part of the animal for savoury ducks (faggots), brawn, heart and so on. The hams and sides were cured by having salt rubbed into them, lying in zinc-lined sinks in the cold larder.

I had two sidelines. In the summer I used to stalk rabbits with a .22 rifle used for Home Guard shooting practice. I have never been a good shot and it was not easy, but I usually came back with two or three which I gutted and skinned before handing them to Mother who made marvellous rabbit casseroles. She rightly refused to receive them until they were ready for the pot. Also, during most of the war I kept about twenty Rhode Island Red hens, which I bought as eight-week-old pullets and reared. I housed them in an unused corrugated iron shed and fed them on tailings from the threshing machine, waste green stuff and some laying mash which I bought. They were free range and were ingenious in finding secret places to lay in the corn and hay stacks. I washed the eggs and sold them to friends. By the time I had finished at Oxford I had earned an income to supplement my pocket money and still had £150 in National Savings Certificates. This was more than a farm worker earned in a year. On being commissioned in the army in 1948 I spent most of the money on a dinner jacket, a London suit and a tropical suit from a West End tailor. I heard that a colleague said I was the best-dressed man in Khartoum. Such a sartorial standard has not been reached since, despite all my wife Brenda's later efforts.

Notwithstanding the hard work, isolation, discomfort and stress from the war and Father's uncertain temper, it was an interesting life. First there were books; the whole family read and talked about them. Father subscribed to Boots' library in Newcastle-under-Lyme and we went there to choose books after selling animals in the market. The charge was, I think, 2d (less than 1p) per book per week. Later I subscribed to the Newcastle-under-Lyme public library, paying an annual fee because we lived outside the borough. Earlier, a great source of literature had been Uncle Arthur Finney; he was Assistant Director of Education for the West Riding of Yorkshire and publishers sent him lots of samples, which he brought over to us on his visits. I would spend hours reading in the box room where they were kept, near the back stairs. It was above the kitchen, so it was warm.

The periodicals coming into the house were the *Daily Telegraph*, the *Observer* and the *Sunday Pictorial* (for Miss Baker, Mother's help), the *Spectator* by post (Harold Nicholson's weekly article being specially appreciated), the *Farmer and Stock Breeder*, and the *Farmer's Weekly*. Farming questions and plans for cropping, breeding and so on were much discussed, and that was when we felt closest to Father. Sometimes, though, he was morose and would read at meals. We all followed his lead until we left the table and put on our boots again to return to work.

Father had a romantic, almost a heroic view of English history and the English countryside. He repeatedly read

Gilbert White's Natural History of Selborne and Boswell's Life of Johnson and Shakespeare. He talked clearly and incisively, emerging as a natural leader in any group. He captained the local cricket team and although without previous military experience, he was appointed to be a lieutenant to command the local Home Guard platoon. It had one section stationed at Baldwin's Gate and another at Loggerheads. Though the television show Dad's Army is of course written for laughs, it has the genuine flavour of the Home Guard. Most of our social life at that time revolved round it. For one thing, there was petrol for Home Guard duties, and we made friendships which lasted for many years. On the other hand, by opening Father to a society outside the farming community it may have encouraged a discontent, which led later to divorce and much unhappiness.

4

MOTHER: MAY LOUISE BOWCOCK, NÉE PARNELL

Mother was a one-man woman. She fell in love with Father when they were at their respective grammar schools in Leek, and I doubt whether she ever fell out of love with him, in spite of all the unhappiness he caused her. She was conventionally loving and dutiful, but with a spark of mischief. She duly went into elementary school teaching in Derby, as her parents wished, and her drawings show how much she loved the children. Thirty years later in Northern Rhodesia she returned to teaching; she said the difference from a school in industrial England was that the English school smelled of unwashed clothes and bodies. It was customary to bath only once a week in a tin bath in front of the kitchen fire, and to change clothes at the same time.

After Father had taken up Riverside Farm they were married in 1925 in Cheddleton. With three sons arriving in the next seven years, the farm and the church opposite, life was perfect for Mother in Chebsey. She exemplified the German ideal woman, devoted to kirche, kinder and küche, but in her case it was entirely freely and happily. In addition she had a kindly but slightly naughty sense of humour. I think Father was sometimes jealous of her because she had a ready popularity, which he, for all his charm and interesting conversation, could not earn. He responded by belittling her, both for herself and as a representative of the female sex. Martin Cotton, a friend all my life, spent a lot of time at Willoughbridge and we had great pleasure wandering the farm or cycling far and wide on roads quite unlike those of today. He once assured me that Mother was not stupid, as Father maintained, but really clever and capable, as well as hardworking, dutiful and amusing. It made me stand apart and realise that Martin was right, for which I have always been grateful. Thereafter I became much more critical of Father's views.

Mother had a straightforward Anglican faith and most Sundays she would cycle two miles up the hill to our parish church at Mucklestone. She tried to get one or more of us boys to go with her, with limited success. Father was a nominal follower: he supported the Church of England as one of the features of Englishness, but his practical support was limited to a £5 subscription when the Vicar, Mr Poole, came on his annual visit.

My confirmation in the Church was left rather late, perhaps because the Vicar was lazy. I was 16 when it was broached, by which time I was reading Winwood Reade's Martyrdom of Man and similar free-thinking stuff. Though doubtful, I decided that I would not hurt my mother and the other good people who wanted me to be confirmed. It was only later at Oxford that I began to understand the faith which has since been at the core of my life.

Apart from the Home Guard and church, which included the Mothers Union, Mother had to work hard for a social life. She was always a keen supporter of the Women's Institute and had to cycle uphill to Mucklestone for meetings. She never learnt to drive and Father usually had something more important to do than to drive her (or us boys) here and there. However, in spite of all her difficulties and frustrations she was quite contented and fulfilled as a farmer's wife with three healthy sons. She had a keen sense of the social hierarchy in the country, and was happy with her position as a substantial farmer's wife, but she was definitely not what was called "county". She was always cheerful and excellent company in those days; although without pretensions, she had a high standard of conduct. She had a sewing room above the kitchen and we would see her working there as we came in from the fields. In the yard below her window there was a pump with a large stone trough, which is now in my garden in Kent, having followed me to various houses since Willoughbridge was sold in 1968.

As the war unfolded Father moved into a more urban society than the simple farming or cricketing community of peacetime, and he regarded it as his right to associate with other more sophisticated women. Mother made every effort to stay with him, but eventually she could not do so any longer in the face of continuing infidelity and contempt. The final crisis came during my last year at Oxford, but Mother unselfishly made no move until after I had taken my Finals in June 1947. Then she left home for some time, but she was persuaded to return. My parents were together for the last time in the summer of 1948 when they came to my passing-out parade on being commissioned as an officer at Bovington in Dorset, and they gave me a marvellous twenty-first birthday party at Willoughbridge soon after. Mother then went on to take various housekeeping/companion jobs, initially in Shropshire with Miss Frances Pitt, a well-known writer on country topics. A farmer's wife is in a particularly difficult position if her marriage breaks up. She cannot stay where she is in the family home and insist that the husband leaves, since he needs to run the farm to provide for the family.

David had already left school after his School Certificate at 16 and was working on the farm – and he was a very good worker too. Michael later left school with his School Certificate after being in one of the finest school rugby teams in memory, and then spent a year at the Kesteven Farm Institute in Lincolnshire. Both of them therefore had to stay at home in a situation where Father was either spoiling them to try to keep their affection, or being harsh to them on the farm. They could not cope with it and both left within a year or two. David married the beautiful Joan Malkin and they went to join Mother's cousin, Bryan Parnell, in New Zealand. Michael got a job planting copra in New Britain, an island to the north of Papua New Guinea, then under Australian trusteeship.

I was homeless, but I had a sort of home in the army and a number of good friends invited me to stay with them in the holidays. I supported Mother without hesitation and did not see Father again for some twenty years. However, I am glad that after Mother's death, on our return to England from Africa, we were reconciled and Father met the grandchildren to his great pleasure. My wife Brenda was a great help in this, always writing to tell her father-in-law about the birth of his grandchildren. He did not reply, but I know that he appreciated it. Divorce at that time was very uncommon, especially among the middle classes; indeed, I cannot remember any other couple in our social circle who were divorced. The experience produced one result: I was determined that I would try to marry a woman who took the marriage vows as seriously as I did, and who would put our children first.

I doubted whether Mother had the best advice in seeking a divorce. She hated the status of divorcée and would probably have been less unhappy with a Judicial Separation, which was then possible. She received only a small income and had to be very careful with money. For some four years she was homeless. After Miss Pitt she shared a Tudor house with a jolly Miss Reynolds in Much Wenlock, and then went to keep house for Martin Cotton's father, Clifford, in Newcastle-under-Lyme, whose wife had died. She was there in 1951 when I came home on my first leave from the Sudan, when I was able to help the situation.

5

OXFORD

I went up to St John's College, Oxford in October 1944 as an open scholar at the age of 17 and a half. Part of the college was taken over by the Ministry of Agriculture and Fisheries (known as the Ministry of Fish and Chips). Only the Front Quad and the Canterbury Quad were occupied by the college, but we had the hall, the chapel and the magnificent garden. I was given a grand set of rooms close to the porter's lodge and beside the passage to the baths and lavatories, which meant I got more casual social calls than was really desirable. I kept this room for two years. One of my first tasks was to buy a scholar's gown, which came down to the knee and was worn at lectures, tutorials and in hall. It was not so long as to be dangerous when riding a bicycle. Scholars wore a surplice in chapel and took it in turns to read the lesson and grace at dinner, which was the Lord's Prayer in Latin. There was a fine in the form of a drink, a sconce, if one stumbled. There was a comfortable junior common room with newspapers, magazines and a bar. The food in hall was better than could be expected, considering that we were in the sixth year of war and had only just begun to win the Battle of the Atlantic by getting the measure of the U boat packs. St John's was a very tolerant college in which all could flourish, and it was easy to make friends. I was lucky to have three school friends at

Oxford with me; Geoffrey Eve was a year ahead of me, also reading history, while Martin Cotton was at Lincoln College, at the time evacuated to Exeter College. Both remained friends for life. I saw less of John Wain, who was living in lodgings near Magdalen and was a pupil of C.S. Lewis.

The first year was medieval history and my tutor was the senior tutor, Austin Lane Poole. I liked him very much and he was always kind to me. Soon after he succeeded Sir Cyril Norwood as President. The following year I did more recent history with W.C. Costin, a kindly and outspoken bachelor whose whole life revolved around the college. After my time he succeeded Poole as President.

I joined many societies, played hockey for the college, rowed for a term (which was quite enough), played squash at the courts in the garden and generally had a great time. On Sunday evenings after hall there was a free music concert at Balliol next door. A cheap record library for 78rpm discs was available: the Marriage of Figaro and Britten's Hymn to St Cecilia were revelations to me. On the other side of St Giles opposite St John's was Pusey House, a repository of the Anglo-Catholic tradition. Eric Kemp, the librarian there, was acting as chaplain at St John's, in place of the permanent chaplain who was in the Forces. He ran a weekly discussion group and invited me to spend a few days during the Easter vacation at his parents' home near Grimsby. During this time we had a day at Lincoln, my first introduction to one of the great cathedrals. I later became godfather to his third daughter Alice to my great pleasure, especially when I attended her Ordination as a Deacon in Bristol Cathedral. Eric retired at the age of eighty, having been Bishop of Chichester for many years.

My principal outside interest for the first five terms at Oxford was politics. John Campbell's biography of Margaret Thatcher contains an accurate account of her time at Oxford. She was a year ahead of me and a term ahead in the Oxford University Conservative Association. After three terms I was elected to the committee and in the fifth term I became

Secretary, succeeding Margaret who moved up to Treasurer, as was the custom. She was elected President in the summer term of 1946 and asked me if I would like her support to be Treasurer. I would have then become President in the autumn term, which would have cut out virtually all interests apart from politics and work. I decided that I would like to make the most of my second summer term, enjoying the river, plays and music in college gardens, parties and balls. This indicated a frivolity and lack of ambition which Margaret no doubt deprecated. I think also that perhaps I felt that I should not push myself forward when I was only 19, while men of 25 or more were returning from the war. An example was Stanley Moss, who was President of the Conservative Association when I was Secretary, and I often went next door to Balliol to discuss the Association affairs. With Patrick Leigh-Fermor, he had captured the German General who commanded Crete in April 1944. He later wrote an account of this astonishing (and cheeky) exploit entitled "Ill Met by Moonlight" which was later made into a film.

I was like everyone else quoted by John Campbell who said that Margaret Roberts of Somerville was the least likely of their contemporaries to be Prime Minister. It was inconceivable then that a woman would occupy 10 Downing Street during our lifetime, and even after entering Parliament she herself expressed the same view. Her later courage in standing as leader was astounding. While I liked her and we got on well, she was never in my sights as a possible partner for the college ball, although girls were in very short supply in Oxford at that time – about one in eight. She was just 18 months older than me.

The attitude of left wing dons towards her has been most unworthy. The Principal of Somerville, Dame Janet Vaughan, said in later years: "She was a perfectly adequate chemist. I mean, no one thought anything of her. She was a perfectly good second class chemist, a beta chemist." Lady Warnock criticised the Thatcher style of dress in a most snobbish manner. These sneers owe something, I think, to the fury of women of the left that the first woman prime minister was not of their political persuasion. However, it was not only the women who behaved badly; I was deeply ashamed when Oxford refused her an honorary degree on the parochial ground that she did not allot as much of the tax payer's money as they would have liked to their particular interest, namely higher education. I found it difficult to contribute to fundraising for Oxford and the university has suffered badly compared to Cambridge – and rightly so. Eventually I overcame these feelings and have supported the college and university, being particularly glad to see that there is a Margaret Thatcher Conference Room at Somerville College.

I attended meetings of all the political parties, including a discussion group led by Tony Crosland, a very superior person who in debate crushed the Communists, then riding high because of the wartime alliance with Russia. The Conservatives continued to make sense to me. They were then in opposition, facing a huge Labour majority, rather as after the 1997 election. The difference between then and now is that under Blair the policies which Labour followed were largely conservative (although the party had bitterly opposed most of them when in opposition for 18 years). After the 1945 election, with the war against Japan still continuing, Churchill, the war leader, was rejected and Labour embarked on a very socialist programme of widespread nationalisation. As a boy on the farm I could see that this could not work. Father argued that the employee of a nationalised farm would not get up in the middle of the night to cover a half-built hay stack in a sudden storm as he, the owner, would. As Aristotle pointed out 2400 years ago, what is everybody's property is nobody's property. All that we have learnt since about Soviet collective farming has proved this to the hilt. It was reported that the 2 per cent of land allowed for private plots produced more than the 98 per cent that had been collectivised (though it has to be acknowledged that there could have been some covert and illegal transfer of produce from public to private ownership).

There were other factors in my thinking. The left denied the murder of 2 million peasants in the Ukraine in 1932–3. Malcolm Muggeridge, who was correspondent of the *Manchester Guardian*, went to see for himself and his paper would not print his reports. We now know that 2 million was a great underestimate. On defence Labour claimed to rely on the Peace Pledge Union and "collective security", voting against conscription as late as April 1939. Then during the war, when there was supposed to be a national government and a political truce, Gollancz brought out a series of yellow books pillorying Conservative leaders as the "guilty men" who had got us into the war. They were indeed blind and had not listened to Churchill and his warnings of the German threat, but Labour politicians were not in a position to bestow blame.

In my final year at Oxford I moved out of college and had to find digs. After an unsatisfactory half-term with a mean man in Park Town with whom Aunt Kath had lodged years before, I was lucky to move to the front room of Tom Purvis, the senior common room butler. It was one of the small terrace houses in Kingston Road, along from Worcester College where my son Oliver went years later. It was a contrast to the grandeur of Park Town, but far more agreeable. Mrs Purvis made me very comfortable and it suited me well for working. I got a ticket for the magnificent Codrington Library in All Souls and used that for most of my reading. The nearby Radcliffe Camera was patronised mostly by women historians so the Codrington was less distracting, being for men only.

The first three months of 1947 were remarkable for very severe weather. For the whole of the Hilary term there was ice and snow on the streets and pavements, so cycling was difficult and dangerous. 1962 was apparently almost as bad, but I was then in Northern Rhodesia. (Since then winters have been comparatively mild until 2010–11.) Many years later, when we moved to North Staffordshire from London in 1968 I assured the children that there would be tobogganing and skating every year, thinking of my childhood at Willoughbridge; it turned out not to be so.

I chose to do the Italian Renaissance for my special subject and went to the house of an elderly retired woman don, Miss Cecilia Adie, for tutorials. It was rather an ambitious choice because the period had little overlap with my other reading and the set books were in Italian, which I had only done in my own time three years before. Miss Adie was a member of a distinguished family of Italian scholars, but she was not a hard taskmistress. I enjoyed the subject and thought I had done the best paper in my Finals; in fact it was the worst. I still remember the relief I felt when, faced with hundreds of pages of Italian to read of the histories of Guicciardini, I found an eighteenth-century translation on the shelves of the Oxford Union. Actually the Italian version would have been more tedious and time consuming than difficult, but I did not have the time. I remember one deadpan remark by Guicciardini referring to the venereal disease brought back from the Caribbean by Columbus's sailors; he said the English call it the French disease and the French name it the English scourge.

In my first two years I attended debates at the Oxford Union and spoke once, but concluded that public speaking was not one of my strengths. I also once engaged in a debate at Pusey House with Tom Driberg, the left-wing labour MP. He wiped the floor with me. Fortunately, in view of what later became known about him as a promiscuous homosexual and possibly a KGB spy, I did not follow up his invitation to make contact in London.

In about March of 1947 I answered an advertisement for temporary Assistant Principals in the administrative class of the Home Civil Service. After an interview I was selected, but as expected I was told that I must do my National Service which had been deferred for two years, so that prospect fell away.

So at a little over twenty I faced my final examinations, an experience which even the redoubtable Mr Gladstone said no man should have to face more than once. There were, I recollect, about ten three-hour papers continuously, morning and afternoon. Fortunately, I was fit and coped, though I was tired at the end. I cannot be sure of my memory but I think I was called for a viva and interview, which were employed to see whether the candidate could raise his grade. Anyway, I did not do so, and a first was unlikely with only two alphas, the rest being beta plus and one beta minor (the Italian Renaissance). It was a fair outcome. I had worked reasonably hard but not as hard as those aiming for an academic career, and I had tasted much of what Oxford had to offer.

Although Oxford had a vast preponderance of men, there were girls to be found here and there. My first woman friend was Gwendoline Williams, another historian whom I had met in lectures. She was two years older, from a London grammar school, and to me she seemed so sophisticated that I rather took fright. She later married another of our contemporary historians, Leo Butler, who became Principal of Royal Holloway College, London University. Their daughter Lucilla was at Cheltenham Ladies' College with my daughter Stella, and they both applied to read medicine at Oxford at the same time. Since Lucilla had a claim to apply for her mother's college, Lady Margaret Hall, Stella was steered towards St Hugh's. Fortunately, both got in; that is how chance dominates our lives. Gwen later made a name for herself as the prolific author of a series of clever detective novels, the hero being an intelligent policeman called Coffin, somewhat on the lines of P.D. James's Dalgleish. She also wrote romantic fiction under the name of Jennie Melville, her grandmother.

In my second year I met Kay, a very pretty blond only child with devoted parents in Devon. She was a graduate of Bedford College, London, evacuated to Cambridge during the war, and was doing a year's Certificate of Education course based in Linton Road in north Oxford. After Kay gained her certificate she went to teach at Cheltenham Ladies' College, and on Saturdays in my third year one or the other of us would travel by Black and White coach along the A40. Then during my National Service we drifted apart, and she later married a fellow geographer who had been one of the Linton Road group.

My three years at Oxford ended on a high note. St John's had its first post-war Commemoration Ball in 1947. The garden was a superb setting for the marquee set up there. Kay was a good dancer and I reserved a large room in the North Quad for my party of about 12, where my excellent scout Harry served supper. Two of the guests were Desmond Cole and Martin Cotton, with whom I had remained in regular touch.

A few weeks later I went back to Oxford to receive my degree in the Sheldonian. As was the custom then, Harry waited outside with the BA gown to robe me – for which he received the traditional reward of five pounds.

Figure 5 Oxford Graduation, 1947.

6

NATIONAL SERVICE

My call up was not until late September 1947. After my finals I learnt of the marital difficulties between my parents, which Mother had concealed from me so as not to distract me from the examinations. Good friends, Joe and Dorrie McKnight, offered me a place to stay. Joe was the manager of a pot bank, as a pottery works was called, in Fenton between Longton and Stoke-on-Trent. Fenton always claimed that it was the sixth town, and "The Five Towns" used by Arnold Bennett was not correct. The pot bank made stilts and spurs, the articles used to support or space the ware while it is being fired in the oven. At this time the industry was changing over from the old coal-fired intermittent bottle ovens to gas-fired continuous tunnel ovens, for which new equipment was needed. Joe gave me a job making a new article for the tunnel oven. I learnt to operate a press that stamped out the article from damp clay, which then went for firing and sale to the trade customers. Joe was hoping that I would arrive at a fair piece rate (the wage per article produced). I was mortified later to hear that my best efforts had been far too slow and the rate I recommended resulted in a disproportionately high wage.

It was a valuable experience to work with the kindly pottery workers, both men and women. At that time the pot banks were nearly all family firms and the bosses were known by their Christian names or nick names. Joe was Mr Mac and his co-director, recently returned from the RAF, was Mr John. Strikes were almost unknown. Wages were low, but all recognised that there was increasing competition from overseas. Among many pottery-working families it was a tradition to go into the same pot bank as one's parents and grandparents.

I realised also how lucky I was not to be going into a repetitive industrial job, whatever it was. My son Matthew had a similar experience between school and university when he did a spell in a chemical depot, which was dangerous, and a butter factory, which stank. He realised that though academic work did not appeal, the alternative would be vastly less agreeable.

In 1947 two years of National Service was accepted as a matter of course, and it was not until the 1960s that it ended. There were eruptions of trouble all over the world and during the next decade British troops, including national servicemen, were involved in Hong Kong, Malaya, Borneo, Korea, Greece, Kenya, Egypt and elsewhere. They suffered casualties, especially heavy in Korea. A year earlier in his speech at Fulton, Missouri Churchill had drawn attention to the "Iron Curtain" which had fallen across Europe. All over the world Communism and free market democracy were competing for power and influence. There were some who said that the atomic bomb had made conventional forces irrelevant, and who were so terrified of the future that they would not have children. I took the opposite view, that so long as the first use of nuclear bombs would certainly bring retaliation there would not be a first use. So it has proved. The Cold War remained cold and we have enjoyed over 60 years free of major wars. I am not now so confident about the Middle and Far East, should fanatical, even suicidal regimes acquire the weapon.

So I reported for six weeks of primary infantry training with the Oxford and Bucks Light Infantry at Cowley Barracks in east Oxford. The drill was rather boring but the experience was not disagreeable, especially as we had a fine Indian summer. The recruits were housed in huts holding about 20 men with a stove in the middle. Most of the intake had just left university or school at Higher School Certificate level, so we had plenty in common. Our hut corporal referred to us as a "f...... brains trust". In time off I was still able to use Oxford facilities such as the Union. One night I wore a dinner jacket for dinner with the First Lord of the Admiralty, invited by a Conservative Association friend, and got a smart salute from another recruit on guard duty as I returned through the gate illegally late.

Among other ranks (that is, non-commissioned soldiers) the use of the F word was universal and unceasing, but it never went higher up the social scale as it does now. There has been a similar decline in music and dancing. The songs of the thirties and forties were far superior to the present day and the ballroom dancing of that time, though more difficult and needing to be learnt formally, was much more enjoyable than today's free-for-all. So it is my opinion that popular culture has degenerated in the last 50 years. Or am I unable to adjust?

There was a boxing competition in which I was knocked about by a brawny butcher's boy, but I was judged best loser and given 48 hours extra leave, which was compensation enough. The weekly pay was £1.20, and it really hurt when one night I was in a pub in Oxford with Dylan Thomas, who was telling black humour stories, and he touched me for ten shillings for a taxi home – which, of course, he never repaid.

After six weeks' concentration on polishing boots, folding blankets in perfect squares and foot and arms drill, we had the passing out parade. This was followed by a party at which much beer was consumed and recruits, corporals and sergeants temporarily became bosom friends. Next day it was goodbye to the light infantry and comfortable Oxford and off to Catterick in North Yorkshire on a potential officer's course – usually referred to as "P f...... O's". It was a ghastly place, bleak and cold and containing huge numbers of miserable young soldiers. The only warm and comfortable spot was the Salvation Army hut – even the NAAFI was grim. I have had a soft place for the dear old Sally Army ever since. It all came back years later when our daughter Stella married Charles and it turned out that his brother-in-law Christopher was commander of the Catterick garrison, which advertises itself now as the largest army base in Europe.

So it was a great relief to escape after three weeks at Catterick to Mons officer cadet training barracks at Aldershot. This gave a small rise in status. Cadets wore a white plastic diamond behind their cap badge, and at the end of a cursing for clumsiness, laziness, dirty flesh etc. the NCO instructor would say "Sir". It was a hard eight weeks and I had no difficulty going to sleep although there was a really bright light directly overhead. But there was now a purpose to it all, which was to get a commission, and the fellow cadets were quite agreeable. The major worry was that I could not get a bright enough polish on my boots. The Regimental Sergeant Major, Brittain of the Scots Guards, was legendary and terrified the lesser non-commissioned officers as much as the cadets.

From childhood I had suffered from fallen arches and discomfort after some of the long hikes in the Scouts. Mother made me wear Dr Scholl's insteps and do exercises. On entry to the army I was graded A3 (feet), so it was sensible to go into the Armoured Corps rather than the infantry. This meant a move from Mons, which trained officers of all branches of the army at the basic level, to Bovington in Dorset, which was the Royal Armoured Corps officer-training establishment. It was like moving from school to university, with a more relaxed discipline and more challenging material to learn. I had plenty in common with some of the other cadets. It was in Thomas Hardy country, on his Egdon Heath (really Wool Heath), and T.E. Lawrence's cottage and the place where he died riding his motorcycle were nearby. The countryside was inevitably ploughed up by the tanks on which we trained. After four not disagreeable months as the weather steadily improved, I passed out satisfactorily and received my commission as a second lieutenant, subaltern – or more properly a cornet, as I was going into a cavalry regiment. (On entry into Parliament William Pitt the Elder was known as "that terrible young cornet of horse, Mr Pitt".)

While at Bovington one had to choose whether to apply for the Household Cavalry, a particular cavalry regiment, or the Royal Tank Regiment. I chose the 15/19th the King's Royal Hussars for the rather selfish reason that they were stationed in Khartoum, which would give me the chance of seeing the Sudan before I applied for the Sudan Political Service. I had the Service in my sights by then as likely to be more exciting than the Home Civil Service, for which I had been accepted on a temporary basis before my National Service. One of the Bovington staff was on secondment from the Regiment and he got me in. As in the choice of St John's at Oxford, chance dealt me the best of cards.

The 15th Hussars were raised in 1759 during the Seven Year War. Their main battle honour is Sahagun in Spain, where in 1808 under Sir John Moore they charged and routed two regiments of French cavalry. Sahagun Day is celebrated every year with various entertainments, and the officers serve meals to the men, as at Christmas. The 15th King's Hussars were amalgamated with the 19th (Queen Alexandra's Own Royal) Hussars in 1922. They had been raised in 1791 for Indian service on loan to the East India Company, which administered British territories in India until after the mutiny in 1857, a very odd arrangement. Their main battle honour was Assaye in Hyderabad against the Mahrattas in 1803. The Duke of Wellington, who was in command, said that it was the bloodiest battle he had ever known, and it was decisive in that campaign. For brevity we often called ourselves the 15th Hussars and I was completely comfortable with them. They exhibited a combination of efficiency, discipline, humanity and fun in the right proportions. The Regiment later became a part of the Light Dragoons.

After my twenty-first birthday party at Willoughbridge, I went out to join the regiment in Khartoum in July 1948. The troop ship stopped at Gibraltar and Malta, still large British bases. We then sailed through the Suez Canal to Port Tawfiq and had to wait three weeks for another ship which would take us on through the Red Sea to Port Sudan. The Canal Zone bases were under virtual siege. The Egyptian Government of King Faroukh and the Wafd party under Nahas Pasha had denounced the treaty governing the British presence and did nothing to discourage pilfering from the British. Almost every night a thief would be shot in spite of numerous warnings. We transients were employed on tedious administrative duties such as pay. It was hot in the bell tent we lived in and we developed prickly heat, a rash usually round the waist where the belt was tight. The politics of the Canal Zone were to return later when they became a big factor in the Sudan 1953 Agreement.

The heat increased as we came to Port Sudan and took the excellent clean and comfortable but slow train, first over the Red Sea Hills with the Beja, often called the "fuzzy-wuzzies" with their "hayrick head of hair", idly using short sticks permanently in position to scratch their heads. Then the train crawled across the mainly flat desert with sparse scrub until it reached the Nile and its irrigated strip of land. The regiment was stationed in the North Barracks, reached by a bridge across the Nile from Khartoum. There are three towns – Khartoum, the government town laid out by Kitchener after the defeat of Mahdist rule, Omdurman, the old Sudanese town built mainly of mud brick, and the newer Khartoum North, which had much of the industry. The barracks were simple but pleasant enough and the officers' mess had a garden looking over the river. On the other side of the Nile was the South Barracks, at that time occupied by an infantry regiment, the Green Howards, and furnished with an open-air cinema called the Blue Nile which was open to all.

The regiment was equipped with Daimler armoured cars, each having a crew of three and a small gun: there is one in the Imperial War Museum. In addition there were scout cars, rather like armoured jeeps with a machine gun. This was not much firepower for a battle and their real use was for scouting and reconnaissance. They could move as fast in reverse as in forward gear, so if one met an ambush, retreat could be rapid. I was troop leader of No. 2 Troop, B Squadron, with a sergeant, two corporals and about a dozen troopers (the cavalry equivalent of privates). They were good chaps from all over the country, mostly national servicemen cheerfully doing their duty, although they would rather have been at home. There was not really enough to do and of course the summer heat in Khartoum is grim without air conditioning, but we managed to keep up morale. (The only air conditioning in Khartoum then was in the house of the Shell manager.) Local leave was taken in Asmara in the mountains of Eritrea, an attractive Italian-built town, but I never went there.

I never quite understood why there was an armoured regiment in the Sudan in addition to an infantry battalion. Perhaps there was a vague apprehension of insecurity so soon after the war. Relations with Egypt were poor and Eritrea was disturbed, then still occupied by Britain and governed by a Sudan Political Service officer, Duncan Cumming. Muslim raiders known as Shifta posed a serious security problem on the plains adjoining the Sudan frontier. The first sign of nationalist unrest had appeared in the Sudan, but British/Sudanese relations seemed excellent. Anyway, when we left in the summer of 1949 we were not replaced.

There were occasional exercises into the desert round Khartoum, where the people were largely nomadic. There was one rather gruesome expedition. My troop had the job of exhuming the bodies of four RAF men who had crashed in the war about 50 miles south-west of Omdurman. We took four lead-lined coffins on our vehicles, found the spot and met the District Commissioner (DC) of the Kababish, North Kordofan, Peter Lumsden,[1] who gave formal permission for the exhumation. This sad affair was probably a consequence of the very important supply line of aircraft flown from Nigeria across the Sahara desert to the Sudan to reinforce the Air Force in Egypt. I believe a number of women pilots took part in this

Figure 6 On a Daimler armoured car of the 15/19th King's Royal Hussars in the Sudan Desert, 1948.

activity, which avoided the long journey round the Cape of Good Hope.

In the winter Khartoum had something of a "fishing fleet" (a phrase borrowed from India) when sisters and daughters came out to visit their relatives. The climate is good from December to March. The residents were kind to us and it was an enjoyable time, with tennis, river trips, swimming and parties. The Mess bought local ponies and there was a frequent officers' riding school at 6 am. I tried to learn as much as possible from Sudan Government officials and decided to apply for the Political Service, having a preliminary interview before the full interview which would be the following September.

The regimental band arrived and played at Mess nights, as well as for parades and for a ball we gave for the Khartoum friends who had been so kind to us. To prepare for this the colonel had the officers learn some Scottish dances on the Mess lawn. In the spring of 1949 the regiment moved to Gosport in Hampshire prior to being stationed at Lübeck on the Baltic in Germany. The whole regiment took the train to Port Sudan and then a troop ship to Blighty. A fellow subaltern public spiritedly volunteered to teach bridge to all who wished, so I arrived home having advanced my education somewhat in equitation, Scottish dancing and bridge.

Gosport was a good place to prepare for a tour in Germany. It looks across the water to Portsmouth and is really a satellite of it. The barracks were quite comfortable, with deep verandahs of tropical design, said to have been intended for Jamaica in the previous century. The principal event was a big parade with the band playing for Princess Margaret, the Colonel of the Regiment, when she presented new colours. I was among a group sent to operate the world shooting championships in Bisley, which was a new experience made all the better by the hospitality of the Guards at Pirbright. Another event was a week on the Armoured Corps yacht, the Theodora, which took a crew of eight if you hot-bunked. We sailed to Ouistreham in Normandy and back in a force eight gale. There was talk of becoming a regular soldier, but I decided that peacetime regimental service was not demanding enough intellectually. However, I was accepted into the Regular Army Reserve of Officers, which meant that I would join the regiment if there was a general call-up. For some 15 years after I had to notify the War Office of my whereabouts and was invited to annual regimental dinners; it was good to remain in touch in that way.

7

LEARNING ARABIC

In September 1949 I attended an interview at the Sudan Office in London before a panel of about six, all serving officers under the chairmanship of the Civil Secretary, the large but not in the least formidable Sir James Robertson – later the last Governor General of Nigeria. I had the impression that I was already half way to appointment following my preliminary interview in Khartoum.

Pensionable opportunities were no longer being offered because independence was already just below the horizon; instead the offer was a 20-year contract with a gratuity of £8,000 when the contract ended, at the end of the term or earlier. The salary was about £600 per year, more than was paid in any other service under the Crown, and there were 80 days of annual leave in Britain. I had no hesitation in accepting.

This method of recruitment would be heavily criticised now as leading to a self-perpetuating oligarchy, but it was probably the best for the circumstances. Governing a remote district in the Sudan meant hardship and loneliness requiring self-control. Only men experienced in the life were properly qualified to choose their future colleagues.

There were eight in my intake and we spent a term at the School of Oriental and African Studies, London University, learning some basic Arabic. The army released me a fortnight

early so that I could start in time, and a few days later as a
civilian I saw the regiment off to Germany from Liverpool
Street Station. I found a large ground floor bed-sitter in
Bramham Gardens in Earls Court owned by a Polish refugee
couple. This was shared with Keith Murray, a fellow national
service subaltern who was starting a career with Watts, the
ecclesiastical outfitter and supplier. Remarkably, he became a
highly respected designer of church interiors, going into
partnership with an architect, Robert Maguire. Their most
famous work was St Paul's, Bow Common, East London
which replaced one destroyed by a wartime bomb and was
listed as Grade II. Keith had a full-page obituary in *The Times*,
although he had little formal art or design training. His elder
brother Simon, a regular, later became commanding officer of
the regiment. I commuted daily on the Piccadilly Line and
tried to comprehend Thatcher's Arabic Grammar, as well as
getting to know my new colleagues, an interesting group, two
of whom had served in India.

At Christmas I spent a few days in Paris. At Ouistreham the
Royal Armoured Corps had invited sailing neighbours in the
harbour to drinks and I had met a sophisticated dark-haired
French girl called Colette Guinard. She lived at St Cloud and
she showed me something of Paris. Mother had asked why I
wanted to visit Paris between London and going overseas
again, and I explained that it was because I had never been
there. She did not think that a sufficient reason, but I still have
the same desire for new scenes, though there are not so many
left now. Even after all these years of travelling, I have a few
more places on my agenda, if time permits. For those too
young to be in the Forces during the war there was no travel
outside Britain. One felt, with John of Gaunt in Shakespeare's
Richard II, that our country was:

"This precious stone set in the silver sea, which serves it in
the office of a wall, or as a moat defensive to a house against
the envy of less happier lands ..."

From the North Cape down to Finisterre the enemy faced
us during the war, and when he was at last defeated there was

little foreign currency for overseas travel. My children and grandchildren have had an immeasurably greater experience of foreign travel than I did, so I wanted to make up as soon as I could once the war was over and I was earning.

Two of our group of eight, Bryan Walters and I, were sent to the Middle East Centre of Arab Studies (MECAS) in Lebanon. We had to go via Egypt because for historical reasons Sudan service did not begin until arrival in the Nile Valley; the Sudan Government was a creation of the Egyptian Army commanded by Kitchener. After my farewells to Mother, David and Michael and a visit to Christopher Fry's play *The Lady's Not for Burning*, the tailor etc., Bryan and I flew to Cairo with a two-hour stop at Castel Benito in Libya which was still under British Military Administration. We stayed in the Carlton Hotel in Cairo for nine days. The Sudan Agent in Cairo, Kit Haselden, looked after us and took us to the Sphinx and the Pyramids at Giza, which we climbed. In the photographs they appear smooth, but close up the surface is jagged, consisting of blocks of stone, so that the climb is a series of huge steps. We were then joined by two colleagues who had already put in some service in the Sudan, Ralph Daly and Michael Tibbs. Ralph and Bryan had both been in the Welsh Guards Armoured Division in Normandy and had gone on into Germany. Ralph had then organised the Royal Tournament before being recruited direct to the Sudan. Bryan had been at Worcester College, Oxford. Michael had served in submarines during the war and then went to St Peter's College, Oxford. We all got on very well from beginning to end.[1]

As well as the pyramids at Giza and the Sphinx we went to the step pyramids of Saquara, the Citadel, various museums and a service at the Anglican Cathedral. From Cairo to Alexandria we took the train through the flat and lush Nile Delta and then a ship, the Al Malik Fouad of the Khedivial Mail Line, overnight to Beirut. This was then a beautiful Mediterranean seaport and capital, with ghastly traffic and crammed with all the good things which were short in Britain where the rationing was still tight. Behind the city the mountains rose up, terraced with citrus, vines and olives.

MECAS was in a Christian village of traditional stone buildings about 3000 ft above the sea. About 200 ft below it was a Druse village from which our cheerful servant Said came. About three months later we were invited to his brother's wedding. We four Sudanis lived in a solid square building with garages and storerooms below. Upstairs was a large room with a stove in the centre and four study/bedrooms opening off it. The main teaching building with dining room was about 30 yards down the slope. The food was provided by a young local contractor and was poor to mediocre; discontent later forced a change. The school had a squash court and the use of a hard tennis court. There were about 24 students aged from 22 (me) to the mid-thirties. Apart from the four Sudanis there were four from the Diplomatic Service, one from the British Council (ex-Ethiopia, Victor Ménage) and the rest from the three armed services.

The language teaching was carried on in syndicates of three or four by four Palestinian Christian Arab refugees. Though they did not push a political line, I suppose that most of us felt great sympathy for these nice and intelligent men. The Arabic teaching was supervised by a retired Danish Protestant missionary, Pastor Nielsen. He was a learned gentleman and one felt it a privilege to read through and discuss the Koran with him.[2]

Shemlan is about 12 miles from Beirut. Most of the distance from Beirut to Aley is on the twisting road up to the Lebanon Mountains, with lots of crashed cars on the rocky slopes below. This is the direct route from Beirut to Damascus, over the Lebanon and then down and across the flat and fertile Bekaa valley, finally crossing the Anti-Lebanon to Damascus on its eastern side. We four Sudanis clubbed together to buy a black 1938 Ford V8 car which carried us far and wide, but not without some skilled attention from Ralph and many anxious moments.

I have found a pocket diary which I kept for 1950, printed for the Welsh Guards and probably a present from Bryan. It records in brief the events of almost every day in the year. Unfortunately, after that year and some subsequent months I gave up keeping a diary of record – only a diary of appointments which was thrown away at the year's end. It is clear that the car was a nightmare, but in spite of that it enabled us to enjoy a full social life in Beirut as well as tour widely. The diary also records all the books that I read. There was quite a good library at the Centre, and many of the books relevant to the Middle East were borrowed from there.

I was put into Syndicate C first, but soon moved to B with an Australian Navy man. However, we could not agree about how to learn. He wanted to press on and learn the language by listening and speaking: I needed to understand the grammar and writing. He was aural and imitative, while I was visual and intellectual. Since the school was teaching more to my method, he sensibly left to live with an Egyptian family in Alexandria. The experience taught me to develop a technique for learning languages on my own. After Arabic, I first learned Nuer in the Southern Sudan, then Nyanja, Bemba and Lozi in Northern Rhodesia, and finally Spanish while in Leek with Brenda. This adds up in the end to 11 languages, with the Latin, Greek, French, German and Italian I learnt at school. Some were not to a very high standard but passed public examinations, except the Spanish which was not entered. The African languages earned a bonus of about £50 for each tongue learned after the first. An exam had to be passed at the higher standard before confirmation of the appointment.

To return to the Arabic, the collapse of Syndicate B was lucky for me as I was moved up to A with our two language stars, Victor Ménage and Alan Goodison, both with Cambridge firsts. Victor had been in the Friends Ambulance Unit during the war and then with the British Council in Ethiopia. He had become an Amharic examiner. Later he went to Al Azhar University in Cairo, and then went to learn Turkish at the School of Oriental and African Studies in

London as part of a special programme to strengthen Turkish studies. He eventually became Professor of Turkish, and on retirement he was awarded an honorary degree at Birmingham University. Victor and his wife Joanne, who met each other in Cairo, are among my oldest friends.

Alan Goodison had just joined the Diplomatic Service and was about my age. He finished his career as Ambassador in Ireland with a knighthood, and then in retirement became an Anglican non-stipendiary minister in North London. By coincidence, another Diplomatic Service student was Christopher Ewart-Biggs who was tragically murdered when serving as Alan's predecessor as Ambassador in Dublin. He was very tall and, having trouble in one eye, he wore a darkened monocle, giving him a rather Bertie Woosterish appearance which may not have gone down well with the IRA. He was in fact very intelligent and with rather left-wing views. To complete the picture, the third first grade Diplomatic man was Peter Wakefield. He later became Ambassador to Lebanon during the Civil War and earned a knighthood, like the other two. After retirement he became Director of the National Arts Collection Fund. I owe it to Victor and Alan that I managed to stay in the top syndicate.

In addition to the regular grind of learning a difficult language, there was an excellent programme of lectures on Middle Eastern and Islamic topics by a variety of speakers, British, Arab, American etc., as well as by Norman Lewis the senior tutor, who was I think a geographer. The Director was Terrence Brennan who was at the end of a career in the old Consular Service in the Levant. He and his wife presided benevolently over the little world at Shemlan.

The Lebanese and Arabs further afield, prone as they were to conspiracy theories, were convinced that MECAS was a school for British spies. Some years later a Foreign Office student called Blake was summoned home from Shemlan, arrested and sent to prison for a long period for spying for the Soviet Union. He was later lifted from prison in a notorious escape and lived in Russia. Of course, the Arabs said that this proved the truth of their belief, ignoring the fact that Blake was a spy for the other side and the British Government would hardly have trained him for that purpose. He has recently come back into the news as the Russian government has been celebrating his ninetieth birthday. MECAS eventually closed in 1978 when Shemlan was shelled during a civil war and the Treasury could at last save money by bringing the Arabic teaching to the UK, which they had long wanted to do.

We Sudanis were helped to settle into the life by two factors: one was membership of St George's Club in Beirut, which had a fine site on the seashore with swimming from rocks and good dining and bar facilities; the other was the friendship of Antoine Hajjar and his family. Ralph brought an introduction from Alfred Atiyah, a Lebanese who had risen high in the Sudan Government. Like him, Antoine was a Maronite Christian, the principal denomination in Lebanon. They have some Eastern Orthodox practices but are in communion with Rome. His wife Annette was Italian and they had three children, Liliane or Loula, a beautiful 17-year-old, and Charles and Emil, who were about 14 and 12. They were a delightful family, kind, interesting and hospitable. Their flat was a refuge from chaotic Beirut. Antoine was a general merchant and could get anything for us at wholesale prices; I remember particularly radios and whisky.

Although Antoine spoke excellent English, I usually talked with the rest of the family and their friends in French. Lebanon, along with Syria, had been a French protectorate from about 1920 to 1940 and the élite were heavily influenced by French culture, as in Egypt. At the fashionable bathing beach, the Plage St Michel, one heard more French than Arabic and my French definitely improved during the year. Charles and Emil were at a French Jesuit School and Loula at a French-speaking convent. The two principal places of higher education in Beirut were the American University, which was largely Protestant, and the French Jesuit University.

On 24 February there was a general election at home. It was very exciting as the results came in, but the Attlee Labour government just survived. They did not last long and the following year Churchill returned to power, although he was probably too old for the job.

Our first major excursion was to the Cedars of Lebanon in early March. The brakes in the car failed, and Ralph had to drive over miles of mountainous roads using only the gearbox as a brake. The weather was wet and cold, but I did get in some downhill skiing lessons (never used again).

There was a fortnight's break for Easter, spent mostly in Jerusalem. We went there via Damascus and Amman, then over the Allenby Bridge which crossed the Jordan, and past Jericho to Jerusalem. Michael, whose father was an Anglican priest and a former naval chaplain, fixed up for us two to stay at St George's Hostel, attached to the Anglican Cathedral, while Bryan and Ralph found a pension. The hostel was perfect, comfortable and decent in the Anglican way with some interesting guests – archaeologists and redoubtable ladies of the British Empire of the kind that one seemed at that time to meet everywhere in the world. The Old City was under Jordanian control and the New City was Israeli. It could not be visited unless one had a second passport. We saw all the holy sites – the Church of the Holy Sepulchre, Bethlehem, the Dome of the Rock, an Armenian service, Orthodox foot-washing on Maundy Thursday, a service in Gethsemane, the Via Dolorosa, an Ethiopian service, and we went to Ramallah to meet the family of Mr Theodory, one of our Arab instructors. Fortunately the Western and Eastern Easters coincided that year, and the high point was the orthodox ceremony of the Holy Fire at midnight on Easter eve in the Church of the Holy Sepulchre. The round medieval church was packed and people of all nations stood with their candles ready. Then the fire appeared in the centre and was spread to all the candles with astonishing speed, with everyone shouting, "Christ is risen" in their own tongues.

On Easter day, after Holy Communion and the Anglican Bishop's At Home we walked up the Mount of Olives to the Russian Convent and then over to Bethany. In the following days we visited Nablus, stopping on the way at Jacob's Well and the pool of Bethesda. On the way back to Shemlam we bathed in the Dead Sea, wearing trilby hats to demonstrate the buoyancy of the very salty water. The final stop was to see Jerash, north of Amman, one of the Roman cities of the Decapolis. I wrote in my diary: "*A wonderful end to the holiday. The country was lovely, quite well wooded, flowers in profusion. Jerash magnificent, extremely well preserved, showing just what the Roman Empire meant. Needed all of four hours there to see it.*" We had the site almost to ourselves.

28 April was my twenty-third birthday and the other Sudanis gave me a traditional coffee pot with a cheerful bird on top, which I still have after all my wanderings. They were very kind to their younger colleague who had not fought in the war as they had.

After the Easter break the work pressure was reduced, and with the good weather there was swimming at the beach south of Beirut. There were some Paris-style night clubs in the city, especially Maxims and the Kit Kat as well as good restaurants such as the Grillon, the Normandie and St George's Club.

During the year there were two very charming girls to take to these places. First was Anne Quarterman, just out of Sarah Lawrence College, who was the neat blonde daughter of an American army colonel who was the military attaché. There were a few US servicemen learning Arabic in Beirut and we saw quite a lot of them. Anne lent me books and her family had a beach hut. It was a big loss when her father was posted to Iran. Later in the year the tall, dark and beautiful Loula Hajjar used to come to dances and parties. About a year later she married Bryan, and after his Sudan service ended in 1954 he went to work in Antoine's Syrian enterprise in Aleppo, selling agricultural machinery in the developing northern plains. He was expelled after the Suez invasion of 1956 and sadly the marriage eventually broke up without children.

At half term we visited Syria, staying in Damascus at Mrs Saadah's pension. She was a Syrian Arab but preferred to

Figure 7 Syria 1950. Ralph Daly, left, and Michael Tibbs, behind me, with our ancient Ford V8 car. Bryan Walters took the photo.

speak French. We visited the magnificent Omayyad mosque and the Street called Straight where St Paul was converted and recovered his sight, lost three days before on his way to the city. At that time the Syrians were very suspicious of foreigners, but less so now, I thought, when visiting Aleppo in 2007.

In mid July after the exams, which had satisfactory results, we set off for a six-week tour to learn as much as we could and speak Arabic. Fortunately it was deemed to be duty, so expenses were paid. We left the car in Amman and took the train to Maan on the line which T.E. Lawrence had blown up during World War I. In our compartment there was a tall fat Jordanian MP returning to his constituency. Michael had with him an account of the Arab Revolt against the Turks, including a picture of Lawrence's ally Auda and his kinsmen. Our fellow passenger recognised himself as the small boy at the front of the group. He was very genial; a most satisfactory encounter.

We stayed in the Arab Legion fort at Wadi Musa, which was under the command of Sergeant Abdul Karim. It was very simple, but clean, and we were well cared for. At this time the Arab Legion was still commanded by Glubb Pasha and there were a number of British officers. It was not until the Iraq revolution of 1958 that things fell apart and the way to Saddam Hussein was opened. The sergeant hired horses and we rode to Petra a few miles away, down the narrow ravine with wild oleander bushes growing beside the track. The site was glorious and we had it almost to ourselves, to explore over two days. Then camels were hired and we went with Abdul Karim to tour the area to the west and visit a Bedouin encampment, where we were generously fed with mutton and rice. We slept on the ground in the open with the camels beside us. The crude saddle was rickety and the hump poked through the frame – very uncomfortable. There followed two nights at Aquaba, then a tiny port on the Red Sea, staying in the Arab Legion mess and swimming and observing the tropical fish.

Back in Amman we prepared for the next stage. This involved seeking help from the Iraq Petroleum Company manager, since the road across the desert to Baghdad is along the oil pipeline. We drove overnight and spent the next day at station H3. The following morning we reached Baghdad across the dead flat desert and stayed at the Semiramis Hotel. Bryan met a Welsh Guards friend who entertained us, and the Embassy got us temporary membership of the Alawiya Club which, according to newspaper reports, still exists. It was the hottest time of the year and the swimming pool was a great boon. We visited the Arab and Iraq museums, the latter founded by Gertrude Bell, which was magnificent. Another day we visited the largest unsupported mud brick arch in the world at Ctesiphon, the holy Shia city of Khadhimain and the site of Babylon. So dominant was the Sunni branch of Islam from 1918 until the fall of Saddam, that I never realised that they comprised only one fifth of the population of Iraq, the Shia being in the great majority.

Figure 8 Jordan, 1950. On patrol with the Arab Legions, spending a night with the Bedouin.

After five nights in Baghdad we left at half past four in the morning for the oil centre of Kirkuk, important enough to have a British Vice Consul and a British Council representative. We saw the installation and the burning oil and gas, said to be the origin of the burning fiery furnace which did not harm Shadrack, Meshak and Abednego in the Old Testament. At that time the various oil nationalisation measures in Saudi Arabia, Iran and Iraq were still in the future, though not far ahead. Throughout we were speaking as much Arabic as possible, although the Iraqi version was rather different from the "modern classical" we had been sensibly taught. We usually made courtesy calls on local governors and were well received. Iraq was then firmly within the British sphere of influence.

We then turned east to Sulaimaniya, an important Kurdish centre. The mountains came closer and there were streams, in one of which we bathed. We had an introduction from a Shemlan neighbour, Professor Christopher Scaife, to visit a

Kurdish chief, Hassan Bek Jaf. We telephoned from Sulaimaniya and he asked us to stay, so we took the track south-east to Halabja, getting even closer to the mountains which marked the frontier with Iran. We arrived in the evening at a high brick-walled circular enclosure on a wide level grassy plain. Going in through the gatehouse, rather like a Cambridge college (it was brick), there was an expanse of turf with dwellings around the circumference. In the centre was a circle of about twenty men in Kurdish costume with daggers in their sashes. Hassan Bek Jaf was a good-looking middle-aged man and a charming host. One man in the circle was different. He was wearing a sports jacket and reading a book, which turned out to be George Elliot's Middlemarch. This was Wilfred Thesiger, just returned from a six-week trek with donkeys in the Rawanduz Mountains to the north.

Thesiger had been in the Sudan Political Service before the war and we knew of his exploits. On one occasion he had left his district Kutum to trek with a caravan of camel traders on the darb él arbain (forty-day road) from Darfur to Aswan in Egypt. Another time he had used his leave to trek to the Tibesti Mountains in the central Sahara, the Touareg homeland. In the war he had served with General Orde Wingate in Ethiopia, restoring his hero, the Emperor Haile Selassie, to his throne, and later he operated behind the French lines in Jebel Druze in Syria. These Druzes were co-religionist with our servant Said in Shemlan. Wilfred was delighted to talk and hear the news of the Sudan and his old colleagues. He told us that he had not returned after the war, since although he respected his colleagues they were "too keen on straight roads and sanitation". He said that his kit was still incurring storage charges in Stores and Ordnance in Khartoum and asked me to dispose of it, which I later did, being able to send him a cheque.

The following day Hassan Bek took us and Thesiger to some sulphur springs under the mountains, where we bathed and lunched and drank gallons of tea. We were enjoying it so much that we did not get back to Suleimaniya and the simple but adequate rest house until nine at night.

There are two postscripts to this enjoyable episode. About thirty years later I was in my solicitors' office in Leek, North Staffordshire when a young man of Middle Eastern appearance came to see me about a passport problem. He wanted to join his mother, who was in Los Angeles. It turned out that he was a Kurd, and I mentioned how grateful I felt to Hassan Bek Jaf for his hospitality, even after such a long time. The young man replied that Hassan Bek was his grandfather!

The other postscript is very sad. My diary mentions that we were in the region of Halabja. I realise now that this is where Saddam Hussein used poison gas on the Kurds, murdering large numbers most cruelly. The Kurds have been restive for many years. Although Sunni Muslims, they are ethnically different from the Iraqi Arabs. The great Saladin who confronted Richard Coeur de Lion in 1192 was a Kurd. They had hoped for a homeland of their own after the defeat of the Turkish Empire in 1918, but they ended up living in four countries, Iraq, Iran, Turkey and Syria, although the parcels are contiguous. There was an independence leader in the mountains in 1950 supported by the Soviet Union, since the Cold War was at its most intense.

Next we travelled back west to Kirkük and then north-west to Arbil and Mosul. Arbil is a very impressive mound on the flat plain, created by 5000 years of detritus. It is thought to be the oldest continuously inhabited town in the world, and was a typical Muslim town with narrow streets, mud houses and veiled women in black disappearing into buildings to avoid being seen by males. We then turned north into the mountains, taking the spectacular road up the Ruwanduz gorge built by the Royal Engineers during the war to transport supplies to Russia (and little thanks we got for it). We bathed in the fast, cold waters of both the Greater Zab and the Lesser Zab, tributaries of the Tigris. At Mosul the British Council representative, who was in Kirkük, invited us to stay in his house. His servant fed us and did our laundry; it was luxury. Even better, we visited the site of Nineveh.

Next day the Syrian customs displayed their usual disagreeable nature, holding us up for hours at the frontier town of Tel Kotchek. Now the land was fertile and the population mixed, because there were many immigrants into what was intended to be a rich cereal belt. There was talk of settling Palestinian refugees in this region, but the politicians manipulating them told them that they must not move out of their tents, as that would be to admit that they were not going to recover their land. Sixty years later they are still waiting.

We were now near the Turkish frontier (then, as now, no love lost between Syrians and Turks). After a night in an Arab hotel we travelled 95 miles south-west across a dusty desert to Deir es Zor, a crossing of the Euphrates for both vehicles and Bedouin. Long ago it had an interesting mixed classical and oriental culture, and there is a good exhibition in the British Museum. We stayed with hospitable American missionaries at the Presbyterian hospital.

A long day took us to Aleppo, since the Iraq Petroleum rest house on the way was closed. Aleppo is a special city, the home of Abraham (or Ibrahim) the Friend of God, revered by Jews, Christians and Muslims, with a fine citadel and walls. There was lots of mail waiting at the British Consulate and we had an introduction to the Altouanyan family. The father was a self-sacrificing doctor who had been a great friend of T.E. Lawrence. The children, whom we met and who are now middle-aged, had been the inspiration for Arthur Ransome's Swallows and Amazons on their annual visits to the Lake District. In the region of Aleppo we saw some fine castles and also former Christian churches, one containing what was claimed to be the actual pillar of St Simeon Stylites. Then we drove through the magnificent Alawite Mountains to Latakia, and so back to the Mediterranean. The Alawites come from this area and are regarded by orthodox Muslims as very heretical, being a far-out Shia sect. The past President Asad was an Alawite and so is his son, Bashir, who had his oculist training in the UK. This explains why the Christians have had a fair deal in Syria, since they are allies of the Alawites against

Sunni Islam. In this area there were Crusader castles, above all the magnificent Krak des Chevaliers. After that we visited Tartous and stayed in the Buffet de la Gare at Homs, and then on to Palmyra, visiting the Temple of Baal, the great colonnade, theatre, forum – a remarkable ruined city in the desert. We then visited Tyre, Sidon, Banias and Beaufort Castle, with the remains of Phoenician, Roman, Byzantine and Crusader occupations, returning via Baalbek and back to Shemlan on 3 September, having left on 16 July just seven weeks before. Everyone had done something different on their travels so there were many experiences to exchange. We had travelled the furthest of anyone.

It was still hot summer in Beirut, which meant that Aley, near Shemlan, was a centre of social life for the Near East. The hotels had dances and nightclubs to which we went with Loula and friends from Egypt and Khartoum. Those from Egypt spoke more French than English. One of the RAF officers at MECAS was married there, and I arranged the flowers in the church. I played squash about three times a week and bridge quite often, though the Arabic work was heavy. Antoine Hajjar came often to bridge and on 14 November I note that I made my first grand slam.

In late November we had our final exams. I was fourth in Arabic with 84 per cent, and fourth in background studies with 75 per cent, Bryan being third. In each case Ménage and Goodison were first and second. This was satisfactory and treated as a pass in the Sudan Higher Arabic examination. After many farewells we left by ship to Alexandria, then by train to Cairo, and by plane to Khartoum on 8 December. Somehow Loula was in Cairo with a friend, Gilberte, and I returned so late from the Halmia Palace that I did not go to bed before catching the Misrair flight to Khartoum.

8

KHARTOUM PROVINCE HEADQUARTERS

It was good to be back in Khartoum after 18 months, but with a different employer, and now as a civilian instead of a soldier. There were similarities though. The Political Service wore uniform when in the provincial headquarters (the mudiria) or the district headquarters (the merkaz). This was a bush jacket and shorts with epaulettes showing the rank for daily wear, white in the office and khaki on trek. The head covering was a pith helmet of the Bombay bowler design, as worn by Churchill in the Western Desert, with the province badge. Khartoum Province had an elephant, a reference to the meaning of Khartoum which is an elephant's trunk, believed, not very convincingly I thought, to stem from the shape of the land created by the confluence of the White Nile and the Blue Nile. Upper Nile had two crossed spears inspired by the Nuer hunting and fishing spears. For formal occasions there was office dress – jacket and long trousers of thin khaki barathea, with brass buttons and the same stripes of rank on the epaulettes. I do not think I ever wore mine except at our wedding. The ceremonial helmet was of the type used by British troops in the Victorian era, having a gilt badge with the royal arms on the front, called the Wolseley helmet after the famous nineteenth-century Field Marshall.

Later, in Northern Rhodesia, the provincial commissioners, district commissioners and district officers did not wear uniform in their daily work. This meant that when they had to deal with an emergency out of the office they could only be recognised as the men with authority by the presence of their uniformed district messengers. I preferred the Sudan practice of uniform on all occasions, since it helped to further the valuable policy of being recognizable and accessible at all times in all places to all people.

After arrival on 8 December 1950 I was taken to numerous places to be introduced, including the legislative assembly, which was beginning to test its strength, and invited to drinks and meals. The service took very good care of its new members. I noted that I understood about two thirds of the Arabic spoken in the Assembly and it did not take long to become familiar with the Sudanese version, which is actually quite good.

A friend I met again on arrival was Frances Delaney, a woman geologist. She had grown up in Kenya and received part of her education in Paris. She would trek on her own with Sudanese assistants, driver and servant in the remotest parts. She wore bush jackets with huge pockets for her specimens, which she would collect with her hammer in the extreme heat of the day. The Sudan had some minerals but no great riches, it seemed. The discovery of oil in quantities in Western Nuer District of all places and in Southern Kordefan, justifying a pipeline to Port Sudan, was 30 years in the future. Frances lent me a bicycle and I then bought one of my own to be my transport for the year I would be in Khartoum. Her fame was such that some years later, when she went to work on the other shore of the Red Sea in Saudi Arabia, she was asked if she really was Umm Sharkush, which was her Sudanese name meaning the mother of a hammer. As a geologist, she always carried a hammer to take rock samples.

I used the word trek for a journey into the desert or bush. It was surprising that the Sudan adopted an Afrikaans usage; perhaps this was because at the time of the reconquest of the Sudan the news was all of the Boer War, and the Afrikaners'

Figure 9 Khartoum, 1951. In the bachelor flat in the Sudan Club Garden. Sudan Political Service uniform was white for the office and khaki on trek.

idea was of the Great Trek as a modern version of the wandering of the people of Israel in search of the Promised Land. So South Africa and the Sudan used the word "trek", East Africa adopted the Swahili word "safari" (in itself derived from Arabic, as are the Swahili words for such articles as nail, gun and flag), Northern Rhodesia (Zambia) used "tour", while Nyasaland (Malawi) was very correct in adopting the Chinyanja word "ulendo".

My living arrangements were ideal. The Sudan Club with gardens, swimming pool, tennis courts and good catering was on the road which ran beside the Blue Nile. In the grounds were two blocks of single flats. I was to take over John Udal's flat on the upper floor of the building known from its colour as the "yellow peril", as well as taking over his job in the mudiria. He was going to MECAS and so was able to leave me his household goods and furniture. This gave me time to have my own furniture made, at the official price, in the prison which was a part of my responsibility. The carpenter was a dear old man who had killed his wife, justifiably by all accounts. My accommodation consisted of a living room, a bathroom and a verandah where I slept. There must have been a communal kitchen somewhere, but I never found it. I engaged a servant, or suffragi, named Mohammed, who came from Dongola, as many did, which was about 200 hundred miles to the north. He was a decent, loyal and fairly honest chap, competent and rather subdued in temperament. He came with me to Western Nuer, but found the place and people so alien that he decided to return north when I went on leave after we had been 18 months together. He shopped and cooked for me as well as doing my laundry and cleaning the flat. He would wake me for the morning tea using the Sudanese custom, by gently rubbing my big toe until I responded.

Khartoum Province comprised three districts: Khartoum, the capital laid out by Kitchener; Omdurman, the old capital of the leader of the Mahdi rebellion containing the prominent dome of his tomb; and Khartoum North which was the industrial quarter. The latter district took in a substantial slice of desert country, and Duncan Waugh the Assistant DC (A/DC) with his wife, Daphne, were stationed for some time at a bleak place called Abu Deleiq which was the headquarters of the local chief or Omda. Housing was often a problem. The Waughs also lived romantically on a boat on the Blue Nile of a type called a gyassa, named the Candace, which was the title of Ethiopian queens at the time of the Roman Empire. Finally they moved into a rented house in Khartoum North.

Like most houses in Northern Sudan the roof was flat with a low parapet and spout for the occasional summer rainstorm. Most people slept on the roof, reached by outside stairs up which the servants would carry the bedding at nightfall. There was often also a black painted tank which captured the heat of the sun and usually provided enough hot water.

About two years later in Western Nuer District I began writing an account of my time there, which included a description of the religious and political situations. This will appear in the next chapter, so I will pass over those matters now. I understood what was happening politically since one of my jobs was to help the Deputy Governor Rex Harrison, a great encourager, to compile the Khartoum Province security report. The Governor of Khartoum had fewer functions than a Governor in other provinces because there were well developed town councils in each of the three towns and a fully staffed judiciary. However, he had overall town planning functions in which I assisted, and I also helped in liaison with the three DCs. I learnt how the government worked because all the departmental headquarters were naturally in Khartoum, and about the Sudanese people from my Sudanese colleagues, particularly the Town Clerk of Khartoum Daoud Abdul Latif, a lively and clever man.[1]

There was an active social life, and as a bachelor of 24 years I was invited out a good deal, not only by the British, but also by the Sudanese, Greeks and Lebanese. During the season, which ended in late March as the temperature began to increase, I often accompanied June Drake, the sister-in-law of Alan Arthur, the DC Khartoum. She was out for a few months on a visit with her parents. Alan had been in the Indian Civil Service before Indian independence. June later married an MP who became a Circuit Judge.

There were certain things one was expected to do. One was to visit the tents of the various Muslim tariqas or sects at the time of their festivals (eids). The hosts were most charming and hospitable, a very far cry from the murderous hostility of Al Qaeda today. Another expectation was that a young man would play polo. I did my best but it was not good enough, and I fear I let my ponies down. I had two, both greys. Aziza, a mare, was so named because it means darling or beloved, which she was. Later she had a foal as beautiful as herself whom I called Samira. The other pony was a gelding and so cheap – £17, I think – that I named him Atiya, which means a gift. The reason for the low price was that he was wilful and stubborn, but he was strong on long treks.

The horses were bought from colleagues who had been posted to Khartoum from out-districts and who were no longer entitled to a horse allowance, as I was. This enabled the employment of a syce (an Indian word) or groom. His name was Mohammed Osman Yassin, and like Mohammed the suffragi, he came with me to Western Nuer but returned to the north when I went on leave, being replaced by a Nuer called Majok. The Nuer do not have the same affinity with horses as they do with cattle, but he did his best. I rode every morning in Khartoum, usually with a friend, at about six, when the syce brought the horses round from the borrowed stables. Then back to breakfast prepared by Mohammed, and at nine to the office by horse or bicycle. The office hours were nine until two, followed by lunch and siesta. From four there would be tennis, squash or hockey – terribly exhausting in the heat. As I was playing once on the Gordon College ground I heard Mozart's *Il Mio Tesoro* coming from an open window. It seemed supremely beautiful and I realised that I was irredeemably Western in culture. Old white male they call me now. So be it.

After exercise there were drinks, followed by dinner and sometimes the cinema. Most of the year dinner would be served in the open on a mastaba or patio area on the lawn. Ten o'clock was the time to leave, made clear by the host calling loudly over the house to the suffragi to bring water. One drank the water and made one's farewells. It was a useful convention, and it is a pity that there is nothing similar in Britain.

An item of local colour was the camel cart collecting human waste buckets. The system was operated by Nuba, strong black men from the rocky hills of Southern Kordafan, trained in their various traditions of wrestling (Leni Riefenstahl later published a celebrated book of photographs of them, bloodied from the contest, which some claimed was infused with Nazi philosophy). Many Nuba went into the army, and they now pose a particular problem since they were allied to the southern rebels but have always been treated by Government as part of the north. There was much criticism as independence approached that the capital did not have a water-borne sewage system. On the contrary, I regarded it as a matter of pride that the maximum funding went to the out-districts. Now, after 50 years of spending on the Three Towns at the expense of the rest of the country, there is a near universal revolt by the regions against the centre, in the north as well as the south.

The Anglican or Episcopal Cathedral in Khartoum played a big part in British life. The day of rest was Friday, the Muslim Sabbath, and Sunday was a working day. (This was reversed in the three southern provinces.) The main service was evensong at six o'clock, to which the Governor General usually came. It was followed by a buffet meal and discussion on the topic of the day. This institution was known as the Cathedral Supper Club and was a meeting place for all comers. The cathedral was a fine sandstone building by an Italian architect, suited to the climate. The Episcopalians have since been ejected on the grounds, whether spurious or genuine I do not know, that the building poses a threat to the security of the nearby Presidential Palace. A replacement has been built on a site provided. Later John Udal's ordained daughter Joanna worked there as the Archbishop's assistant, a remarkable record of three generations serving the Sudan since John's father Douglas was Principal of Gordon College which later became Khartoum University. Joanna was later appointed as the Archbishop of Canterbury's secretary for the Anglian Communion. After the British left the Sudan a number formed the Sudan Church Association to provide support for the continuing Episcopal Church. Because of the Civil War and persecution of Christians, later the need for support became so great that the Association is still active some 50 years later. Indeed, it provided the principal means for the financial maintenance of the administration of the church and reassured the suffering southerners that they were not completely forgotten by the world.

One had to serve a full year before the first leave. It was the practice to take either early leave in April, May or June or late leave in July, August or September. Wives usually stayed on leave for a full six months, avoiding the worst of the hot weather. My leave was ambitious. I had arranged with David Eales, a bimbashi (major) in the Sudan Defence Force, to travel home by road in his 1938 two-seater Morris 12, sharing the expenses. The weather began to heat up in early April and we left by train to Wadi Halfa, the northern frontier town on the 11th, with the car on a flat wagon behind us. Some people had said that the journey was not practical, but senior colleagues were in favour and gave us letters of introduction. A farewell party at the railway station, including Mohammed, my suffragi, and David's clerical staff, saw us off. We travelled across the increasingly bare desert in single compartment comfort, arriving in Wadi Halfa the following afternoon. When I saw Michael Palin on television doing the same journey in reverse 40 years later the contrast could not have been greater. I noted in my diary that Wadi Halfa was "a pleasant place, Arab rather than Sudanese in character, clean and plenty of trees". It was a compensation station for a senior DC who failed to get promotion and was known as "the Halfa Hundreds". By the time of Palin's visit the old settlement had been submerged by the Higher Aswan Dam and a new town had been built.

There was neither road nor rail north from the Egyptian frontier and everyone had to take the paddle steamer to Shellal, a day and two nights, stopping at the temple of Abu Simbel, since moved by UNESCO to save the impressive statues from flooding. Then on through the Egyptian customs, helped by the Sudan Railways agent who had been telegraphed beforehand, and along the rough rocky desert road to Luxor, 120 miles in eight and a half hours. There were very few tourists. We crossed the Nile in a traditional boat without mechanical power and walked through the lush fields of wheat and sugar cane. Some cheerful peasants were having their breakfast of onions and bread on the ground and they asked us to join them, which we did. Then we went on to the amazing temples and tombs of Thebes, and back to the great temple of Karnak in the afternoon.

From then on the journey was on dirt roads through the intensively cultivated irrigated strip along the Nile. There was barely a wheel to be seen, let alone an internal combustion engine, except in small sugar processing plants. Loads were carried on the head or back, mostly by the women. At one point we had a puncture, luckily near the farm of a royal princess (King Faroukh was still on the throne), and the manager had it repaired in his workshop. He was a white Russian who spoke atrocious French and gave us an excellent lunch. We had written beforehand to Dr and Mrs Skellie of the American College in Assiutt, to whom we had an introduction, and they were extremely hospitable when we stayed the night.

The following day we reached Cairo, through increasingly developed country with better housing, garages, shops and so forth, with the last 100 miles of road being tarmac. In effect there was a MECAS syndicate reunion as I stayed with Victor Ménage and Alan Goodison, who were sharing a flat. Victor was on the staff of Al Azhar University and Alan was at the British Embassy. I was introduced to Johanna Maxwell of the British Council library, and it was clear that a marriage to Victor was a happy prospect. There was a lot of business to be done in Cairo, getting Western Desert permits from the RAC and visas for the onward journey from the British, French and Spanish Embassies, but there was still time for lunches with the deputy Sudan agent Gawain Bell and his wife Sylvia, and with Willie Morris, a St John's contemporary at the embassy, later to be ambassador to Egypt. I even fitted in tea at Groppi's with three of Loula's girl friends and a film called "Gone to Earth", which rather bizarrely was set in rural Shropshire. The author, Mary Webb, who in her time was well known, came from Much Wenlock. (The hunting crowd could never understand how she got the title so wrong; they call it "gone to ground".)

It was a four-hour journey to Alexandria through the Nile Delta, where David knew Colonel Stirling, the Times Middle East correspondent. We had a drink with him at his hotel and he was most interesting. Our dismissal was the best I have encountered: he apologised by saying that he had to leave us to play bridge with King Zog. Zog was an Albanian warlord who had seized the crown, the same crown that had earlier been offered to C.B. Fry the cricketer. He was deposed when Mussolini invaded at Easter 1940. The English papers concentrated on the plight of Queen Geraldine who had given birth two days before. The family went into exile in Alexandria.

So far we had been travelling north but now we turned west, along the length of the North African coast, through the places which had meant so much in the war only a few years previously. First night was at Mersa Matruh, a pleasant resort with a good simple hotel. We had a coffee with some Sudanese workers who were homesick and disliked Egyptians. On the way the road had passed through the El Alamein battlefield. At the Libyan frontier we entered British-administered occupied enemy territory, governed at the time by two Sudan Political Service colleagues, de Candole in Cyrenaica and Travers Blackley in Tripoli. I had letters of introduction from Khartoum, but as things turned out I could not deliver de Candole's. There were a number of British army garrisons and we stayed at the NAAFI Officers' Club in badly battered Tobruk. The port was being developed for a proposed British base in Cyrenaica and a friendly government was expected in the future under King Idris, but his tenure was to be short as he was deposed by Colonel Gaddafi. Continuing west, rain-grown crops began at Derna and we stayed in a pretentious Italian hotel in Cyrene. The Greek and Roman remains were extensive and the site very beautiful, with not a tourist in sight.

The Barca plain leading to Benghazi was covered with Italian settlements. The 16/5th Lancers were stationed there and we called in for tea, then reached Benghazi and stayed in the Officers' Club. David was entertained by friends and we all had a cheerful dinner at the Club. Next day we saw more of Benghazi, which was not very exciting, and looked up a Sudan contact who was a financial adviser while the car was serviced.

Our route had been following the successful advance of the Eighth Army from El Alamein, over country that had earlier been won from the Italians and then lost after Rommel and his Afrika Corps arrived. Everywhere there were the relics of war. Now we were travelling along the southern shore of the Gulf of Sirte at no more than 20 miles per hour over a dreadful road, following the route of the German retreat to Tunis and their eventual surrender. The road passed Mussolini's grandiloquent monument, which the British troops called Marble Arch. Sirte was a sordid night stop, but we found spaghetti and local wine in a little Italian café. Sirte was later to enter the news as Gaddafi's final redoubt and place of death. Next day the desert gave way to palm trees, rain-grown crops and neat white Italian settlements, leading to Tripoli. Leptis Magna, the Roman port, was visited on the way, which was as impressive as Cyrene but there was only a single guardian there. We had two nights in Tripoli, a fine clean town in those days, staying in a British army officers' mess with a friend of David's. I cashed in one of my letters of introduction to Travers Blackley, the Military Governor seconded from the Sudan Political Service, who was living in vice-regal style in the Villa Volpe, the palace of the former Italian governors. The Blackleys were very hospitable and glad to hear news from Sudan.

Moving west again we came to Sabratha, the third of the magnificent Roman/Greek cities of Libya. Soon we passed out of the influence of the British Army, which would not be felt again until Gibraltar. All was now French – language, currency and food. It was difficult to get the local people to understand that we were speaking Arabic to them: they would always respond in French. The road crossed the French-built Mareth defensive line where Montgomery's famous left hook manoeuvre through the mountains outflanked the Axis defences and opened the way to Tunis. Now we could depend on hotels, restaurants, tarmac roads and garages all the way home, though not on French banks to change Barclay's travellers' cheques. After a night at Sfax we reached Tunis with two stops, one at El Djem where the huge lonely coliseum rises unexpectedly out of flat olive orchards and the other via a diversion to Kairouan, one of the holy cities of Islam, full of white mosques and suspicious faces. After a night in Tunis we visited the old site of Carthage and then pressed on into Algeria through mountains covered in cork forests and intensive cultivation on the plains. A night in the port of Bone was followed by a diversion inland to the magnificent site of Constantine, straddling a deep ravine. The next nights were in Algeria, then a fine city, and Oran where we asked for a bath at our hotel and were given a key which entered straight into public baths next door, to our surprise.

In Morocco we were back in the desert for 100 miles or so. Fez, another holy city, had a huge suq, very picturesque, in which we got lost, but as in Kairouan the people did not seem to like Europeans. However, on the surface there did not seem to be the bitterness which fuelled the terrible war in Algeria a few years later. Morocco and Tunisia, being protectorates with traditional native rulers, fared better. Algeria was a Département of France and in theory could never be independent. It was the second African territory to be invaded for permanent conquest and settlement of the interior in 1838, the first being the Sudan, invaded by Mohammed Ali, the Khedive of Egypt in 1821.

After a night in Tangier, in rooms let by an Italian lady, we just got a place on the Blandy ferry which took three hours to arrive at Gibraltar. There David's contacts got us rooms in a new Toc H hostel, converted from a prisoner of war camp by the sea, and dinner in the garrison mess. Next day we climbed the Rock, enjoying being back in a British atmosphere. The Morris Motors agent gave us coffee to deliver to a friend in England. He was the charming owner of a sherry factory at Puerto Santa Maria.

Spain was then little visited. It was still recovering from its civil war and Franco was a pariah to many. But we should remember that he resisted heavy pressure from Hitler, to whom he owed gratitude since without German military help he would probably not have won the civil war. The Germans wanted Spain to join the war on their side, or at least to allow them through it to Gibraltar, which would almost certainly have fallen. Britain could well then have lost the war.

Our route took us through Seville and Cordova to Madrid, where a tyre was cut by a tramway rail and we had to change the wheel on a main road in the rush hour. Next day we drove out to Toledo and back. The town has a superb cathedral, but many of the villages were poor and dirty. Continuing north we stayed in Burgos with its magnificent Gothic cathedral and crossed into France, passing Biarritz and Bordeaux. After a stop to see Chartres cathedral we spent five nights in Paris on rather a social round, as well as some sightseeing for David, including the opera and the Folies Bergères. I saw a lot of Lillemor Mannerheim, who was studying sculpture with Zadkine, as well as Colette Guinard and her family and Clive Howson, a school friend who was a First Secretary at the British Embassy. David knew Claire Hollingworth, the war correspondent, but she was away and we had a most interesting dinner with her husband, Geoffrey Hoare, also a journalist. Claire's autobiography is well worth reading: she was one of the earliest women journalists, making her way in her profession by her strength of character. She was the first to report the German invasion of Poland in September 1939, which precipitated World War II.

We drove overnight to Dieppe and slept in the car before crossing to Newhaven. This was before the days of roll-on roll-off ferries and the car was loaded by crane. I arrived back in England after 18 months away and spent a night with friends of David in Sussex, and then went to visit June Drake and her kind family in a beautiful country house in Harlow in Essex; the new town was little more than plans then. David and I parted at Mill Hill Barracks. During our six weeks together we had got on remarkably well in spite of the problems with his 13-year-old and much travelled car, which were to be expected. We forget now how unreliable and capricious cars were until the eighties, when the Japanese taught the world about quality control. David and I had each contributed to the success of the adventure in the way of contacts, knowledge and languages. In the course of one and a half years I had visited all the Arabic-speaking countries except those on the Arabian Peninsula.

From the Drakes' I was able to go to London to visit tailor, hatter, barber, the Sudan Agency and numerous friends from Oxford and the army. I went to one great coming-out party in Essex for the daughter of August Courtauld, who had spent a winter under the Arctic snow in the thirties when rescuers could not reach him.

Mother had been lent a delightful cottage in Cheddleton, near Leek in North Staffordshire, and we had a most enjoyable month there entertaining lots of relatives and old friends. My brothers David and Michael were able to visit and Mother took great pleasure in being able to feed all her sons together again. My brothers were both living at Willoughbridge and working on the farm, not very happily. There were breaks from the time in Staffordshire to take my MA degree at Oxford (no damned merit – time and money alone were required), go to more great dances in Essex with June and to the regimental Old Comrades' Association Dinner at the Connaught Rooms in London. I also spent a weekend with Desmond Cole at Bedales School, where he was teaching. It was very interesting to see co-education for bright children. In London I ordered prints of Canaletto and Van Eyck paintings, and in Stoke-on-Trent some Carlton China, all to be sent to Khartoum.[2]

Our tenure of the cottage having ended, Mother and I spent some days with kind farming friends in Uttoxeter and Stafford before my last hours with June in London, going to the ballet at the Festival of London (which was very successful and far superior to the Millennium Dome) and to the Café de Paris and Pigalle. Dinner dancing with a French accent was the fashion then and far more civilised than "clubbing" appears to be now.

The Sudan Government had a contact with a charter air travel company, which flew from Blackbushe in Hampshire. My journey was fine, but a year later a plane came down in the Mediterranean and some lives were lost, including the wife of the Provincial Education Officer of Upper Nile. Anne Driver, who had been an air hostess (a superior job in those days), was credited with saving lives and keeping up the spirits of the children as they floated in their life jackets in the dark sea. On another occasion a propeller fell off, and on the following journey John Udal made a point of testing the propeller's firmness at each of the four stops – Nice, Malta, El Adem in Libya, and Wadi Halfa. There was an overnight stop at the Phoenicia Hotel in Malta, which was luxury.

Duncan Waugh met me off the plane in the Governor's car and I took the job in the mudiria back from him. Three days later my diary reads: "To drinks for the Civil Secretary's calling night along with David (Eales). David Jacot and a new nurse Brenda Stephens came up (to my flat) for drinks after." I remember that occasion well. David and Brenda were dining on the Sudan Club lawn. I stopped to greet David, a friend who worked for Shell, on my return from leave and so was introduced to Brenda. I invited them to drop in after they had finished their meal.

For some reason not explained, the diary stopped a few days later. There is a reference to a parade for prison warders, at which the Governor gave medals for gallantry during the police mutiny which had occurred during my leave. This had been a nasty affair. It was the former Labour Government's policy to encourage trade unions. Unfortunately the World Federation of Trade Unions (WFTU), a Communist-dominated movement controlled and financed by Moscow, had penetrated the Sudan. In many parts of the world there was a struggle with the International Confederation of Free Trade Unions (ICFTU), which was Western-sponsored and had largely lost the cause in the Sudan. The WFTU was, as one would expect, completely ruthless and aimed to damage the most vulnerable sections of society. A police mutiny was frightening, opening the prospect of widespread crime and disorder. Fortunately the public remained calm and other government servants loyal. Later the union of Sudanese male nurses, the mumarridin, was targeted. Strikes caused suffering among Sudanese patients, which was alleviated by the efforts of European nurses and volunteers.[3]

The final entries in the diary for July 1951 mentioned that I finished reading Orwell's 1984 – "very clever and quite horrifying". How the man who went to Spain to fight for the republicans in 1937 and found their cause taken over and betrayed by the Communists would have rejoiced in the collapse of the Soviet order in 1990.

Finally I see that I was visited by Suleiman, the former servant of the Regiment's commanding officer. Somehow, over two years after the regiment left the Sudan he had heard that I had returned and tracked me (a mere subaltern) down. I was able to give him all the news picked up at the recent Old Comrades' Association dinner.

In the very, very hot days of summer social life was low. From April until October the average maximum temperature in Khartoum is over 100°F and the minimum over 70°F (38°C and 21°C). New arrivals were told that they were not allowed to complain until the temperature was over 100°F. Shortly after meeting Brenda for the first time I was driving through Khartoum in the heat of the day when I saw her cycling and stopped to have a word. She was on her way to the zoo to sketch the animals and birds, having come off night duty. I was impressed. We next met at weekly Scottish dancing practice at the house of the Director of Surveys, "Jumbo" Wakefield, brother of the Scottish Rugby International and Conservative Minister Lord Wakefield (whose initials were W.W.W.). This was almost the only summer social activity. The men wore white shorts, socks and tennis shoes, the women long cotton dresses, and we danced on the mastaba or patio in the open.

If it fitted with Brenda's shifts we rode at six in the morning, she on Aziza and I on Atiya. She was quite a good rider, having learnt from an expert when doing a holiday nursing job at a Butlin's holiday camp. We played tennis and swam at the Sudan Club; at both of these she was also good, indeed better at swimming than I was, with a good crawl, which was not surprising from a girl who had spent summers by the sea. At all sports she was graceful and elegant. Her height, just under six feet, in no way inhibited her movements. I record this as so many friends will remember her only after she was afflicted by rheumatoid arthritis at the age of 37. We also met at cathedral services and then the Supper Club. We found that our tastes in music, books and poetry were very similar or complementary.

Brenda's upbringing had been almost entirely in Brighton, though her parents came from the Isle of Man, where she was born on 21 April, 1924. Her father Albert Stephens was described in official records as a general dealer. He had served in a Guards regiment as a private soldier during the 1914/18 war, but had been invalided out of the army after contracting rheumatic fever. He then started a business selling surplus forces' equipment, which prospered. In 1927 with four children he moved to Brighton, believing that a drier and sunnier climate would be better for his health.

Brenda's mother, Doris Mamie Bell, had only the minimum education required at the time but she made sure that her children had all the opportunities within reach. Both Brenda and her sister Norma joined the Girl Guides and took a leading part. Brenda won a scholarship to Varndean Girls' Grammar School which she left after getting a respectable school certificate, the GCSE or O level of the time. In normal times Brenda would have gone to an art college, as art was her great passion, but as it was wartime she took a clerical job in the Council offices writing out ration books until she reached 18. She wanted to go into the Wrens (the Women's Royal Naval Service) but her father persuaded her that if she was to train for war work she might as well do something

Figure 10 Khartoum 1951. Brenda Stephens on Aziza.

which would be of use in peacetime as well. In 1942, in the middle of the war, she was accepted as a probationary nurse at the London, now the Royal London, Hospital.

After the war ended Brenda, who by then had completed her training, nursed at the American Hospital in Paris where she was plied with chocolates and cigarettes by grateful American servicemen. She then had an appointment at the hospital of the Anglo Iranian Oil Company in Abadan, Iran, before the nationalisation by Mossadeq. Then Mary Charles, a friend with whom she had trained at the London Hospital during the war, suggested that she apply for the Sudan Medical Service. Mary had joined the Service and nursed in El

Easher, the provincial headquarters of Darfur, where she had married Arthur Charles who was DC of Kutum.[4]

By the end of the year kind friends were beginning to invite Brenda and me out together; Mary and Arthur Charles, and the Waughs on their boat. A/DC Khartoum was usually a year's posting and I was delighted to be sent to Western Nuer District in the Upper Nile Province (now known as Unity State), almost as remote a post as one could find. John Udal returned from MECAS and took back his household goods, in good order I hope. He was posted to be A/DC Malakal District with a semi-independent command responsible for the Shilluk tribe based in Kodok, 460 miles south of Khartoum. This was formerly called Fashoda but had been renamed in deference to French sensibilities and the courage of Major Marchand and his men, who had made the remarkable journey from the Congo to the Upper Nile in 1898. After recovering the Sudan on behalf of the Khedive of Egypt and so regaining virtual control of the Nile waters, Kitchener was not about to cede what had been so hard gained. Eventually France abandoned its ambitions to establish a presence in the Upper Nile and Marchand withdrew. With Britain controlling the only feasible supply route, namely the Nile River from the north, a French military post was not sustainable. To make the situation even more difficult internationally, France's claim to the Upper Nile would have been in defiance of Egypt's rights. Kitchener flew the Egyptian as well as the Union flag, a practice which continued throughout the condominium until 1956. His campaign was a re-occupation of the Sudan by the internationally recognised right of the Khedive and not a conquest by a third party. This does not alter the reality that Kitchener and Britain were in charge. The situation remained so for whole period of the Anglo-Egyptian Condominium, notwithstanding frequent friction.

9

UPPER NILE PROVINCE: WESTERN NUER DISTRICT

The railway runs south from Khartoum to Kosti where it crosses the Nile and continues west to what was then the rail head at El Obeid, the provincial headquarters of the Province of Kordofan. Those going south transferred at Kosti to the regular post boat paddle steamer. Like the trains, the post boats were clean, smart and efficient. Sudan Railways ran the best monopoly nationalised industry I have experienced. With me were Mohammed, the two horses Aziza and Atiya and Mohammed Osman, the syce. The horses were led without trouble up the gangplank onto the open lower deck of a barge. There were two or three of these barges lashed to the actual paddle steamer carrying people, livestock and goods of every kind. Wood was stockpiled at intervals along the river and when we tied up local men would carry it aboard. The further south we went the less clothes they wore as we moved steadily against the current into Dinka country in Upper Nile Province.

One other passenger with whom I had interesting conversation was a slim bearded man of about 28, a French Canadian. He had been at a Canadian university and then the London School of Economics. He was now travelling widely to complete his education. His name was Pierre Trudeau. He wrote to me later from India and we corresponded for a while.

I was as myopic then as I had been earlier with Margaret Roberts (Thatcher) in my failure to forecast his future job of Prime Minister of Canada.

John Longe, the Governor of Upper Nile, based in Malakal, was very welcoming. He and Mary became good friends to Brenda and me in future years. I did the round of the provincial officers and met a unique group, the Jonglei Investigation Team. The Upper Nile is a vast evaporation basin. If the White Nile could be channelled in a direct line so that it does not form the huge swamps there would be much more water available for irrigation in the Northern Sudan and Egypt. However, this would have a dramatic effect on the ecology and the way of life of the Nilotic people, so a multi-disciplinary team was set up to examine all the implications. It was led by Paul Howell, the former DC of Central Nuer and author of 'A Manual of Nuer Law', along with hydrologists, an agronomist, a vet, a surveyor and so on. Some years later the independent government started the Jonglei canal from the south in Bor district. A French company imported a colossal trenching machine and made impressive progress through the deep black cotton soil, but the local people had not been consulted and became hostile. The French withdrew and left their huge machine to rust. It is very much to be hoped that when peace does come to the south the valuable research done by the Jonglei Investigation Team will be resurrected, but it will be many years before a mutually beneficial agreement to proceed is reached. Fortunately, the Jonglei Investigation Team's reports and findings are carefully preserved at the Sudan Archive in Durham University library.[1]

It was encouraging to find that there was a vacancy for a nursing sister as assistant to the Matron, Betty Tucker. Brenda wanted to move out of Khartoum and nurse Sudanese people, and two months later she duly arrived. The province was full of young bachelors, but by having known Brenda in Khartoum I was a step ahead of the competition.

The journey out to Bentiu, where I would be based, was by the district steamer, the Tamai, taking some two days. After the wide expanse of Lake No one enters the Bahr el Ghazal, the Gazelle River. It was now January 1952. In October 1953 I began to write a full account of the political situation and the work (see Chapter 12), so again I will limit this chapter largely to personal matters.

The only other British official was the DC Pat Garland. He was and remained a bachelor, who had previously been in the army and then became an administrator in British Somaliland. He had been appointed as A/DC and promoted when his DC was transferred to be Police Magistrate in Khartoum because of sickness, not improved by gin. Pat was very precise and everything highly ordered. I always thought that the skin of his servant was more polished than that of any other Nuer. He was kind to me and we got on well, though we were not really fellow spirits. I had a fairly independent command in the south of the district and Pat always backed me. As we went on trek at different times we did not overlap very much in Bentiu. The only other Europeans in the district were two Mill Hill Catholic Fathers, one Dutch and one Lithuanian, at a mission school five miles away, and two Church Missionary Society medical missionaries at Ler, my centre 85 miles to the south. Jim West was a doctor born in Kenya and Betty his wife was a nurse. I have kept in touch, and it was Betty who told me that the American Presbyterians had re-opened their hospital in 1979 after the first civil war and the expulsion of the missionaries. My daughter Stella was able to go there on her elective term from St Thomas's Hospital nearly 30 years after her parents had left. Many Nuer came in to greet her as the child (gat) of Bilrial (me) and Nyaok (Brenda), our Nuer names.

Pat announced that he was taking early leave, so in April at the age of 24 I was left in charge of the district nearly 200 miles from Malakal. The Sudan Almanac of 1952 states that Western Nuer District covered 14,175 square miles, which would have been accurate, and held a population of 168,000 which was stated to be approximate and was probably an underestimate. For comparison, the area of Wales is 8,015 square miles. Soon after Pat had left a chief's policeman appeared at my house in the afternoon. He held out a stick with a paper in a cleft for me to take. It was a letter in Nuer from a chief clerk about 80 miles away to say that there had been a fight in which five men had been killed, so I had to get there as soon as possible with some police and arrange the necessary investigations and trials by a chiefs' court.

Evelyn Waugh's novel "Scoop" has a very amusing account of innocent young Boot in London buying cleft sticks to send his dispatches, but if you wear no clothes how else do you carry paper? The Nuers' other solution to the problem was a cylindrical shield carved from ambatch, a sort of balsa wood, the material we boys used to make model aeroplanes during the war. It was hollowed out at each end for native tobacco and perhaps a few coins. (The Egyptian piastre was the currency, which greatly assisted Egyptian bribery.) The only other equipment for the Nuer traveller apart from the shield were two spears, one broad-bladed for hunting animals and the other barbed for fishing. If his wife followed she would have a Moses basket on her head containing a baby, some grain and a cooking pot. Being married she would wear a cotton fringe round her loins with her breasts uncovered. If there was an unmarried girl in the party she would wear nothing at all, except the family beads if she was on the marriage market.

I never felt a moment's fear during my two and a half months' isolation, and nor was I surprised at having so much authority so young. It all seemed quite natural, probably because of the self-confidence induced by growing up in a country which had ruled the world's largest empire and had stood alone against Hitler. We did not realise how weak the sacrifices of two world wars had left our country.

Brenda had taken early leave, probably to show that she was not in my pocket, and we overlapped for only about five days. When I took my leave I went to stay with her in her mother's flat on Brighton seafront. She had bought a green 1936 Austin 7, old but little used. She had arranged a visit to Glyndebourne and we took a picnic. In a beautiful evening it

Figure 11 A young Nuer man with ivory bangle, wire corset and beads.

was like heaven. In London we saw Peter Ustinov's *Love of Four Colonels*. Being straight from the lonely swamps I laughed inordinately and embarrassed Brenda. We drove to Blackbushe for her return flight, and I hired the car and drove north to see Mother again after a year.

Mother had been asked to keep house for Martin Cotton's father Clifford after his mother had died. There was room and I based myself there. In Brenda's green Austin Mother and I toured Scotland, ending at the Edinburgh Festival. I was fairly sure by then that my future would be with Brenda, but I looked up various girls who had been friends to be certain. Before marrying I had to ensure that Mother had a more stable home, and we bought a traditional cottage behind the street in the pretty village of Abbots Bromley, near Uttoxeter in East Staffordshire, called Spring Cottage. It was my British address and base for the next six years. Mother was as happy as she could be in her circumstances, and she took a job which she enjoyed as a matron in the girls' boarding school in the village, the School of St Mary and St Anne, part of the Woodard Foundation.

I now had no doubt and immediately on return to Malakal I proposed to Brenda in the sisters' mess, a pleasant house which she shared with Betty Tucker, the matron. She accepted the following morning, as always refusing to be taken for granted. I was 25 and she 28, an age difference which never caused a problem. There was a rule in the Political Service that one could not marry under the age of 27 without the Governor General's permission. I went straight to see John Longe, the governor, and he said, "There is no one I would rather see one of my officers marry than Brenda. I will recommend it and I am sure it will go through." He also said later, "If your wife were to be anyone other than Brenda, I would move you from Western Nuer District. Also, if you have a baby I will move you."

Our home circumstances made it difficult to envisage a wedding in England, so we decided to have it in Malakal at Christmas when the Province and the chiefs would get together for meetings and festivities. George Martin, the Provost of the Cathedral in Khartoum, who we both knew and liked, was to come to take the Christmas services and he agreed to marry us on 27 December. John Longe suggested that Brenda should come on the steamer with me on my return from leave to Bentiu to see her future home. As she opened the mosquito wire door a snake fell on her arm from the thatch above. It slipped to the ground and slithered away. Her cool reaction then and later showed that she really did want to marry me and could cope with Western Nuer. She returned to Malakal on the Tamai and set about the wedding preparations which almost all fell on her.

In December I was in Ler preparing for Tony Polden, the vet for the three Nuer districts, to come with his team to inoculate for rinderpest. This was a terrible scourge, and if we could control it the benefit to the people would be enormous. However, it was a major task to convince the Nuer to trust their precious cattle, worth as much as life itself, to the needle.

Virtually the whole province met in Malakal for Christmas. Officials had meetings, usually addressed by provincial officers, on such policy matters as agriculture, marketing and livestock, and there were parallel meetings usually devoted to trying to harmonise customary law across the Nuer regions. There was also a round of parties, tennis and swimming.

We were married in the inter-denominational church. The five-year-old bridesmaid and page were Jane Longe and Tim Clerk (known as Timsah or crocodile), the son of the Provincial Medical Officer. The reception was in the Governor's garden looking over the Nile. The guests included the Catholic and Sudanese nurses from the hospital and the senior chiefs from Western Nuer – about half each of Sudanese and British. Although it was not in the plan, after the Governor had spoken Head Chief Gatkek of the Leik Nuer summoned my interpreter Malual forward and announced that he would make a speech too. He said that they were very glad that one of their DCs was getting married as they considered a man only half a man until he took a wife. Bilrial had found a very long woman who must have cost many cows (Brenda was over 5'11" tall). I was not sure how Pat Garland, who was my excellent best man, took this, but he never followed Gatkek's advice to marry.

One of the Province's steamers, the Gordon Pasha, was to make a visit to the sawmill at Tonj, a Dinka district in Bahr el Ghazal Province, to collect sawn mahogany. The Upper Nile had virtually no building timber except dom palm poles. The Governor said that we could travel on the steamer to Bentiu and beyond, so the steamer was moored beside the garden. I carried Brenda up the gangplank and we waved goodbye to all our guests. We wanted the crew to share the cake and asked how many there were. The answer was 22.

There was an unexpected postscript to the wedding. In January 1980 I was on a RAF VC10 aircraft taking the first wave of election supervisors to Zimbabwe. The captain came past after we had flown over Khartoum in the dark and I asked him where we were. He looked at his watch and said that in one and a half minutes we would be over a little place I had never heard of called Malakal. I told him that not only had I been married there 27 years before, but our daughter was at that moment in the same province. He took me to the cockpit and showed me all the maps of the area.

Figure 12 Wedding, Malakal, 27 December, 1952. The bride made her own dress and the groom is wearing officer dress, used for formal occasions such as parades.

The Gordon Pasha called in at Bentiu for a few hours and continued south to Lake Ambadi. The river winds so much in the swamps that at one stage the same single tree was visible for a whole day. At Tonj we stayed with David and Vivien Biggs and loaded the timber onto a hired merchant's lorry. This broke down and we decided to walk in the heat of the day to join the steamer. Again there was no complaint from the bride. What a gem I had married.

We were soon off to Ler for the rinderpest inoculation programme. Would the Nuer respond to our propaganda? In the morning the plain was dotted with cattle being driven in by their singing owners. Tony Polden and his team were almost hidden by cattle, Nuer and dust as they worked throughout the day. There was one minor perquisite: since the vaccine had to be kept refrigerated Tony had a large mobile paraffin-fuelled fridge in which he kept his beer cold. The Food and Agricultural Organisation of the United Nations declared rinderpest extinct in 2011 and has ceased its field operations. I wrote an article on this and my memories of the first inoculation campaign in *Sudan Studies*.[2]

Meanwhile court and administrative business were continuing. Brenda was introduced and the following day we were told that her name would be Nyaok, which means daughter of the cattle, to remember the occasion on which a record number of cattle had been assembled – an excellent name. Pat had introduced me a year earlier on my arrival and the chiefs decided on Bilrial, which is a black bull with a

Figure 13 Tony Polden, the vet for the Nuer District, inoculating cattle for the first time against rinderpest (cattle plague), now declared extinct.

a white band across the middle and black spots on the band. I was told that Nuer has a vocabulary of 1000 words, of which 400 describe cattle. When a bilrial came up in the next cattle fines auction I had to buy it. It was kept in a byre behind my house and a man was paid to take it out for grazing and to sing to it.

We went on leave in May 1953 and spent our time between Brighton and Abbots Bromley, being introduced to each other's families and friends. For our second honeymoon we drove Brenda's Austin 7 to Italy, visiting Florence and Venice principally. The car was like a little green box on wheels with wire spokes: wherever it stopped it was surrounded by Italians muttering "antica!" in either sympathy or admiration. The top speed was a juddering 60 mph, even on the Lombardy autostrada. Neither of us had been to Italy before. Brenda wanted to see pictures and I to follow up my Oxford Renaissance studies. It was all that we hoped. There was one particularly agreeable incident when we were having an evening drink on the deck over the water at Pensione Calcina

Figure 14 Home and garden at Bentiu. We slept in the meat safe on top of the store room. The Bahr el Ghazal river is just behind it.

on the Zattere in Venice. I could not remember the Italian to ask the waiter for a match to light Brenda's cigarette. A charming American came to our aid, a Mr Milliken, who turned out to be the director of the museum of art at Cleveland, Ohio. His mother had been a Venetian and he had the use of her gondola. He invited us to take a tour of the city in this the following evening after dinner. He knew all the great buildings and many of the people who had lived in them. It was magical. Mr Milliken sent us Christmas cards with reproductions from the Cleveland collection for many years afterwards. He said that as an American one thing he envied us was "your beautiful young queen".

Queen Elizabeth II had recently been crowned, on the day that news arrived of the ascent of Everest. She was indeed beautiful and determined to do her duty, which she has done faithfully for over 60 years. We had a radio and also a record player, which was powered by a 12 volt car battery charged up on the Tamai. This was before transistors. The Tamai came into Bentiu from trek as we listened to the short wave commentary. The naked prisoners came to carry the trek equipment to the house and office. Each one insisted on greeting us in turn and waiting for a reply. This was disruptive and tantalising, but each man had to receive attention.

A word about the prisoners: they did have a simple white uniform of tunic and shorts, but to avoid getting them dirty they would hang them on the bushes. In any case they believed that a free man goes naked and clothes are a badge of servitude.

Another word about smoking: as I grew up almost everyone smoked. In the Forces there were cheap cigarettes and the common order was "Fall out for a smoke break". There was no idea that smoking was harmful to health, except a vague idea that one should not smoke when in serious sports training. I myself did not smoke because Father did heavily – and died of cancer at 67. Every time there was an increase in tax on tobacco, which happened every year during the war, Father would swear to give up. For the next fortnight he was

Figure 15 Two young Nuer girls on their way, with their belongings, to cattle camp between Ler and Ganglil, Western Nuer District. There is no protection from molestation or wild animals for miles around.

even more difficult to live with than usual and it was a relief when he reverted. This was clearly a drug which controlled him. Brenda took up smoking as a student nurse like all the others, as part of the process of growing up. In Northern Rhodesia, a tobacco producing country, cigarettes were good and cheap, part of the way of life. However, by the time of our final return to Britain in 1965 doubts were appearing and Brenda knew I did not like the mess and smell, though I never made an issue of it. As our Holland Afrika ship made its way up the Solent approaching Southampton Brenda took several hundred duty free, walked to the stern and threw them into the wake.

10

THE VIEW AT THE TIME

On our return from leave in the summer of 1953 it was clear that great events were afoot. I have found forgotten papers which show that I decided to keep a record at the time. It was over 50 years ago and some of it might seem odd now, even politically incorrect, but let it stand as it was written to form the rest of this chapter. There is an occasional pencil note by Brenda and she began to type it (but did not finish), so presumably she agreed with it.

THE OVERALL PICTURE

October 1953. Bentiu

It will be of interest perhaps to make a record of the events in this country during the next two years, as they strike and affect an Assistant District Commissioner working in one of the most primitive areas. Next month the Sudan is to hold its first elections under a self-governing constitution. Whichever party or group wins a majority in the House of Representatives will form a government possessing almost complete power in internal affairs. Reserved to H.E. the Governor General, Sir Robert Howe, will remain the powers of foreign affairs and defence, and a special responsibility for the public service and the backward parts of the country. In three years from the date of the inauguration of the new parliament the Sudan must exercise self-determination that will choose its future international status.

Egypt is pressing the Sudanese hard to unite with her. She is interested in gaining control of the middle reaches of the Nile and in recruiting good fighting men for her army. She also suffers from the delusions of greatness which impel immature nations to assert themselves at the expense of others. She imagines it her duty to recover the "rights" which she possessed as conqueror of the Sudan before Britain entered as usurper, as she sees it. Thirty years of propaganda and subversive activities directed particularly at the young intelligentsia have produced a small but vociferous party demanding complete unity with Egypt. This group would have little influence on the illiterate masses who do not get the free trips to the luxuries of Cairo, and did not the Sudan suffer sadly from a bitter rivalry between the two great religious sects, the Khatmia and the Ansar, which gives Egypt a foothold.

At the head of each of the sects or tariqas, which means path (by which one may find God), stands a very holy man, and between the two the feeling of antipathy is deep and personal. The Khatmia leader is Sayed Sir Ali el-Mirghani, who so long as the Codomini of Britain and Egypt stood together was the close supporter of the Government. His people come from the north and east of the Sudan, and many have always had commercial and cultural links with Egypt. The head of the other sect, the Ansar, is Sayed Sir Abdel Rahman el-Mahdi, the posthumous son of Mohammed Ahmed, the Mahdi or the Divinely Guided One who in 1880–4 overthrew the Egyptian government of the Sudan and in the process killed the Khedive's representative, General Gordon; he was not, it should be noted, a representative of the British Crown though appointed with British approval.

Mahdism in the early days of the Condominium was naturally a suspect force. A resurgence was always thought possible, and the intelligence reports were chiefly concerned with Ansar activities. Sayed Abdel Rahman, who had inherited his father's "baraka" or power of blessing, was regarded as the probable focus of any rebellious movement. He was made to live in a remote part of Blue Nile Province on a small government pension. After World War I the Government decided to forget the past and to reward SAR, as he is always called, for his quietude and loyalty. He was given land at Aba, an island on the White Nile near Kosti where his father first made the astonishing announcement that he was the Mahdi. He was an intelligent and able man, and quickly took advantage of the encouragement which the Government was giving to the growing of cotton. He was helped by the practice which his followers have adopted of stopping for a while to work in the fields of their holy leader, thus gaining baraka to help them on their weary pilgrimage from West Africa to Mecca.

As SAR grew more wealthy and more powerful, so Sayed Sir Ali el-Mirghani, or SAM, became jealous and afraid. He suspected the Government of playing false with him, its true and trusted supporter. In fact the Government was doing no more than magnanimously raising the defeated enemy, and inviting all citizens of the Sudan to share equally in its development. However, the terrible memories of the Mahdia, of the unspeakable atrocities committed by the war bands of the Khalifa Abdullahi upon the riverain and town-dwelling people who were largely Khatmia, went far too deep to be appeased by such a simple explanation. The Ansar comprise most of the fighting tribes of the Sudan, in particular the brave and brutal Baggara. The Khatmia feared that the British were permitting, perhaps actively encouraging, a resurgence of the Mahdist power which would in the future put the settled lands with their Mirghanist inhabitants once more at the mercy of the wild men from the desert.

Disturbed and piqued, SAM began to flirt with Egypt, which by this time, the thirties, had been deprived of any real share in the governance of the Sudan and was only too glad to do anything which might embarrass its British rulers. It so happened that the majority of the Sudanese intelligentsia which the Education Department produced from the thirties onwards were Khatmia, since they naturally came from the more advanced and settled areas, the Three Towns (Khartoum, Omdurman and Khartoum North) and Northern Province. They were encouraged by Egyptian politicians, and in particular by Ali Maher when he was Prime Minister in 1942, to develop their natural aspirations, but in the direction of a close union with Egypt. These Unionist intellectuals knew that they had no chance of gaining a popular following without the backing of a holy man, so SAM was dragged along half-reluctantly in their train. The result, after many splits, conferences and consultations, is the present National Unity Party which is standing at the elections, as far as can be gathered, for a form of dominion status in relation to Egypt. However, the pronouncements by various wings of the party are so conflicting or so vague that one must conclude that the real raison d'être of the NUP as it stands at the moment is the fight to get an anti-Mahdist majority in parliament.

Meanwhile those of the educated class, who had no love for Egypt but preferred to work for independence in their own way, were forced into alliance with SAR who founded the Umma or People's Party, of which his son Sayed Siddik became chairman. This party has co-operated throughout in the Government's programme of constitutional development and declares that it aims at the establishment of an independent Sudan, free of ties with Britain, Egypt or anyone else. In the eyes of its enemies it is doubly tainted; first, it is said to be a puppet of the British who use it to fight Sudanese national aspirations embodied in the Unionist movement; and second, it is believed to aim at the establishment of a monarchy with SAR as king. It seems likely indeed that this ambition has been entertained in the past, for it is only in the last month that the Umma party has declared unequivocally that its purpose is the establishment of a republic.

In the autumn of 1951 a new movement arose among a number of men of substance and tribal leaders who were weary of the barren and bitter rivalry between the two Sayeds. These men started with high hopes that they would win to themselves the most worthy on both sides, the moderate Khatmia who had no love for Egypt and appreciated the real virtues of the Sudan Government, and those on the Umma side who did not wish to aid the establishment of a Mahdist monarchy. The new party called itself the Socialist Republican Party – not a very happy title, but it was explained that it had to be Socialist because it was opposed to the cotton capitalists who led the Umma Party and who threatened to form themselves into an upper class of pashas as has happened in Egypt, and it was Republican because it was opposed to a Mahdist monarchy.

The Socialist Republicans (the SRP) began by incurring the hostility of SAR who feared, quite rightly, that many of his followers might desert. He accused the Government of encouraging the new party and then betraying him who had been its most loyal supporter. Meanwhile SAM was said to have given his blessing to the new party. He has always claimed – indeed, he still does claim – that he allowed his followers to join the Socialist Republicans if they wished. Many did so, stimulated by the recent activities of Egypt whose Government had in October 1951 abrogated the Condominium treaty and promulgated, without even an attempt at consultation, a servile constitution for the Sudan.

There were many outsiders, and many British officials, who saw in the SRP the best hope for the future peace and stability of the Sudan. It brought together members of the two rival sects into one political party, and, just as promising, it offered a chance of co-operation with the black south, for Ibrahim Bedri, the Secretary General, had served with great success as an A/DC in all three southern provinces. Unfortunately it seems that the sectarian pull has proved too strong. SAM probably became afraid that his followers would be badly split with the result that the Umma would romp home as easy winners. He has therefore brought practically all the Socialist Republicans within the fold of the National Unity Party, which has had to water down the pure wine of unity in order to accommodate the moderates. Many Ansar followers of the SRP have also returned to the Umma fold as a result of sectarian, financial, or family pressure. The SRP is thus much reduced in strength and the leadership consists now of a few strong-minded men, backed by a number of tribal leaders so secure in their positions that they can ignore the displeasure of both Sayeds. The party will probably win a few seats at the election and act as a centre force, though inclining to support the Umma as it stands for independence and heartily dislikes Egyptian ways.

The fourth factor in the new parliament will be the south. The Southern Sudan is an entirely different country from the north, the two being joined together only by the accident of conquest. The north is largely desert or semi-desert, the majority of its people possess skins in various shades of brown, its language and culture are Arab and its religion is Islam. Thus, although many diverse racial strains can be found in the five northern provinces there is an overlying unity provided by a common language, culture and religion.

In the south in the other land the people are black, pagan and split up into many tribal groups, each speaking its own language or dialect. Between the tribes traditional enmities exist and the memories of ancient wrongs go deep. The country consists of savannah, swamp, bush or forest. Communications are difficult and only maintained with great labour, mobilised by the personality and energy of the district commissioners. Before the Government came here the country had suffered appallingly from the activities of Northern Sudanese slavers. During the Egyptian period slave raids were encouraged by the officials of the government. The Khalifa took over and developed this thriving business. In such a poor country the human crop was almost the only wealth that could be exported. As a result the first British administrators who came to the south found people demoralised, without traditional authorities such as existed in the north, and with a terrible hatred for the Northern Sudanese.

For all these reasons, differences of race, colour, culture, language and religion, poor communications, administrative backwardness and ancient fears, the south will remain a special problem for as long as can be foreseen. It is more than the common minority question, for the south has a population of 3 million out of a total of probably 8.5 million. Thus the southerners comprise more than one third of the whole, and an active policy of assimilation to the north would probably cause a strong reaction and perhaps a demand for secession.

Politics entered the south only a few years ago, when representatives were sent to the old legislative assembly in 1948. But it is only during the last two years, when the pace of advance towards self-government has been so rapid, that a few southerners have begun to understand that their political actions will affect their whole futures and that they can no longer rely on the protection of their district commissioners. There have been a few who have tried to form a Southern Party to will support candidates who will best defend the interests of the south. These interests they interpret in three directions: the extension of education and economic development, in order to raise the standards of the south to match those of the north; maintenance of the present standards of administration, by which is meant retention of the British officials until there are Southern Sudanese trained to take their place; and resistance to possible attempts at exploitation by the north.

The Southern Party is still trying to organise itself and it seems that it will have little effect on the electioneering. However, it will probably form a nucleus around which Southern MPs may gather when they meet in the House of Representatives. At the moment most Southern candidates are standing as independents and the voting will be based upon their character, professions and record.

The Umma and the SRP, realising the resentment they may cause, have wisely not tried to run their own candidates. Instead they have been giving discreet support to the Southern Party, since it is strongly anti-Egyptian. The NUP, on the other hand, are trying to build up support by influencing certain important southerners in their favour. By a judicious combination of bribes and threats they may succeed in getting a few candidates returned. After the election the pressure on the successful candidates will be terrific. It will be painful to watch the strain which material temptations will impose on simple and unsophisticated characters who are untrained to bear such a responsibility. Few realise how great the responsibility will be. It may well be that the Southern Members will hold the balance between the two northern sects, and on the vital question of the union with Egypt their votes will be decisive.

THE LOCAL PICTURE

It is nearly two years since I was posted to Western Nuer as Assistant District Commissioner, or A/DC, and they have been the most full and profitable years of my life. The Nuer are one of the group of Nilotic tribes who inhabit the upper reaches of the Nile and its tributaries, chiefly in the Sudan but extending also into Uganda and Kenya. The principal tribes are the Dinka, Shilluk, Nuer, Anuak and Acholi. The Nilotic race has characteristics of its own which distinguish it from the other main ethnological strains of the Sudan – the Arab, Hamitic and Negroid. Though close to the Negro in culture, physically the Nilotic differs greatly, being tall and slender with only moderately full lips and a fairly high-bridged nose. Each Nilotic tribe has its own language, albeit with obvious affinities with the rest. It seems to be easy for a member of one tribe to learn the language of the others, but at inter-tribal meetings an interpreter is always necessary. Oddly enough the languages which are most readily mutually understandable are those of tribes living at the periphery of the Nilotic homeland, namely the Shilluk, Anuak and Jur.

The Dinka are the most numerous and the best-known of the Nilotic tribes, since they number over 1 million souls and adapted themselves early to the demands of the administration.

They extend over much of the Upper Nile and Bahr el Ghazal Provinces, inhabiting country which is either scrub, forest or flat open plains.

The Shilluk are much smaller in number, about 120,000, and live chiefly on a narrow strip of land on the west bank of the White Nile extending 300 miles north, south and west of Malakal. They are known chiefly for their politico-religious system, with their chief, the Reth, being one of the last of those priest-kings who first inspired J.G. Frazer to the studies which resulted in The Golden Bough. There is something of the atmosphere of the sacred grave of Nemi in the position of the Reth, who before the government came resembled very much the "Priest who slew the slayer, and must himself be slain".

It was the belief of the Shilluk that when the Reth's powers began to wane the tribe would lose its fertility, the women would become barren and the crops would fail. When the elders became convinced that this disastrous condition was imminent the ageing Reth would be approached and warned of his end. A grave would be dug, he would lie in it alive and the soil would be replaced. The spirit of the late Reth would hover uncertainly for a space, and would then descend on some member of his family who would be acclaimed as the new Reth. Of course, the Government forbade this custom, but it is only 20 years since the A/DC of the Shilluk last heard that the Reth was about to be buried some miles away from where he was at the time. He jumped on his horse, and riding for all he was worth he just succeeded in forestalling the murder.

The Government works through the Reth, who has vast influence among his people. The Egyptians, who have an irrigation station in Malakal, are trying to undermine his position as he is a strong supporter of the Government, but he is intelligent enough to understand what they are doing and has resisted the paid troublemakers very firmly.

The Shilluk are an interesting people to work with, but they have an aloof and detached manner, which can be rather irritating. Their country is dull – a bare hot windswept ridge parallel with the river, and the only features are the clusters of huts and isolated dom and doleib palms. It is difficult to discover a norm in facial types, but any Shilluk is easily recognised by his tribal markings, a row of knobs of raised skin above the eyes stretching from ear to ear.

The Nuer are the most warlike, independent and proud of the Nilotic tribes. They number about 450,000 and form a solid block across the central part of Upper Nile Province. Most of this land they have conquered from the Dinka during

Figure 16 Nuer man and Atar Dinka women, recognised by their type of skirt.

the last hundred years. The tradition of the Nuer is that they came from a comparatively small area between the Bahr al Jebel (the White Nile) and Bahr el Ghazal, and spread east in search of good grazing. They conquered the Dinka who were in occupation and absorbed them into their own society, imposing the Nuer language, custom and culture. This was not difficult as the two peoples are very much alike and acknowledge each other as cousins, but the Nuer possess a consciousness of being superior.

The visitor would wonder why the Nuer chose to extend eastwards, for their land has little obvious attraction. There are great stretches of permanent swamp and practically the whole area is liable to flooding during a year of high river or heavy rains. The grass grows eight feet high, snakes and lions abound, and the mosquitoes are a constant torment. In the dry season from November to April the grass turns brown and is burnt off, and the scene is of endless flat plains of baked cracked cotton soil, stretching away in every direction until they meet the harsh metallic blue sky. One may go miles to find shade, and yet more miles to find water. When a belt of forest is reached on the higher ground, it is usually of poor thorn scrub and useless for building. Yet the Nuer believe that this unfavoured land is the best on earth, for it yields what to them is the priceless gift of fresh green grazing all the year round for their cattle. At the end of the dry season in March and April before the rains break, fresh pasture may be found on the edges of the diminishing swamps and on the flood plains called toiches.

The Nuer are divided into three administrative districts, Eastern, Central and Western Nuer, with their headquarters respectively at Nasir on the Sobat River, Fanjak on the Zeraf and Bentiu on the Ghazal. It has been necessary to place all the headquarters on the rivers, because although the people have their permanent habitations inland on the ridges of higher sandy ground, the roads are impassable for six months of the year and then all surface communication is by steamer and foot.

These Nuer districts are probably the most backward in the country. They are also the happiest, by a paradox which is no longer surprising. Administration started during the early twenties, but 1927 to 1929 was a time of troubles. The first DC of Western Nuer, Vere Fergusson, was murdered and there were two revolts in Central Nuer. Military patrols and punishments followed until the Nuer learnt that the Government meant to be master and was not to be put off by the inaccessibility of the country as previous rulers had been. The methods were harsh but the lesson was learnt, and hand in hand with the punitive measures went a policy of rebuilding tribal life under Nuer local authorities. Slowly the people's confidence was won until at the present time the Government enjoys tremendous prestige. Its actions are assumed to be beneficent and the people will usually promise co-operation, even though conservatism or laziness mean they do not always carry out their promises. Yet as recently as 1936 a DC of Central Nuer was complaining that all he saw of his parishioners was their bare bottoms as they fled into the bush to avoid paying the taxes.

Western Nuer was the most backward of the three districts because its communications were the most difficult. Perhaps also its people are the wildest of all the Nuer since they are the purest strain, unmixed with conquered Dinka. The murder of Captain Fergusson in 1927 naturally slowed down progress since the next few years had to be devoted to settlement and pacification. Until 1947 the District Headquarters was on a steamer which cruised on the Bahr el Jebel and the Bahr el Ghezal. The DC and A/DC lived on the steamer between treks, and kept the office and stores on board. There was no administrative centre for the district, no prison, no police headquarters and no store. The steamer would tie up at a landing stage constructed to serve a particular tribe. The carriers would be collected and the DC then walked inland until he came to the court centre, which might be one or up to seven days trek away. If it was during the rains he would have to wade and the journey would take twice as long. Having arrived at the court centre the chiefs would come in. For a month the DC and chiefs would sit together and all administrative affairs and judicial cases were settled. Then the DC would return to the steamer and move on to the next landing stage, or meshra, to repeat the process.

The system suffered from the same disadvantages as the medieval English monarchy which was similarly peripatetic. Plaintiffs with appeals never knew where to find the appellate authority, and might follow him around for many months before defendants could be obtained and the case heard. Financial affairs were difficult to administer when the treasury was not in any fixed place, and revenue could easily go astray. An emergency could find the executive authority far away in some inaccessible part of his domain – and yet the instinct which inspired both the Norman kings and the early DCs was the right one in the circumstances. It was essential that authority should be shown to the people so that they should learn to know its ways and to fear, respect and trust it. This the ruler could only do by coming among the people and living with them awhile. As J.S.R. Duncan has said, the early DCs, by means of great energy and force of personality, succeeded in imposing their will on a virile and proud people. We are now reaping the benefit of our predecessors' efforts and have inherited the prestige which they built up.

The file of hand-over notes makes interesting reading. B.J. Chatterton, who was A/DC from 1932 to 1937, describes the administration of those days as "trying to keep nine obstreperous monkeys up nine different sticks. (There are nine tribal areas.) As soon as one is left alone it immediately tries to climb down. After the leave season it is usual to find most of the monkeys on the ground. One of the main reasons for this is that there is nothing permanent and material to keep the monkeys up. As soon as the DC returns from trek to the steamer all the Nuer say: 'The Government has gone. Let us play.'"

Chatterton was the first to demand a land-based, permanent district headquarters, yet even he thought it necessary to split the district into two, making a sub-district headquarters at Ler. He did not think it possible to make a road from Bentiu to Ler. That road is now, after much toil, the administrative axis of the district.

The war held up the development which otherwise would probably have come in the early forties. As it was, the building of the district headquarters at Bentiu did not start until 1946. Then the development of the road system began in earnest. The Nuer learnt how to work, and if they were slow in learning they lost their bulls in great numbers. It was a harsh but necessary discipline. The DC and A/DC, Douglas McJannet and Donald Rae, drove the Nuer hard and themselves harder. They laboured in the heat of the day making earth ramps and constructing bridges, showing the people how the job was done and how much could be achieved by one man who worked hard. By 1950 the system was almost complete and every tribal area except one, the Nyuong, could be reached during five months of the year. McJannet and Rae handed over to Will Thompson, Pat Garland and myself an adequate and viable administrative system. What has been done in the last four years has brought many changes. The country has been opened up and great benefits brought to the people, but the form of administration built up in the years 1946 to 1949 has remained fundamentally unchanged, and the task of recent years has been to enlarge and improve.

BENTIU AND ELECTION ARRANGEMENTS

We returned from leave almost four weeks ago and the local atmosphere has again become part of us. I had at first intended to begin immediately with the writing of a diary but decided that the introduction was necessary, at the risk of dullness, in order that what I say might have relevance. Further, I was, I felt, out of touch, and must wait until the influence of Italy, France and home had been replaced by the Sudan and Western Nuer.

It was a great pleasure to return and find so many smiling faces obviously pleased to see us. We had expected that with the approach of the elections the propaganda of lies and slander, which is the main tactic of the pro-Egyptians, would have penetrated to Bentiu. We thought that many, even among the Nuer, would be watching us carefully and wondering whether we were really such benefactors as we had always appeared. Even worse, perhaps our most loyal supporters would be afraid to show their friendship in case it might later get them into trouble if a pro-Egyptian government came into power. Indeed this has been the strongest Egyptian line in the south: "You had better give us your support because we are going to replace the British and it will go badly with you if you are friendly with them." Major Salah Salem started this odious form of attack on simple people during his mischievous tour last December, and it has been faithfully copied since.

So we were relieved to find that Bentiu's happy atmosphere had not changed. The station looked fresh, colourful and neat, and a crowd was gathered at the landing stage to meet the steamer consisting of officials, police, workmen, prisoners and merchants. Some of the merchants have formed a Unionist Party committee, but one feels that they are acting more out of sectarian loyalty than political conviction. Certainly it does not seem to have affected their attitude towards ourselves personally, whereas the fervent Unionist will usually employ rudeness, at least in public, as a proof of his political faith. The local NUP Chairman, a Bentiu merchant called Mekki Mohd Ahmed, came into the office the other day to ask me to get him some bamboos from Shambe when I next go there in the steamer. As he was leaving I said half-jokingly to him, "You wouldn't get all this help from an Egyptian mufattish (DC), at least not without a consideration." He went out laughing his head off at such an absurd idea as an Egyptian in Bentiu: "No, no, that would never happen!" It never occurs to him that if his party gets into power Egypt will expect a return for all the money she has spent on propaganda and bribery. Egyptian officials and adventurers will flood in and acquire powerful posts. They will only be dislodged by a rebellion, as in 1881–5. Yet Mekki and people like him see the political picture only in terms of sectarian loyalties. He is Khatmia; Sayed Ali has backed the NUP; therefore, he believes that to do his religious duty he must work for the NUP. He has no understanding of the consequences which would follow from NUP success, and even if he did have such foresight, he could hardly go against the wishes of the Sayed.

It has been a pleasant month in Bentiu, spent mostly in the office organising and planning for the trekking season and catching up with all that has happened during our leave. October is a month of preparation, getting everything ready for the opening of the roads when the wheels will begin to turn. We have started to dig a well in the native lodging area, finished a deck tennis court, brought all police, prison and financial administration up to date, put the electoral organisation into being, and warned all workmen who are to go out on jobs away from Bentiu. Meanwhile work on the roads has been going ahead. Messages have been coming in continually from the chiefs, reporting progress and asking for help in dealing with headmen and people who shirk the work. The answer is to seize a bull from every defaulter and hold it until he appears for work, which he does very soon. When the road is finished he will appear before the court and get his bull back, usually on payment of a small fine. Each tribe has to maintain a certain length of road and the work is classed as a civil duty. A man may work thirty days, but as he only turns out once every four or five years, it is no hardship and is within the ten days' civic duty a year allowance specified by the International Labour Convention.

There have been a few amusing or interesting legal cases. One concerned a policeman's wife, a pretty Zande girl who saw a bicycle outside a hut and could not resist the temptation of trying it out. Her husband who was escorting a working party of prisoners was astonished to see his wife, who he thought was at home making his lunch, riding unsteadily but happily through Bentiu. He raced after her, shouting, and eventually pulled her off after a scuffle. The girl was not at all abashed, even when the case came for trial and she had to pay a 10s fine and £1 damages to the owner of the bicycle.

Another case was of a Dinka thatcher who had stolen the wife of the Nuer farrash (caretaker) of the steamer. The Nuer, Reth, was quite prepared to part with the woman, who turned out to be the subject of one of my wife's drawings and who we knew to be barren. The dispute was over the amount of the bride price, which I got them both to agree to be £11, to be paid in eight instalments with no deposit. So much easier than buying a television set.

These personal cases should really be settled by the native or chief's courts, and they usually are. With detribalised government employees and hangers-on, however, it is sometimes simpler and more satisfactory to see the case oneself. Unless both parties are amenable to tribal discipline an appeal from the chief's court is very likely, so that much more trouble is caused in the long run.

Our newly arrived clerk Saad Farag is in trouble. (The last one, who rejoices in the name of Gabriel Beriberi Atalla, has resigned to stand for election to the Senate. He is quite capable but rather unstable. His faults of character have prevented him from becoming an administrative officer, and as a result he has become pro-Egyptian.) Saad Farag came with us on the steamer when we returned from leave, and seemed a quiet inoffensive little Zande about 40 years old. A fortnight later a letter arrived from the Kadi (the judge of Muslim law) of Malakal. It appeared that Saad was a Christian in spite of his name, and had gone through a form of marriage with a Muslim woman in Malakal in June. The wedding was in accordance with Muslim custom, which is pretty free and easy, and the divorce which took place a month later was also by Muslim custom and even simpler than the marriage. Now information has been laid against Saad by one of his colleagues that he had concealed the fact that he was a Christian. The Kadi says that marriage between a Christian man and a

Muslim woman is forbidden, which is true of Muslim law, but not of course of civil marriages. The offence under the Sudan Penal Code is of "dishonesty or with a fraudulent intention going through a ceremony of being married knowing that he is not thereby lawfully married", which is punishable by imprisonment of up to seven years. Since Saad went through a form of marriage without revealing that he was a Christian there is a prima facie case against him, and I had to make a preliminary enquiry. He put in a statement beginning, "Since I did not wish to contract V.D. in the future I asked Mohammed Eff Farag the Head Accountant to find me a wife in Malakal." He admitted that he was a Christian and that he had a wife married in a Christian ceremony in Wau. His defence was that the sponsors of marriage knew perfectly well that he was a Christian and did not warn him that he was committing an offence. The information, he claimed, was lodged because it turned out that the woman he married had a lover, who thought of this method of revenge for the loss of his mistress. Saad has certainly been foolish and immoral and is probably guilty of the offence, but, he says, if these Muslim friends of his were so disturbed that he, a Christian, should marry a Muslim woman, why did they not advise him to take a concubine in the first place? It certainly does seem that the motive for the complaint is animus against Saad, partly because he married a woman who was another man's mistress and partly because he is a Christian. If the case comes to court he will call the Head Accountant (now posted elsewhere) as a witness for the defence, and no doubt some dirty washing will come to view. I have commented in the letter forwarding the enquiry that it may appear in the course of the trial that Mohamed Farag the Head Accountant should be charged with abetment. This will be seen by the clerks and may have the effect of causing the complaint to be withdrawn, in which case Saad Effendi would make a public apology and the affair would close. It is not a case I should like to try. There are only two classes of cases in which the impartiality of the British as Magistrates could be challenged in this country – those concerning other British, or Muslim against Christian. In practice the magistrate usually leans over backwards in order that justice should appear to be done.

My wife has been very busy getting the house in order and making sure the servants now fully realise that leave has ended, and with it the lazy life of the cattle byres. We brought a few wedding presents of silver from England and have enjoyed giving our home some civilised touches. Silver brings mellowness to rooms and tables in this country, minimising the ordinariness of cheap painted furniture. It has the great advantage that it does not break during transfers and here it does not suffer from its English disadvantage, that there is no one to clean it.

We are fortunate in our house, which was built by F.D. McJannet, the DC in 1947, for only £1,200. The present DC Pat Garland had a new house built for him for £3,400 while he was A/DC and decided to stay in it after his promotion, which proved to be just as well since I with the larger house am now married, and he is still a bachelor.

It is a long low bungalow with an enormous thatched roof, which gives it the appearance of an old-fashioned English farmhouse. The eaves reach far out so that the walls are always in the shade. The rooms are large and high with concrete block floors polished to look like stone flags. Through high brick arches one passes from verandah to sitting room and thence to the dining room. Beside the verandah I have constructed a small fountain, which plays during the heat of the day. The impression is of spaciousness and coolness, a tremendous relief when coming in hot from the burning sun at midday. Off the dining room is a large store, and a covered, mosquito-wired passage leads to the pantry and kitchen. The sitting room opens on the other side into the large bedroom and then into a bathroom almost as big, decorated in blue and black with red and white curtains. It contains a large built-in wardrobe and serves as my dressing room. I have put in a door leading from the verandah so that servants do not need to go through the bedroom, a refinement made necessary by marriage. The bucket lavatory connects with the bathroom by another mosquito-wired covered passage, so that the building has the shape of a hollow E with one projection shorter than the other. In the garden is a small room with outside steps leading up to a large meat safe on its roof. Here we sleep during the dry months, overlooking the garden and the river, where we can hear the fish splashing and the hippo grunting.

The garden looked beautiful on our return from leave, the lawns a bright green and the shrubs and climbing plants well grown and in flower. The annuals sown in seed boxes were a disappointment, and only the balsam has got away. Germination seems to be difficult here and even when seeds come up they often die away when only half an inch high.

Figure 17 On the veranda at Bentiu. Brenda is painting Nyador, the wife abducted by Deng Duot, our cook when we were on tour in the river steamer, Tamai. He was ordered to pay the bride price from his salary for years thereafter. Their first child was called Philip Babur – babur being the Arabic for the steamer which facilitated the abduction.

Yet when flowers have a good start they usually thrive, producing prolific blooms, seeding themselves and giving pleasure for months. Fortunately the roses are doing well, and along with the gardenias which enjoy the rains they provide plenty of flowers for the house. The free-growing lantana with its variety of colours is also very useful for small posies, combining well with the coral creeper and a delicate blue creeper whose name I cannot discover. We were particularly pleased with a border of cannas which we planted on the river's edge before we went on leave. They had grown to seven feet in height, a forest of brilliant red and yellow blossoms, masking an untidy area of rushes and coarse grass as we had hoped they would.

GANGLIL, 31 OCTOBER 1953

The first trek of the season started six days ago, when we left Bentiu on the steamer "Beatrice" at eight o'clock of a Sunday morning. Now we are installed for six days among the Nyuong Nuer, the southernmost tribe of the district, 150 miles away from Bentiu. Ganglil, their court centre, is the least accessible and most uncomfortable of the villages which have to be visited regularly, yet at the same time I enjoy coming here because anything that can be done is so obviously useful, and what is more, appreciated.

Half past seven in the evening finds us seated in our mosquito room, which is a net eight feet square supported on a bamboo framework. Suspended outside the room on a tripod is the pressure lamp, offering a quick and giddy death to thousands of insects of apparently infinite varieties. The netting wall nearest the lamp is strewn thick with them: moths of every size, praying mantis and grasshoppers over two inches long, huge armour-plated beetles which come to rest as heavily as thrown pebbles. Inside the mosquito room we have an old goat hair rug from Aleppo for greater homeliness, the radio, two tables for our drinks, books and evening meal, and

Figure 18 Ganglil, the most southerly court centre in Western Nuer District. Two girls bring gifts of fresh milk. The gourds had been cleaned with cows' urine.

the collapsible chairs in which we are sitting. It is so hot and the mosquitoes are so persistent that we have taken the easy path and after our baths have changed straight into long sleeved pyjamas – let no one blame us for being slovenly unless he has himself lived in Ganglil.

There is no breeze. It is the end of the rainy season and the damp is still with us, sticky and stifling. Lightly clothed though we are and two hours after sunset though it be, we sit and gently sweat. The air is so humid that the clothes on our bodies will not dry but hold to the skin like soaked blotting paper. We drink our whiskies, warm and strong, and feel better. By a recurrent miracle we switch on the wireless and hear Sir Harold Nicholson's urbane voice discussing world affairs and realise clearly that we, hidden away in the most backward part of Africa, are playing a very small part. A servant hands in roasted peanuts. Too tired tonight for chess and too uncomfortable to read, it has been a long day; seven in the morning to six at night, amid the flies, the heat and the shouting people. The pressure lamp burns low and a servant pumps it so that I can see to write again. A few mosquitoes, some formidable beetles and a high-jumping cockroach are sharing the room with us. We take a turn with the flit gun and fly swatter. The insecticide sold by the Sudan Ministry of Health is a great boon, being much cheaper than the proprietary brands. This country would be almost unbearable without flit; it means much more than refrigerators and fans, which in any case one is without when on trek, which is rather more than half the time.

At half past eight the dinner arrives. It is in conditions such as these that our Nuer cook, Deng, makes up for his roguery and roughness. However bad the mosquitoes, rain or wind, somehow he manages to give us a well-cooked three-course meal. Tonight there is onion soup, then roast partridge with spinach and rice. We forgive him for taking the easy course with the sweet and serving paw paw and grapefruit salad. Garwec, the suffragi or waiter, passes the dishes through a window in the netting and we serve ourselves.

By nine we are in bed, as even if sleep does not come soon, which it usually does, it is the best place to read. The mosquito net is a much smaller area than the room and therefore easier to keep clear of the insects. We had a shock yesterday when just as she was going to sleep Brenda saw a black scorpion crawling up the net – inside. Our empty-headed assistant cook Latjor had left the bedding on a small pile of timber for a while. The scorpion had crawled among it and Latjor had not noticed it when he made the bed. We think with horror of what the night might have brought had we not seen it before turning off the light. The sting is agony, but not fatal to adults.

The first day out from Bentiu on the steamer brought us to Lake No at eight in the evening. Professor Arnold Toynbee and his Study of History has taken the following description from Sir William Garston in his report on the Basin of the Upper Nile in 1904.

The scenery of the Bahr el Jabel (White Nile) throughout its course through the Sudd is monotonous to a degree. There are no banks at all, except at a few isolated spots, no semblance of any ridge on the water's edge. Reedy swamps stretch for many kilometres upon either side. Their expanse is only broken at intervals by lagoons of open water. Their surface is only a few centimetres above that of the water level in the mire when at its lowest, and a rise of half a metre floods them to an immense distance. These marshes are covered with a dense growth of waterweeds, extending in every direction to the horizon.

Throughout this whole region, more especially between Bor (to the south) and Lake No, it is extremely rare to see any sign of human life. The whole region has an aspect of desolation beyond the power of words to describe. It must be seen to be understood.

As one becomes more familiar with this scenery, however, the horror of the desolate changes to a fascination with the grandeur of spacious peace. The waste of grass and water gives a feeling of liberation. The world "of telegrams and anger" seems utterly remote. A sense of isolation may well steal on one, but it is an isolation not fearful but splendid. There is a sense of unreality, of detachment from the earth; it is as though it were the end of the world.

In the late afternoon we take tea on the roof of the steamer. The air is still and the gorgeous colours of the setting sun bring an extraordinary beauty to the swamps. A few cormorants swim and dive; a startled hippo grunts; an occasional fish splashes and deep blue green shadows spread across the waters.

121

Figure 19 The paddle steamer Tamai, used for touring when the roads were closed. The barge we lived on is on the left of the picture, usually pushed in front of the paddle unit to get more air.

This evening as we were looking from the steamer we surprised a hippo in very shallow water. It ran away with unexpected speed, its body an almost indecent pink, and found refuge among tall rushes. Hippos are very common in the Ghazal and Jebel but it is unusual to see them out of the water. Normally they show only their nostrils and tiny ears, as they snort with half-fearful indignation at the invasion of their domain.

The hippopotamus is a peaceful beast but very dangerous when aroused. Nuer give him a wide berth in their dug-out canoes, because although he will not attack a canoe without reason he can easily become frightened and upset it. He is then liable to snap angrily at the bodies squirming in the water. The Nuer say that they fear the hippo more than the crocodile. The crocodile may be cunning and cruel but a grown man usually loses only a limb; a hippo can bite a man in two with one chomp of this jaws. I was myself once in a canoe in a narrow stretch of the Ghazal; Majok the ferryman was resting and his son paddling. We saw a hippo's snout cruising slowly towards us, about 20 yards away. I have never seen Majok move so quickly as when he seized the paddle from his son and turned the canoe into the papyrus, to allow the hippo to pass serenely by.

We took with us on the "Beatrice" to Lake No the electoral committee, which was to carry out the primary elections among the Dinka at Riangnom. We have three Dinka tribes in Western Nuer, who call themselves as a whole the Ruweng – that is, those living in Panaru, the Land of the Dawn. They number about 35,000 and inhabit a huge dry almost treeless

Figure 20 Dinka girls drawing water from the Bahr el Arab river.

plain, stretching up to and merging with the Baggara Arab grazing lands along our northern frontier.

One of the more extraordinary provisions of our International Electoral Commissions is the method of indirect elections. It was a triumph for the advocates of common sense that the Commission agreed to any indirect elections at all, though it must surely have been obvious, one would have thought, that among a backward and illiterate population with no knowledge of parties or policies, or indeed of anything outside their own districts, direct elections on the British model must be a farce. Yet the Commission cut down the indirect constituencies to the absolute minimum, permitting thousands of unsophisticated voters to be exposed to glib politicians ranting about matters which to the electors have no meaning or relevance. The capacity of the voter to make a choice seems to be of no importance; so long as a decision which can be hailed as the will of the people is obtained, democratic theory will have been observed and the Sudanese will no doubt live happily ever after.

Indirect elections do have the virtue of ensuring that the electorate knows something of what is going on. The method is to obtain delegates from each tribal section who will later form an electoral college to carry out the actual election of the member. The candidates are thus able to meet and speak to the whole body of electors, who will themselves be presumably men of enterprise and intelligence above the average. Indirect elections have three other advantages; they ensure that the whole electorate is represented, where if the direct method were used the ignorance and laziness of the population and the difficult communications would mean that only those living near the polling stations would exercise their vote – some 10 per cent at most. The second advantage of indirect elections is their simplicity, a virtue greatly to be sought after when government is everywhere becoming more complicated. This leads on to the third advantage of the indirect method, which is that the risk of fights is almost eliminated since the electoral college can be expected to consist of persons of intelligence and substance.

At the end of May the Electoral Commission eventually agreed on which were to be the indirect constituencies. Fortunately the two constituencies of this district, Western Nuer Jebel (west of the Bahr el Jebel) and Western Nuer Ghazal (north of the Bahr el Ghazal), were included. Then the debate began about the method of electing delegates to the electoral colleges. Our first plan, before the Cairo agreement of February 1953 and the commission which it set up, was to form the college from the chiefs, who would certainly constitute the most representative and intelligent body to be found. However, it was objected that chiefs would be under the influence of the DCs, which is probably true and very flattering, since the chiefs are open to our influence not because they fear us but because they have found in practice that to follow our advice is to the benefit of their people. Anyway, an electoral college of chiefs could obviously not be democratic, so the next proposal would be to form a college, a much larger one this time, from the headmen of the clans or gatwots. The gatwot is the senior active member of the family group. His title means literally "son of the stud bull", and he is the leader and representative of the ordinary Nuer in his public social or economic pursuits, whether it be making roads, collecting taxes, discussing marriage cattle, holding dances or migrating to the cattle camps. An electoral college consisting of gatwots would therefore be completely representative of the people and far too large to be subject to the much publicised, but quite fictitious, secret pressure by the DC. However, it seems that gatwots are not known in New Delhi or Washington, so this method also was ruled out as undemocratic.

We were thus saddled with that greatest of all absurdities, the election of delegates by universal manhood suffrage, with the whole paraphernalia of electoral rolls, polling booths, voting boxes and the rest – and this in areas which are among the most backward in the world, where the majority of the population goes naked and only one in a thousand can read, and where the roads are only open for six months in the year.

The preparation of the electoral rolls was in itself a difficult job. The tax lists were used as a basis, but they contain many boys under 21, and exclude the old and infirm who are unable to work. No Nuer knows his age, so all had to be asked: "Were you born before run koriom, the year of the locust, or run Coriat?" (the year Mr Coriat came to Western Nuer). Very often they did not know, so the second test was: "Were you garred (i.e. did you receive the marks of initiation into manhood) before Dhuorian left and Makwerial came?" Dhuorian is Mr Wedderburn-Maxwell who left in 1946, being succeeded by Makwerial, Mr McJannet. It was not a very certain method of compiling accurate rolls, but it was the best that could be devised.

The Returning Officers all over the country are Sudanese, it having been decided very rightly that they must do the actual hard work of running their first elections. For the Jebel constituency we nominated the Administrative Assistant, an intelligent young Dinka called Andrew Wieu.[1] The Ghazal constituency Returning Officer is Mohammedd Tigani Sollum, the accountant, a gentlemanly and balanced northerner. They each devised a plan whereby the electoral committees would split and the separate parts go to a tribal centre, staying there for several days to persuade the people to come in before holding the primaries. Since the polling stations will each serve an area of about 30 miles radius a 10 per cent poll will be very satisfactory, but the Commission has been warned to expect this. It does not seem to mind absurdities so long as it is "democratic" – the magic word.

Fortunately, when the day for the closing of nominations arrived there was only one candidate in the Jebel constituency, Joshua Malual Mut, my interpreter. He is a pleasant young man, quite intelligent but unsophisticated. He is perhaps rather weak, but he is a Christian and has enough public spirit I think to put the interests of the Nuer before his own comfort. The other candidate was five hours late for his nomination and had to be rejected. It seemed hard as he had walked 85 miles through water, but the rules were rightly inflexible. This man was a policeman called Bruno Mub Liveng, a sound but rather simple fellow. He is not nearly so well suited for the position of MP as Malual, but he has the advantage of being a local man. I have several times been told by chiefs that they do not want a "foreigner" as their representative: Malual is of the Lak tribe in Central Nuer. There will be some feeling over Bruno's rejection in his home area of Dok, especially as there is some incipient political activity in Ler, its court centre. However, it is worth dealing with that to be spared an election, and to have the more suitable man returned into the bargain.

The Ghazal constituency, being the northern part of Western Nuer District, has four candidates, three independent and one National Unity Party (NUP), put up by Mekki and his committee. Typically, the NUP candidate is the son of a sacked head chief and one of a family well known for drunkenness and dishonesty. His father, Tivil Ran, was a great man before the Government came, and he himself, Joseph Gang Tivil, was Jack Wilson's clerk and was with him when he was speared by a mad Dinka woman in 1941. In the fracas he seized Wilson's shotgun and shot a man standing nearby. I am told confidently that he can expect no Dinka votes. He was sacked for being drunk, and for some years has lived in his village and cattle camp without clothes. His brother Buth threw the court books into the river in 1950 when fighting drunk and then disappeared to Cairo where many of the disappointed find refuge. From there he has persuaded Joseph to emerge from obscurity and fight the election on behalf of the cause of unity with Egypt.[2]

The other candidates are Yunis Thinath Liep, our only Nuer merchant who served in the Sudan Defence Force during the war and rose to the rank of corporal. Until recently he was the obvious favourite, but many are now saying that he is too much influenced by northern customs and habits to be relied on to promote Nuer interests. The other two in the field are Mamun Muyan from the Leik Nuer, a medical dresser, easygoing and rather lazy, and Michael Cang de Bilkwei, brother of the Head Chief of the Ruweng Dinka, a person of position and influence, perhaps the soundest of them all. He only just qualifies as a candidate under the literacy rule, however, and is so ignorant of the world outside his people and cattle that I fear that he will be only a cipher at Khartoum. It will be interesting to see what the result of this quadruple contest will be, and afterwards how the successful candidate of a not very encouraging bunch behaves in parliament.

11

ZERAF DISTRICT:
THE FINAL SUDAN CHAPTER

The 1953 contemporary record ended abruptly as new events occurred. Bill Carden, the DC of Central Nuer, had been offered a post in the Diplomatic Service along with two or three other colleagues. Apart from recruiting good men, there may have been the intention of improving morale in the Political Service whose members were now naturally worried about their futures. Bill decided to take the bird in the hand and left forthwith, sacrificing the expected compensation for loss of office. Central Nuer was a very large district and the Governor, John Winder, who had himself been DC there during the war, divided the district into Zeraf to the west and Lou Nuer to the east. The Lou were a large tribal group who occupied a vast, bare and inhospitable plain which had always presented problems of access and administration. Bill Carden began his handover notes: "The joining of Lou to the old Zeraf Valley District in 1946 was a mistake". He pointed out that in most years there was an eight-month gap when neither DC nor A/DC was in Lou. The reason for this was simply that it is 155 miles from Fanjak, the district headquarters, to Waat, the headquarters of the Lou Nuer, and from April to December it has to be walked. Philip Lyon Roussel, who had been A/DC of Waat Sub-District, was to become DC of Lou Nuer District with his headquarters at Akobo on the River Pibor.[1] This is a tributary of the Sobat, itself a tributary of the White Nile which it joined south of Malakal. Akobo was actually the centre of its own district for the administration of the Anuak along the Ethiopian border. They obtain sustenance by sucking blood from straws inserted into the necks of their cattle.

Bill Carden told me years later that Lyon was not pleased at being moved from Fanjak to make way for Bowcock who was married. He was entirely justified: I not only had a wife, but I was also to get the better station. "To him that hath it shall be given." Neither then nor in all the years since, when we have been good friends, staying with each other in France and England, has Lyon given a hint of how unfair he felt it at the time. But what else could the Governor have done? Anyway, it could be argued that Lyon, who knew the Lou, was better equipped to establish a new administrative district for them. So Brenda and I were lucky because Fanjak was an attractive established merkaz and I was promoted, as was Lyon, of course, though it was still something of a battle to get the pay that was supposed to go with the job – £1,400 a year.

Because of meetings arranged over Christmas in Malakal and tribal meetings at the extremities of Western Nuer, Brenda and I went to Fanjak in November to be briefed and introduced by Bill. We would return to Bentiu, and after fulfilling the commitments made to tribal meetings before learning of the transfer, move to Fanjak for the handover. These inter-tribal meetings were essential dates in the calendar and were of the first importance. Cattle theft, animals damaging crops, fishing disputes, abductions of girls – all traditional practices – could soon lead to open warfare unless the perpetrators were brought to justice without too much delay. When the complaints were between Nuer and Dinka in the south of the district, or Dinka and Humr Arab in the north, a joint chief's court was assembled and made to sit until judgement had been given in all cases and confirmed by the DC or A/DC of the two districts. Then the execution of the judgements and penalties was as important as the court hearing, or self help would lead to further trouble. Laying on these meetings involved a good deal of preliminary organisation, and once a date had been fixed it had to be kept. So we adhered to the programme, meeting first with the Yirol Dinka at Shambe on the White Nile, then holding provincial meetings at Malakal at Christmas and finally meting with our Dinka and the Kordofan Dinka and Arabs at Abiemnon on the Bahr el Arab, a tributary of the Bahr el Ghazal. Western Nuer DC was the host, and it was also a provincial meeting with the Governors and Deputy Governors of each province. Some wives arrived, including Brenda who came on all treks, however tough, so there were a dozen officials and wives at a long table, made up of all the trek tables of the participants put together, under the large fig trees in the centre of the encampment of tents and grass huts beside the river. There were plenty of duck and geese for shooting and food. The Nilotic men did not consume milk or birds so wild fowl were numerous, especially knob nose geese, whistling teal, francolin partridge and guinea fowl. The Humr Arabs, or Baggara, are cattle, camel and horse-owning nomads. Their women, then bare-breasted unlike most Muslims, travel on the backs of bulls with their possessions as they follow the grazing. Thinking that there would be milk in the Arab encampment, our servants went over to ask for some. The Arabs regretted that all their cows were dry and sent a tin of Carnation milk instead. They would never be defeated in fulfilling the obligations of hospitality. Regrettably they are the same people, among those now known as Janjawid, who have caused such suffering to the Fur and other black tribes of cultivators in Darfur from 2003 onwards.

We all suspected that this would probably be the last such occasion and wondered whether the peace and progress could be maintained. We would have been astounded to be told that twenty-five years later Chevron would discover oil in commercial quantities in the Ruweng Dinka country north of Bentiu, as well as in Southern Kordofan. Stella, our daughter, stayed a night at the Chevron camp when on her medical elective at Ler Hospital in 1980. However, the second civil war broke out three years later and it was not until 1999 that oil was exported through a pipeline constructed for 1000 miles to the Red Sea.

It was time to move on to our last lap in the Sudan as DC of Zeraf District. I was too busy to maintain my record, to some extent because there was not so much steamer trekking as in Western Nuer, but I have found to my delight and surprise that Brenda kept a diary from February to July 1954, probably with a view to continuing my Western Nuer diary. It begins with our departure by steamer on 3 February, with a police guard of honour and a crowd of northern merchants, government employees and Nuer waving us goodbye from the Bentiu landing stage or meshra. Then we called on the Mill Hill Fathers at Yonyang, their mission and school five miles downstream. They had been good friends during our time in Bentiu and had given us the mahogany for our bed, which we later passed on to the graduate Dinka administrative assistant, John Warabek, as a wedding present. The Fathers quite liked visitors: they kept a bottle of whisky but were only permitted to touch it when dispensing hospitality. They could be seen going for the drinks cupboard as one approached the house. They had often come in their tiny boat with tiny outboard motor to play homemade croquet on our lawn.

We arrived forty hours later at Fanjak to hear that Bill Carden had been called to deal with the consequences of a fight among the Dinka to the north in which 14 were reported killed. He arrived back home after dark, having set the legal processes in motion. The next day we went south to a place called Ayod, which has since become known as a major feeding centre for the relief of people suffering from the civil war. On the way we inspected a well which in the course of five years had reached a depth of 160 feet without finding water. The chiefs agreed that it was pointless to spend more money on it, not to speak of the danger for the well diggers, a specialised class of bricklayers. At dusk we saw a leopard in the headlights and heard lions at night.

We continued south into Bor District for an inter-district meeting at Duk Faiwil, staying in temporary grass huts. The DC was Major Jack Cumming, the last of the "Bog Barons", that doughty class of officers, usually from the Army, who were recruited to administer the most uncomfortable districts in the south. He was a very good host and entertaining company, but Brenda was astonished and amused to see his dictatorial manner with the Dinka. The following day Lyon Roussel arrived to report that his former Administrative Assistant had been made a minister and was going round the district saying that he would get rid of the DC if the people were displeased with him. Things were falling apart.

The next move was north-east to the ferry over the Sobat river. The private lorry had broken down and by luck we got a lift in another which was passing. This broke down in turn, and we walked four miles before the original lorry, now repaired, took us to where lunch was awaiting. It was now 6.30 p.m. and we had been lucky to arrive at all. As Brenda wrote: "so foolish to leave one's bed and food behind anywhere in this country." We went on into Malakal where Bill completed his handover and farewell parties. He went on to a couple of deadly dull years with the Foreign Office, but then to Muscat, Qatar, the Lebanon as Director of MECAS, Yemen and finally Khartoum, in each case as head of mission.

I was briefed by all departments and Brenda went to the hospital to discuss dispensaries and "visited some of our Western Nuers whom I'd packed off to hospital from isolated spots where no medical attention was available". Later she records: "Reports of Nuers invading Dinka fishing grounds came through this evening. Philip very busy organising police to go out from Malakal that evening as a fight was imminent."

During the dry season Fanjak was much more accessible from Malakal than Bentiu, so it was easy to return there on 17 February by lorry, halting to check on the 200 prisoners who had been given six months' labour on the roads following the fatal fight which had coincided with our arrival in the district. Stopping for lunch at Atar we bathed. "A lovely spot for a swim where green grass runs down to the water's edge and though the water is shallow and muddy it is free from crocodiles." But was it free from bilharzia? Brenda was later diagnosed with it, and in 1959 had to undergo a course of injections in the Hospital for Tropical Diseases in St. Pancras, London.

The comparative accessibility of Fanjak was a great difference from Bentiu. Only once in the two years I was there did I travel by wheels from Bentiu to Malakal, first going 100 miles north into the Nuba Jebels (hills) before turning south-east to Malakal. But a mail runner from Fanjak to Malakal was possible even through the rains. A police corporal called Tiptip Pec took three days to travel the 90 miles to Malakal and three days back. He then rested a day at home in Fanjak while the mail was answered ready for him to take back to Malakal. This fitted with the Nuer walking range. If they said that such and such a place was a day's journey away, that would be about 30 miles.

By the end of February 1954 the special court of independent chiefs had been assembled at Atar, south of the east-west stretch of the White Nile between Fanjak and Malakal. This was to deal with the serious fight which had called Bill Carden away just as we were arriving in Fanjak. My memory tells me that the final total was 21 killed and 42 injured. It was the worst incident during my time in Upper Nile. The chiefs dealt with the very complicated case thoroughly, going into all the causes and not hesitating to blame the chiefs of the two Dinka sub-tribes involved. They passed sentence on all who were found guilty, and it was for the DC to confirm the sentences or otherwise. Fortunately I had the very experienced Governor John Winder, who had himself been DC of the area, to advise me. Many of the fighters, perhaps about 80, were given six months' labouring on the road, a number were imprisoned for five years, and the chiefs were fined and imprisoned in Fanjak for six months. It was decided that to deprive them of office, though fully justified, would be a mistake.

Figure 21 Nuer prisoners, sentenced by the chief's court for taking part in a fight, working on a new road.

At the same time there was a cerebro-spinal meningitis (CSM) outbreak at Atar. This very dangerous disease was frequent in the Sudan and decisive action had to be taken to bring sufferers into isolation camps and draft in medical attention. I was able to leave this to Brenda, who records: "Went to the quarantine where we have 14 cases of CSM. Two pleasant nurses are managing very well under difficult circumstances. Small grass huts have been set up by the side of a khor (stream) and masses of sulphathiazol is being injected and taken by these miserable fever ridden patients. Miraculous results – only four deaths out of 97 patients who have been in quarantine, though there are rumours of other deaths outside."

On 3 March Brenda records: "Tony Polden (the Vet for the Nuer districts) came for one night. He was very pleased with Samira (the foal) but thinks the other two horses are still far too thin and perhaps have worms. On the world news heard of riots in Khartoum at opening of Parliament." This was a dreadful affair. President Neguib, the military ruler of Egypt and Nasser's predecessor, was there as if to take over the Sudan, where he had a following because his mother was Sudanese. The Ansar, the Mahdi's followers, were transported in from Kordofan and Darfur in the west with the blades of their spears hidden under their loose clothes. Many people were killed in the riots, including the British commander of police. It should have been a warning to the politicians who came after to respect the views and interests of the people in the outer parts of this vast country, but the present military/Islamic government has taken no notice. The dreadful Darfur oppression which began in 2003 probably had its motivation in the statistical report called "The Black Book", showing that some 70 per cent of the top jobs in the country are filled by men from three clans north of Khartoum. The situation was rather like Saddam Hussein's favouritism towards his clan round Tikrit in Iraq. It is not only the black Muslims of Darfur who are disaffected. The Beja of the Red Sea Hills, the Fung of Southern Blue Nile Province and the Nuba of Kordofan are likewise now hostile to Khartoum. In January 2011 the south chose independence as South Sudan by an overwhelming majority in a referendum.

After Atar we went on a trek to the south of the district. Here is Brenda's full description, with my interpolations:

Wednesday, 3.3.54: Just before leaving for Falagh found Garwec drunk. Terrible scenes in the house. Garwec quite mad, fighting with Latjor. All servants brought by the police sergeant to office and Philip dealt out large fines to Garwec and Latjor. Left Fanjak very angry and upset. Falagh frightful place. No water, rest house filthy and ramshackle, half the people of the police post sick and must be taken into hospital tomorrow. Both tired and bad tempered. Garwec feeling very sorry for himself. Arrived late and went straight to bed after Philip had dealt with workmen's queries over dinner.

I had inherited Garwec – which means child of the cattle camp – from a predecessor in Bentiu. He was very loyal and attentive, almost obsequious, and in that respect unlike a Nuer. Drink was his problem, taken probably to cover his social inadequacy. A few months later he died without warning, probably caused by his drinking. Latjor was the complete opposite, a magnificent, laughing young warrior who joined my team as I trekked on foot through his country, Jagai. He announced that he was coming to work for me and I told him there was no vacancy. He said he would come anyway if he just got his food, so he was taken on, paid of course. Brenda did a portrait of him, now on my wall, rightly without his servant's tunic and wearing a necklace. He was soon joined by two beautiful younger sisters. The elder, aged about 15, was covered with the family beads because she had come onto the marriage market. If she brought plenty of cattle, 40 being the standard for Nuer and 20 for Dinka, then he could use them to marry in his turn. Latjor was one of those I found it hardest to leave some months later.

Friday, 5.3.54: Called at 5.00 a.m. with tea and biscuits. Left Falagh at 5.30 and drove about 10 miles on road to where 40 prisoners, police and horses were waiting. Songs from prisoners.[2]

Unloaded lorry, all luggage distributed among the prisoners (pity the men with the wireless and battery) and set off on foot at 6.45 a.m. across country that was very dry and uninhabited. Two tribal policemen, who wore laus, just a piece of cloth tied over one shoulder, walked with us carrying spears and water and my little French bag containing oddments perched precariously on the head of one of them. We walked for an hour, drank at the well, as the horses were very thisty, then changed to horses. Reached our camp at Fashudil, twelve miles from the road, and sat under the trees until Deng (the cook, Deng Duot, an engaging rogue) had produced a delicious breakfast and lunch combined. Rested for three hours then set off walking and riding alternately. Passed through some cattle camps where the boys and girls came out in full force to see us. They wore few beads but looked attractive nevertheless. *The cattle camps are a major feature of Nuer life. As the swamps dry up in the dry season and the permanent rivers are once more within their banks the cattle are taken to fresh grazing, usually near permanent water. The older people are left behind in year-round dwellings and cattle byres or luaks on the low ridges inland. The cattle camps are temporary grass shelters and the young people have a great time. There is plenty of milk for the girls and fish for the boys, so they grow plump and glossy. If a visitor appears they run out with foaming milk in gourds. These may be scoured with cattle urine so the flavour is not always as expected.*

Reached Nyalok at 5.30 p.m. The police had erected grass huts for us by the side of the stream. In a very short time the wireless was set up and we were enjoying drinks and a good meal. Very exhausted but pleasantly so. All the local chiefs and head men came to see us while we sat back. A bull was killed for the prisoners who sat round the camp fire looking very contented, especially after I had administered dabs of iodine and a few bandages to their minute wounds. Wonderful bed and sleep.

Saturday 6.3.54: Managed to keep ourselves cool by getting prisoners to throw water on the grass hut. The temperature inside fell considerably. Philip finds these people, the Radh Gaawier, a great problem. They are very scattered owing to geography of the country which is liable to flooding. The collective administration seems very difficult. Many of the people who have come in to the court have tropical ulcers and infected eyes. They present their wounds to me and expect a miraculous cure. They must learn to visit the dispensary 16 miles away, not a great distance by Nuer standards.

Sunday 7.3.54: The local young girls came to see me today. I made them pose in turn for a quick sketch whilst the rest curiously picked up and looked in to our possessions lying in the hut. They were most amused when they found the mirror. They wanted to see the reflection of their neat little bottoms and beads around their waists.

Figure 22 Dry season cattle camp. Dinka at Lake No.

At 7 pm another large group of 55 prisoners came into the camp for the road making. Much singing could be heard in the distance on the far side of the stream and then to hear our own prisoners singing in reply. More bulls were killed and everyone was happy.

The dietary customs of the Nuer were surprising; men did not drink milk, which was reserved for women and children. They were very fond of meat and whenever a herd of kob or thiang (types of antelope) was seen, there would be cries of "ring ring" – that is, meat. If time allowed one would then shoot an animal for the party. I had a Holland and Holland .375 magnum rifle. Men would not eat birds, which were plentiful, so with a shotgun I was able to get whatever Brenda needed – goose, partridge, guinea fowl, duck or bustard. All the people ate a grain porridge called "asida", made into sticky balls. The cereal was maize, brought to Africa from the

New World by the Spanish and Portuguese, or a form of millet called dura. Further north in the Sudan this is the only cereal crop as it is very resistant to drought.

11.3.54: Returned to Gagh across country. Hotter than ever when we stopped to rest. Camp invaded by bees. Used a luak (cattle byre) as my boudoir since there was no rest house or tent. Exhausted at end of the journey, asleep by 8.30.

12.3.54: Left Gagh at dawn and drove 85 miles to Awoi. Stopped on the way to inspect a well and police post and for breakfast. Found the rest house very dark and primitive. The governor (John Winder) and his sister arrived at tea time. The main reason for the Governor's and Philip's visit is to bring back an influential witch doctor, Dwal Diu, to the district. He was exiled many years ago for causing a fight but returned unofficially a year ago.

13.3.54: The Governor stayed until tea time. Left before Dwal arrived. Deng coped admirably with meals prepared on a camp fire. No eggs or meat to be bought. Water supply from a well half a mile away and getting short.

Water was a major problem – too much in the rains when the Nile flooded, too little during the dry season. At that time water had to be obtained from perhaps several miles away by digging pits in the river bed. This meant much toil for the women, bringing water in gourds or safihas (five-gallon petrol containers) on their heads. The DCs mostly regarded wells as a priority, but the Nuer chiefs did not always see it that way. Well diggers and liners were a scarce and valuable resource with a hard and dangerous job. Awoi was not too far from Ayod, which became a large United Nations feeding centre.

Sat. 13.3.54: I held court with the local village women. (By this time Brenda could speak Nuer reasonably well, but I cannot remember whether she took the exam.) One wanted to know if my husband beat me as hers did her! One woman turned the sewing machine handle very satisfactorily and asked to return to Fanjak as my servant (shades of Latjor a year before). All very happy souls.

Dwal arrived and everyone rushed out to meet him. Lots of singing and dancing, quite frightening. One realises what an important man he is to these people. Trouble might easily occur when they know he is to be taken back. Thank goodness the mounted police are here. He's an impressive old man, between 50 and 60, very tall and broad, clothed in a large shell-studded leopard skin with ivory-pronged rings on his fingers and heavy bracelets and beads.

Sunday 14.3.54: A good pile of mail arrived by lorry from Fanjak. Dwal was not too pleased when he was told to return with us, making excuses that he was sick. But Philip thinks he will come without trouble. (There is nothing more about him so presumably he did. John Winder had had dealings with Dwal when he was DC some twelve years before. He had been exiled to the Shilluk area across the White Nile to the north. John must have felt that he should come to support me as a new DC and tell Dwal what was expected of him.)

Tuesday 16.3.54: Returned to Fanjak. Left Awoi at 6.00 a.m., arrived at 1 p.m., 115 miles. Stopped under some trees half way for breakfast, surrounded by lovely birds. (Bill Carden had bequeathed his "Birds of South Africa" by Roberts which seemed to cover the Sudan quite well and it was a great stand-by. The big fig trees usually had a flock of green pigeons. There were many rollers, sunbirds, waxwings, weaver birds, flycatchers, shrikes, egrets, ibis, storks, crested cranes, marabou storks, vultures, hammerhead storks. Where dura was grown the tiny quelea were a pest and the agricultural department tried everything to control them, without much success.)

Sunday 21.3.54: John Warabeck came to tea. He is longing to get married to his nurse friend in Khartoum. He feels lonely here. (John was an A/DC on probation. He was a handsome Dinka and one of the first to go to the university, formerly Gordon College, in Khartoum. He was anxious to learn social skills and asked Brenda to teach him ballroom dancing. She

*began, but I suppose it became redundant soon afterwards.
With independence he gained rapid promotion, which was
expected, but I heard that he drank too much and died
prematurely – a great loss.)*

*Monday 22.3.54: Philip's holding a major court on the
verandah. A young man who beat a man on the head who has
since died is being tried for possible murder.*

Actually, if it was murder it was probably a magisterial enquiry,
and if there was a case to answer the matter would have been
referred to the High Court in Juba for trial. Neither Bentiu nor
Fanjak had a separate court house since the vast majority of
cases, including homicide where there was no "biem" or settled
intention to kill, went before the chiefs' court.

*Called out to a woman in labour. Arrived to find child still-
born. Nothing I could do except for some medicine.*

*Thursday, 25.3.54: Went to Wathkec to investigate brutal
treatment by chiefs' court of a merchant (a northerner) selling
grain at a high price. A long drive across parched country.
About 50 young Nuer boys and girls flocked around the lorry
to meet us: they have brought their cattle here for the dry
season. Dispensary very neglected and patients few. Tried to
organise a grain and milk supply.*

*Wathkec is a dirty fuelling station on the main Nile. Shilluk,
Dinka and Nuer collect there each year for grazing and
fishing, living in small grass huts. They also earn money
cutting wood for the steamers. Post boat called late at night.*

*Friday, 26.3.54: The merchant had been beaten and left in
the sun, so the Executive Chief was arrested and dismissed
from office.*

The northern politicians and many academics since have
blamed the British policy of what they call "divide and rule"
for the rift between North and South that led to over 40 years
of civil war. In my experience the Closed Districts Ordinance
was essential to maintain peace, such was the legacy of hatred

resulting from centuries of raiding for slaves and cattle. That merchant must have been approved by the Governor as a resident, but he still suffered ill treatment from the Nuer.

Monday, 29.3.54: The new A/DC (Sudanese) from Bentiu visited Fanjak with his Egyptian wife and four children and came for breakfast. Seems sensible and experienced (though only in the north). It will be interesting to see how the Nuers take to him.

Drove to Atar to clear up remainder of cattle fines from the big fight last month. CSM epidemic subsiding but the prisoners are breaking out with chicken pox, not seriously fortunately.

Brenda continues to describe our activities and treks by steamer, lorry and police horse, one of which rolled over on her and injured her arm. Then, on 8 June, she records:

My friend "dysentery" has returned so we decided I shall go to Malakal when the steamer arrives and I will try to go home as soon as possible for some treatment.

The next steamer had to be diverted to Bentiu but the Governor sent one a few days later with the radio engineer. Everyone looked after Brenda well and she was fortunate that John Udal from Kodok, who was to be Stella's godfather later, was on the plane with her to Khartoum and then on to England on 19 June, with the usual night stop in the luxury of the Phoenicia Hotel in Malta. She was well again when she met me off the plane on 2 July.

What now touches me is that there was no complaint in the diary. She mentions the Atar rest house, but does not tell that one evening at about 7 o'clock she was in her four feet square by nine inches deep canvas bath in the centre of the floor, in an otherwise unoccupied room of mud walls and thatched roof. The hurricane lantern was on the floor – but when I lifted it up the light showed dozens of scorpions all over the walls. The Sudanese scorpion will not kill an adult, but causes very severe pain for two to three days. A child is in great danger from a bite. All I could do was to patrol the floor to keep the scorpions away until she had dried herself and dressed. On another occasion a policeman was bitten on the ankle by a poisonous snake. The South African serum had not then reached the Sudan, and Brenda undertook the traditional practice of cutting the wound with a razor so that the blood flowed, getting a friend of the patient to suck and spit out the poison, rubbing in potassium permanganate crystals and applying a tourniquet. The policeman was fit again in a few days.

There was a herd with some large bull elephants which from time to time came within reach of Fanjak and made a nuisance of themselves. I had a licence to shoot up to three of these at £15 per beast. One famous bull had such large tusks that Lyon Roussell named him "roller skates", fantasising that they were too large to be moved without wheels. One day the game scout (this was before the word "game" was replaced by "wildlife") reported that the herd was within range, so I set off with him and a crowd of volunteer prisoners. As it happened the elephants were moving steadily away and we must have walked about 40 miles before catching up with them. They were a big herd, about 50, with the cows and calves in the middle as they rested on their feet in the heat of the day. We watched them from downwind, about 40 yards away, for an hour or so, trying to get a view of roller skates. Then I saw one with a really big tusk and shot him from about 20 yards. The most merciful technique for a mediocre shot, as I am, is to shatter the front shoulder from the side which brings the animal down. Then one closes in quickly and places a fatal shot into the brain, usually through the eye, causing immediate death. The rest of the herd melted away and the butchering began. Soon women appeared with their Moses baskets and little fires were lit to roast favourite portions of meat. The tusks were hacked out, their roots nine inches deep.

I had never done such a long walk and the following day I could not even stumble a little. I had to get back to the office and was carried for a while on a stretcher. Then the horses arrived with Majok the syce, and so I rode home with the prisoners carrying the tusks and tons of meat.

One tusk weighed 119 lbs and was, I think, a record for the Sudan, which has big elephants. The other was broken but still weighed 87 lbs. I regret not having had the big tusk shipped home, but with independence approaching one could not have coped with the export documentation necessary from afar, nor dealt with the situation if the tusk had disappeared on the way. Ivory then sold for about £1 per pound and there were always merchants ready to buy it on the spot. So even after paying for the licence and generous tips to all who had helped, there was still a good profit. My record only stood for five days. Not knowing of my bag, Lyon arrived to pursue roller skates again, rather like Captain Ahab and the great white whale. Deservedly he got him and the bigger tusk was 124 lbs – 5 lbs more than mine. Typically of the time, one of the pro-Egyptian merchants in Fanjak sent a sensational account of the episode to the vernacular press.

I took two working days off for some rest, but I had ample leave credit because when I was on trek and often in the station I worked on a Sunday. All the prisoners who came were volunteers and they got lots of meat; this is the sort of affair that the Nuer loved.

Shooting elephants is very exciting and I got five altogether in Western Nuer. People now think I should feel guilty, but I do not. If they become too numerous elephants will move into human settlements and a family's sustenance for a year can be destroyed in a single night. Away from villages they can cause severe devastation to the tree cover. The South Luangwa Reserve in Zambia provides a case study. At the time of independence there were 60,000 elephants there, seriously damaging the environment for other wildlife. Culling was proposed with meat being distributed to local people, but this met with great opposition. Then came independence and the resulting destruction of much of the fauna. The elephants were reduced to about 10,000, which is thought to be the optimal number. So, by an irony the poaching produced a desirable result, and with protection the numbers have stabilised. The option of controlling excess numbers by culling or other suitable methods must always be available when the scientists so advise.

12

THE END OF THE SUDAN CONDOMINIUM

Handing over to an experienced Dinka A/DC called Manasseh Pec, I followed Brenda on leave after three weeks, and she met me at Blackbushe Airport, Hampshire. Brenda's mother was sick and spent some time in hospital while mine had been busy getting Spring Cottage in Abbots Bromley into shape. The Foreign Office was holding interviews for a few posts and I foolishly drove down from Staffordshire (no motorways then) in the Austin 7 on the morning of the interview and was unprepared for it; I was unable to give a coherent assessment of the French problems in Vietnam. Eventually about eight of the Political Service joined the Foreign Service and all became heads of missions in due course. At first the Foreign Office took the view that former Political Service staff would not be acceptable in the Sudan, perhaps embarrassing the Ministers whom they had known only too well. This proved to be a misreading of the situation. Eventually the independent Sudan Government asked specifically for ambassadors who knew the country and were known friends.

We returned after leave to receive a letter giving two months' notice under the terms of the Anglo Egyptian Agreement of the previous year. In Malakal I met my successor, a well-built but somewhat arrogant northerner called Hassan Dafallah who had been at the School of

Administration and had a few years' experience. We went to Fanjak on the steamer together, calling in on various places and introducing him. He was to stay in the rest house until his family came – I do not know whether they ever did.

We went into the handing-over routine as I had done with Bill Carden. I drafted a note to staff to say that I would be touring the district with Hassan to introduce him everywhere, and I would hand over on my departure which was fixed. I showed Hassan the draft and he said it did not accord with his orders. All Sudanese DC designates had been instructed verbally by the Prime Minister to take over immediately on arrival in their new Districts. I had no means of knowing whether this was true. It did not seem out of character with Ismail el-Azhari, who was neither a sensible nor an honourable man. At about the same time I received a letter sent by Azhari to all the dismissed administrators thanking them for their devoted service to the Sudanese people! I could not discuss the problem with the governor on the radio telephone, which was insecure, and so I decided that it was in the interests of the people to accept Hassan's word and do my best to make the arrangement work. I therefore issued a notice, which he agreed, to the effect that he was taking over and I would spend the next seven weeks visiting the district with him and writing my handover notes. My report on the episode is in the Sudan archives at Durham University, probably typed by Brenda on the steamer on our journey north. These handover notes appear here at appendix 4.

The district was in a febrile state. A distinguished southern politician had been to see me to discuss the possibility of the British DCs supporting secession of the south, but I had to discourage such plans. It would have meant the civil war starting a year earlier than it did, with massive international ramifications. After much suffering, in January 2011, after discovery of large oil reserves, the south opted for independence with the benefit of half of the oil revenues. The growth of air freight has vastly altered the outlook for landlocked countries, but in 1954 the south could have been blockaded and forced to surrender in a very short time.

Tragically South Sudan now seems to be collapsing into civil war, mainly caused by rivalry between the Dinka President, Salva Kir, and the Nuer Vice-President, Riak Machar. The latter married the aid worker, Emma McCune who was killed in a traffic accident in Nairobi in 1993, aged 29 and pregnant. She is buried at Ler in South Sudan. I suspect, but have not been able to confirm, that Riak Macher is the son or grandson of my old friend, Head Chief Riak Dong.

I toured the district in 1954 with Hassan, introducing him to significant people and showing him round. Shortly before leaving, all the chiefs came in to Fanjak for the formal handover. I still vividly remember sitting with Hassan and the chiefs in a great circle under the neem trees. I had taken care in preparing what I was going to say. I said that Hassan had been trained at the School of Administration by Political Service officials, and had then worked under others for several years in district administration. The systems of government would carry on as before. Then the chiefs spoke in turn, interpreted into English. Each said much the same, that this was not of their doing. They listed the DCs by their bull names and said what good things had been done. They, the Nuer, after first being hostile, had grown to understand how beneficial kuma (the government) was. They did not understand how it was that I, Bilrial, wanted to leave. They did not wish me to go and the decision to return to my country was mine, not theirs. They did not know what they had done to upset me. As for this man (poor Hassan, having to listen), they knew Jallabas (northerners who wear the jallabiya – a sort of long shirt), and they would not change. They were prepared to give him a chance to prove whether my words would be justified, but if he turned out to be like other Jellabas and his kuma was not good the people would return to the life they had before the British came, retreating to their swamps and other inaccessible areas. They had lived like that before and would do so again. This was of course no empty threat, since only a generation had passed since that had been their condition.

Hassan did his best to reassure them but they were not convinced, and rightly so in the light of later events. I was deeply unhappy but I could do nothing more. Matters decided thousands of miles away would have to take their tragic course, and the Northern Sudanese were left with an appalling colonial problem, though in their arrogance few of them realised it.

So now it only remained to auction the belongings which were not going home, pack the rest and say our last goodbyes. We had bought a colour cine camera on leave and I took some very poor reels of a unique life, now kindly arranged by my son, Matthew, onto video and DVD. Not having the chance to see my mistakes I was filming blind, but I am grateful for what has survived. So we said our goodbyes and a big crowd waved as the steamer left. In Malakal the other administrators gathered and most of us travelled on the steamer "Beatrice" to Khartoum. Our servants were with us, so apart from the sadness of leaving it was an agreeable journey, talking about what the future might bring. In Khartoum we were all put up by senior colleagues; we were with Sir John Carmichael, the Financial Secretary, and his wife, whose fourth child Brenda had helped to deliver. A superb final party with a brilliant cabaret was put on in the Deputy Civil Secretary's garden, and so a magnificent and honourable enterprise came to an end, far too early as most Sudanese now acknowledge.

13

NORTHERN RHODESIA: BROKEN HILL URBAN

So it was back to England for the winter of 1954/55, my first since 1948. I was 27 and probably not too old for the recent graduate recruitment market. We were based at Spring Cottage in Abbots Bromley, East Staffordshire, where Mother had taken a job which she enjoyed as a matron at St Mary and St Anne, a girls' independent boarding school in the village.

When the end of our time with the Nuer came into prospect we were able to think about starting a family and this affected our decisions. A resettlement bureau was established to help us find jobs, and I also registered with the Oxford University employment service. I was quite open-minded and had interviews with the record company "His Master's Voice" and, through my St John's friend Rex Allen, with Macmillan the publisher. I was offered a post with MI5, then coyly called a department of the War Office, and invited to an interview with what we now know as MI6, the Secret Intelligence Service. Although several Sudan colleagues joined MI5 and did well, I was not sure whether I had the right temperament for very secret work. Several colonial territories were also recruiting, and we did a lot of research on them.

I said at first that I was rather sickened by African nationalism and the harm it was doing to the people it claimed to lead. The Solomon Islands was a possibility, and we went

151

to see a nice Australian district officer and his wife on the Colonial B Course at Cambridge (a sabbatical year for officers of some years' service). When asked about their salary they said that after a three-year tour they had managed to save enough to buy a radio. It was clear that there was a vast difference between territories which were grant-aided from the British Treasury and those which must live from their own taxation. It seemed humiliating to us that British civil servants could treat overseas officers drawn from the same graduate recruitment pool so contemptuously in matters of pay, so if I wanted to continue with district administration, which I enjoyed so much, it almost certainly meant Africa and a territory with a healthy revenue of its own.

I briefly accepted a job with the United Africa Company, a major part of Unilever, then a greater power than now. It meant half the year in Nigeria and half in Unilever House in Blackfriars, London, as assistant to the Deputy Chairman, with a salary twice the going rate in the public service. As I got out the map of Greater London to consider where we might buy a house using the Sudan compensation, Brenda said, "You don't really want this job, do you?" I had to agree and immediately sent a letter withdrawing my acceptance, with apologies, the same day as I had accepted.

We settled on Northern Rhodesia (later to become Zambia), which had a good climate for a family and adequate revenue from the Copperbelt. It had recently been combined into the Central African Federation with Nyasaland (later Malawi) and Southern Rhodesia (Zimbabwe). The idea of a partnership between the races, distinct from the apartheid of South Africa and the black nationalism to the north, was attractive in theory. Northern Rhodesia (NR) was developing fast following the expansion of the copper mining industry during the war, and seemed to offer the prospect of a full and interesting career. There was no thought of not offering pensionable terms, as had been the case in the Sudan.

We now had to move quickly as Brenda was expecting our first child and would not be allowed to travel by sea after the seventh month. The Colonial Office booked us with the Union Castle line on the "Dunnottar Castle", which called at more places and took longer than the same company's mail boats, which boasted that they left Southampton every Thursday at 4.00 p.m. and took 14 days to reach Cape Town. Our ship set off from London and then called at Rotterdam. It was surprising on a winter's evening to see all the living rooms uncurtained for the world to see what was going on inside. The Dutch are like the British in so many ways, but quite different in this. I wonder why. It still applies.

The Rotterdam stop meant that we took on board a large contingent of Germans emigrating to South-West Africa (Namibia). The white Nationalist Party had taken power in South Africa and refused to put the League of Nations mandated territory of South-West Africa under the United Nations after 1945, so they had a free run there for the time being. A significant element of the Nationalist Party were Nazi sympathisers, and I suspect were encouraging Germans who did not like their new democracy to settle in South and South-West Africa (now Namibia).

The younger Germans displayed more than a hint of the "strength through joy" attitude seen at the Nazi rallies. There was constant friction between the Dutch and the Germans, especially in the deck game competitions where the Dutch insisted on a British umpire, even in the early stages of a knock-out tournament.

I was caught up in this as I found myself in the final of the men's singles deck tennis against a lithe young German of about 18. (I was nearly 10 years older.) His compatriots were all at one end of the court, with the British and Dutch at the other. We reached two sets all. In the final set I went to 4–0. Then the German boy fought back with his greater fitness to 4–4. The tension was tremendous. I just managed by slowing the tempo to win the next two games to take the match. At the prizegiving dance that evening not a single German turned up. This was just 10 years after the end of the war.

Germany is now a most valued partner in Europe and thoroughly democratic, a great achievement. I suspect that the group on the ship were out of sympathy with the beliefs of the new democracy and hoped to perpetuate Nazi ideology in the former German South-West Africa, now controlled by those they saw as their allies in South Africa. They all left the ship at Walvis Bay while the Dutch and British continued happily to Cape Town.

In the expectation of a baby we had brought with us a Hillman station wagon. It provided the carrying capacity we needed but was a little under-powered. However, its main fault was that when the engine became hot the petrol passing through the pipe to the carburettor vaporised and the car stopped. This was particularly embarrassing in wildlife parks, especially when we were once chased by an elephant in Wankie (now Hwange) Game Park which is between the Victoria Falls and Bulawayo.

From Cape Town we drove through the Karoo and Johannesburg, marvelling that an African country could be so greatly developed. Surprisingly in Cape Town there was no sign of apartheid on the buses, perhaps because Rhodes's slogan of equal rights for all civilised men was still influential, but it was rigorously applied in the Transvaal.

When we crossed the Limpopo River we came to the strip roads, a feature of both Southern and Northern Rhodesia at that time. On a gravel base were laid two strips of tar for the wheels. When meeting an oncoming car each one had to move over to the left so that only the right wheels were on the tar strip. Overtaking was impossible unless the car in front pulled right off its outer strip to let one pass. After about 2000 miles and 12 days we reached Lusaka, the capital of Northern Rhodesia, moved from Livingstone near the Victoria Falls some years before. We had averaged less than 200 miles a day and the Establishment Department were wondering whether we would ever arrive, since most people took half the time.

Lusaka looked well laid out and cared for. It has a good climate, lies at about 4000 feet above sea level, and was a great contrast to Khartoum. We were booked into a comfortable Government hostel, but were not looked after as well by our new colleagues as we would have been in Khartoum.

The people responsible for postings knew of the forthcoming birth and we were sent to Broken Hill, which had a fine new hospital, about 90 miles north of Lusaka on a tarred road. Broken Hill owed its existence to the lead, zinc and vanadium mine which had been discovered soon after Cecil Rhodes's Chartered Company had arrived. It was named after Broken Hill in Australia, also a lead/zinc prospect, but actually the Northern Rhodesia ore body turned out to be much more complicated to process. The African name was Kabwe, to which it has now reverted.

The town was also known for Broken Hill Man or Homo Rhodesiensis, the remains of a very early hominid discovered during mining in 1921. He is believed to be over 125,000 years old and a very early specimen of homo sapiens (i.e. us). He is now kept in the vaults of the National Science Museum in Kensington.[1]

At that time the town had a population of about 5,000 Europeans, 50,000 Africans and a few Indians. At the mine there was a cinema showing fairly recent films, as well as sports grounds and a swimming pool. In the centre of the town there were all the necessary shops and bars but not yet a hotel. Around the town there were European-owned farms, many of the farmers being Afrikaners. They were largely decent fellows but with a few apartheid sympathisers. The railway passed through the town on its way from Victoria Falls and Lusaka to the copper belt further north. Virtually all the development in Northern Rhodesia was along this line of rail.

Broken Hill was a railway as well as a mining town. Roy Welensky, who was to be Prime Minister of the Federation of Central Africa and a tough but fair opponent of British policy, had been an engine driver and had his home in the town. It is significant that a Lithuanian Jewish immigrant did such a job. The higher paid manual jobs were reserved for whites (and in the copper mines they were very highly paid), protected by ruthless unions who had nothing to learn from the London Fleet Street print unions when it came to extortion.

The Broken Hill Urban District, to which I was posted, consisted of the town and the European settler farms in a circle of about twenty miles' radius. Surrounding the district was the Broken Hill Rural District, which roughly included the Lenje tribe and ran south as far as the Lusaka municipal boundary. I was the second most senior official in the urban district, responsible to the District Commissioner, Peter Clark, an experienced officer with a great sense of humour and a winning human touch. He was very welcoming and we became good friends. He was a Scot and a son of the manse. He and his equally charming wife, Noreen, had four children.

Broken Hill held the headquarters of the Central Province with the Provincial Commissioner, F.M. Thomas[2] and his staff, and all the provincial departmental officers, agriculture, education, police, labour and so forth. Also, sitting sometimes rather awkwardly with the Colonial Service Officers were the Federal staff; health, European Education, European agriculture called Conservation, Posts etc. There was also a full-blown municipality of Broken Hill with a town clerk from Richmond, North Yorkshire. It could scarcely have been a greater contrast to the loneliness and discomfort of the Upper Nile.

We had been allocated a three-bedroomed Public Works Department house in a street called Marshall Avenue. It was rather uninspired architecturally but well built, as could be seen when we revisited it in 2000.

There was a servants' quarter for our first cook, a tiny old man called Teapot. He was quite insistent on the name. After some months he decided to retire to his village and by great good fortune our wonderful Absent Ngoma came looking for a job. Thereafter our domestic and touring arrangements worked with the utmost harmony and reliability. Later, Absent's sweet-tempered wife Joyce appeared, and then their two children Efrida and Barnabasi, who grew up playing with ours.

As our baby's arrival became more imminent, another expectant mother came to stay. She was Joan Andrew, whose husband Roger, also from St John's Oxford, was District Officer (DO) at Serenje, about 170 miles north-east. She and Brenda both went into hospital at much the same time, sharing a room in what was then the European Wing. The next day, 31 May, I visited Brenda after work ended at 4 p.m. and Joan was in the labour ward. As a midwife herself Brenda knew that her time was near, but all the staff were occupied with Joan. I got someone to hear my calls at last and Stella was delivered on the spot, about half an hour after Joan's baby girl Terry. When I visited the following day I was allowed to go into the nursery and bring out the baby labelled Bowcock. I brought her into the room where the two mothers were and remarked how much prettier she had become in twenty-four hours. Brenda said, "But that isn't our baby." Fortunately maternal bonding had detected a labelling mistake, and Joan could reflect that she had the prettier baby, at least to my untrained eyes. A few days later Stella came home to the lifelong care of a perfect mother.

With so many functions in the hands of specialist departments and the municipality, the DC's role was that of co-ordinator and filling any gaps in government coverage, as well as most African affairs. There was an idea among many Europeans of South African extraction that the Provincial Administration dealt with Africans and the town council with Europeans. This was given credence by the fact that the head of the Provincial Administration was called the Secretary of Native Affairs. There was a good deal of racial discrimination, in spite of all the talk of partnership in Britain and Salisbury, the Federal capital. The centre of the town was entirely white and the Africans were not admitted through the main doors of the bigger shops but directed to a hatch at the side, where they had to queue for the privilege of spending their money. I am glad to say that shortly after my arrival the Northern Rhodesian Government (NRG) set up a commission to advise on ways to end discrimination and things greatly improved. I gave evidence of how the situation had struck me on arrival from the Sudan, where discrimination between white and coloured (as distinct from between brown and black) was rare except where Muslim custom required it – for example, with alcohol.

One of my responsibilities was the native court, which sat with an African president and two assessors in a thatched shelter behind the Boma. In Northern Rhodesia the District Commissioner's office was referred to as the Boma, which was the word for an encampment with a protective wooden fence. It was the equivalent of the Arabic zariba, which was usually constructed of thorns. (In the Sudan the DC's headquarters was the merkaz, meaning the centre of activity and communication.)

The native courts played a very important part in the government of the country, with powers to fine or imprison for up to six months. The local legislation recognised the validity of customary law so long as it was "not repugnant to justice, equity and good conscience".

Naturally, case law grew up round the doctrine of repugnancy. There was an appeal from the native court to a native appeal court, then to the DC and finally to the High Court. Broken Hill, like other mining towns and Lusaka, had a great mixture of tribes and the court administered an amalgam of their laws. At the Federal level, the Supreme Court had a similar problem. It applied the English Common Law for cases from Northern Rhodesia and Nyasaland (Malawi) and Roman-Dutch law for cases from Southern Rhodesia (Zimbabwe). The native court had a clerk who kept a brief record in either English or the vernacular, which had to be reviewed and the fines checked.

The 50,000 Africans lived in simple permanent houses in two principal housing areas or locations, one provided by the mine and the other by the municipality. Both had a cinema, a dance hall, a beer hall and some sports facilities. I was co-opted onto the football league committee and also to be Assistant District Commissioner of the Scouts.

The mine was owned by Anglo American, the large mining group controlled by the Oppenheimer family. It moved its headquarters to London in about 1998 and continues to be a powerful force in much of the world. It was a fairly liberalising influence, trying to advance Africans against the opposition of the white unions. With the encouragement of the Government, the Mines' policy on African housing was quite different from South Africa's. There the mine workers were housed in single-sex barracks and their wives and families were left behind in their villages. The social consequences were inevitable. Although the Northern Rhodesian arrangement was far preferable, there were still great problems caused by the men working sometimes over 500 miles from their home villages. A good deal of my time was taken up in raising African problems with the African Mine Personnel Officer and the Municipal African Location Manager.

It was widely recognised in the Provincial Administration that African urban society was lacking a middle class of responsible, educated Africans with a stake in the country, making up what is now called civil society. One way of encouraging its emergence was thought to be the provision of serviced plots of land where people could build their own homes. This was in direct opposition to the South African principle that Africans had no permanent place of abode in the towns, being merely migrant workers who would return to their home villages. As urbanisation progressed and Africans became more educated and pursued European-style career patterns, a South African style policy became increasingly unrealistic and oppressive.

Land was found about two miles from the centre of Broken Hill for what was designated Mukobeko African Township. Its development became my principal responsibility, with considerable input from the departments for Local Government and Surveys. There was a town plan, building regulations and an advisory panel intended to become a municipal authority in due course. Temporary buildings were not permitted, but the large dried mud blocks made in moulds, known as Kimberly bricks, were allowed.

Like most new projects it was slow to take off and there was some political opposition, on what grounds I could never discover. Probably the main obstacle was that most Africans just did not have the money at that time, even though self-build was promoted.

In 2000, 44 years later, I went back to Mukobeko. It had become a suburb of Kabwe but had an identity of its own. The town plan was still to be seen and helped to mitigate the scruffiness which seems always to characterise African urban living. Unfortunately it was evening by the time of our visit, so I was not able to speak to the town officers to find out what their successes and problems were.

After 18 months we were able to take some local leave. We had met Tom and Margaret Dow, who had been in the Sudan Forestry Department. Their first child, Malcolm, had been born soon after Stella and Margaret offered to look after her so that we could get away on our own. Accordingly, we set out to explore Central Africa.

First we went straight up the Great North Road, stopping with the Andrews at Serenje, a beautiful district with waterfalls and fine views from the escarpment on the watershed between the Zambezi and the Congo. We had been advised to call on Sir Stuart Gore-Brown, a member of Legco, the legislative council, as a representative of African interests. His estate, Shiwa Ngandu, has been described in the book *The Africa House* by Christina Lamb.

After mile upon mile of similar and apparently empty African bush the English gentleman's country house was astonishing. Sir Stuart was extremely welcoming, and as he was obviously lonely it did not seem to be taking advantage of his hospitality to stay for a comfortable night. Then we travelled on through Chinsali and Isoka Districts (where I was later to be DC for a short period) to Tanganyika, not yet Tanzania, which it became after the post-independence merger with Zanzibar. The first settlement over the border was Mbozi, lying at over 5000 feet with good red soil. We were guests of Tommy and Judy Thompson who had earlier stayed with us in Broken Hill when having medical treatment. Tommy had been in the Indian Police and Judy a nurse. They were establishing a coffee farm, having built an attractive wooden house and planted their first coffee, a beautiful plant in a beautiful setting.

Unfortunately for them, independence came unexpectedly early and harassment by local Tanganyika African Union officials forced them to sell for an insignificant price and live in straitened circumstances in England. However, in 1956 there was still optimism in Africa, though Tommy did say that he feared that when they bought the farm their hearts ruled their heads.

We turned south towards Nyasaland (later Malawi) for a stay at the Northern Rhodesia guest house on the Nyika plateau. This is a remarkable open upland area, rather like the English South Downs, with great herds of zebra and various kinds of antelope. It was very beautiful. One part was in Northern Rhodesia, managed by the Northern Rhodesian Game Department.

From the Nyika we went down to Lake Nyasaland at Nkata Bay, staying at the guest house on a narrow strip of land jutting out into the lake. The guest house was clean and comfortable with superb views over the lake, but the sheets had holes in them. In the NR guest houses everything was in good order. It was a small indication of the effect of being dependent on the UK Treasury for a grant in aid, as Nyasaland was. This was one reason why the UK was so determined to push Nyasaland into federating with the Rhodesias against its will, thus relieving a burden on the British taxpayer.

We happened to be at Nkata Bay for the Queen's birthday celebrations. The DC was very hospitable and the whole population seemed to throw themselves fully into the events, with all kinds of competitions, including canoe races across the bay. Although the people were undoubtedly poor they seemed cheerful, and it was a shock that one year later Nkata Bay should be the site of the first disturbances which led to the Devlin Report and ultimately to independence and oppression by President Banda and his successors.

We travelled on to the capital, which during the British period was at Zomba, half way up a mountain planted with forests of conifers and eucalyptus. We stayed with David and Stella Boughton. Stella had been on our boat coming out to Cape Town to join her husband, who was a major in the King's African Rifles. I took the opportunity to meet the DO who was undertaking in Blantyre, the commercial capital, the establishment of a town like Mukobeko. He gave me a tour of his much larger project which was largely building houses for rent, which in Broken Hill was the responsibility of the municipality.

Then we turned west through Lilongwe, which has since become the capital of Malawi, and Fort Jameson (Chipata), the headquarters of the Eastern Province, Lusaka and home.

14

BROKEN HILL RURAL

Later in 1956 I was transferred to the Broken Hill Rural District, the boma of which was situated within Broken Hill Urban. It was in a park of about 30 acres with simple offices, a few officials' houses, district messengers' quarters, a tennis court, a cricket ground and a swimming pool. At the rear of our house was an outside kitchen reached by a mosquito-wired corridor. The house had originally been the prison. In the garden was a rondavel, a round hut of mud brick and thatch that served as a guest room, which I also used for my law studies. In 2000 the house and rondavel were still there, though much dilapidated. It was an ideal posting. I could get back into rural district administration and we still had the hospital and shops nearby, an important factor since our second child was on the way.

Matthew was born on 9 December 1956, eighteen months after Stella, so life was perfect. Brenda had warning of the impending event when we were in the Mine cinema watching Grace Kelly and Cary Grant in a film set on the French Riviera called "To Catch a Thief". I had to take her to hospital before the end and we never knew who the villain was. Matthew arrived very quickly, in his typical good-tempered way, and I celebrated on the town with the DC of Mkushi who was staying with us.

The move raised the question of language. Northern Rhodesia has over 40 languages, which are more than dialects. It was compulsory for the Provincial Administration to learn one of the main four to higher level. On arrival Peter Clark had advised me to learn Chinyanja, as it was the lingua franca of the army and police, though it was only widely spoken in the Eastern Province and Nyasaland. Fortunately our servant Absent came from the Luangwa Valley in Eastern Province and I was able to speak with him, always in the vernacular, and after leaving Zambia to correspond with him. All the main languages had been put into writing, mostly by missionaries. I passed the higher exam, so was eligible for confirmation in my job. I decided to miss out on learning Lenje since it was spoken by not more than 50,000 people and the leaders of the community usually understood the major languages. The Zambians are remarkable in mutual comprehension. During the 2000 trip our driver Rodrick, a Bemba, when asking the way, would lean out of the window and after greeting a stranger would ask, "What tribe are you?" Then he would communicate in the required language.[1]

The Northern Rhodesian Government (NRG) policy on language was, I think, enlightened, as in the Sudan. The first higher language was compulsory, but after that additional languages earned a bonus of £25 for achieving the lower standard and £50 for the higher. Wives also could earn the bonus, an extra gleam of enlightenment. I subsequently passed higher Bemba in the Northern Province (actually more spoken in Broken Hill than Nyanja) and lower Lozi in Barotseland, now Western Province. Brenda passed the lower Bemba in 1960 and later learned some Lozi, but was sick for the exam so never took it.

When, in 1963, I transferred to the Judiciary in the Southern Province, the home of the other main language, Tonga, I decided not to learn it since I spoke Nyanja at home and always had an excellent interpreter in court. Even though I knew a language fairly well I would always use an interpreter in court. Not to do so would, I thought, be unfair to the parties concerned since it takes many years to appreciate the nuances in a language. On the other hand, it is a good discipline for the interpreter to know that the magistrate speaks enough to monitor his interpretation.

Anyway, I thought I had probably learnt enough languages by this time. In Africa these had been Arabic, Nuer, Nyanja, Bemba and Lozi. At school I learnt French, German, Italian, Greek and Latin. Brenda and I did a year's Spanish in about 1975.

The language policy was, I believe, one of the successes of British colonial administration. It made the people understand that their rulers were genuinely interested in them and it demonstrated a degree of humility quite different from the attitude of the official who always speaks through an interpreter. It was the key, however imperfect, to an understanding of the culture of the people and engagement with them. Reports coming from Africa now show that of all the nineteenth-century colonisers, the British were preferred. The language policy may be one of the reasons.

Unfortunately, though, there were few, if any, outsiders who spoke the language, but like the Dutch, the Lenje understood that being a small tribe this was inevitable. The independent Zambian government took the bull by the horns and made English the sole official language. This was very wise. One only has to see the experience of India trying to make Hindi the sole language, or Sri Lanka ousting Tamil from its status under British rule, to appreciate the terrible consequences of language discrimination.

The Broken Hill Rural district was quite compact, with the main road from Lusaka to Broken Hill and the Copperbelt running through it. In the centre there was a big block of European farms known as Chisamba. There were two interesting geographical features, namely the Lukanga swamp teeming with mosquitoes and fish to the west and the Luangwa Valley at the bottom of a steep escarpment, very hot and full of game to the east.

There was a Game Ranger in the district as poaching was a problem with two nearby towns full of South Africans, who were often enthusiastic but not always ethical hunters. Night hunting with powerful lights which dazzled the animal was forbidden and brought heavy punishment, including the confiscation of any vehicles used.

It is worth mentioning two cases in which opinion has completely reversed. Crocodiles were regarded as vermin and there was a good luxury market for the skins, if well cured, for shoes and ladies' handbags. Many whites from the south got permits to hunt crocodiles until it was realised that the stocks of the best edible fish, the bream or tilapia, were diminishing. Professional research was commissioned in the late fifties. It was found that barbel or catfish were the principal food of the young crocodiles. When the crocodiles were killed the barbel increased, and they in turn fed on the young bream. So the crocodile was moved from vermin to protected status. It has to be recognised that the result was the loss of some young children.[2]

Wild dogs were regarded as dangerous vermin, so much so that there was a bounty of £1 per dog. One Saturday in Broken Hill Rural (we worked Saturday mornings), a man brought in five tails and I duly paid the money against his thumb print receipt. It transpired that the pack of dogs, frightening creatures, had fallen into the fast canal of the Mulungushi Dam hydro-electric scheme and were swept up against the grille and drowned. Not perhaps what was intended or expected when the scheme of bounty was designed, but the conditions were satisfied and it must have been like winning the lottery for the villager. Now wild dogs are highly valued and protected.

The Mulungushi Dam, about 30 miles east of Broken Hill, was constructed by the mine to provide water and electricity. It was a favourite place for picnics and boating, but not swimming on account of the crocs. I had a theory that if one went to the middle and had a boat circling around the crocs would be frightened off. I tried it once and survived, but it caused Brenda such stress that I did not think it fair to repeat the pleasure.[3]

Although Broken Hill Rural District headquarters was in a town with the urban district all around for some twenty miles, the touring was just the same as for any other rural district. There were considerable differences from the system of "trek" in the Sudan. In the first place the Sudan was much hotter and more uncomfortable in almost every aspect. Trekking was by camel, foot, horse, lorry or steamer while in NR the bicycle was almost universal, using bush paths where local people had gone before. These were rather like the tracks between villages in England that the English have inherited from their ancestors.

The people were largely concentrated in villages, each under a head man, whereas in most of the Sudan they were much more scattered. Many in the Sudan were nomadic, like the Kababish in Northern Kordofan, or semi-nomadic like the Nuer and Dinka. In Northern Rhodesia also, the soil structure and climate were much more suitable for wheeled vehicles. In 1956 one could engage and pay for 22 carriers, and later when there was an economy drive because of low copper prices the number was reduced to 19. Most men had bicycles and the porters usually carried loads on their own bicycles, either riding or pushing.

When the family came on tour, as they did once or twice, Brenda of course had her own bicycle, while Stella was on a seat behind a district messenger. We had a sort of meat safe made for Matthew and this was tied on to the carrier of a porter's bicycle. A touring officer had a bicycle allowance of 10 shillings (50p) per month.

There was a well-ordered routine going from village to village, carrying the tax registers and the cash box for the tax which was something like 10 shillings per year. In the Nuer districts it had been seven shillings (35p) or the equivalent in Egyptian piastres, which was the currency there.

In NR, one went to the starting point by the district five-ton lorry. On arrival a long procession of bicycles was formed with two or three district messengers under either the head or the second messenger, the DO, the Chief, two or three court assessors, and several Kapasus or chiefs' policemen. As one arrived on the outskirts of a village it was the custom for the women to be waiting outside and clap gently as the party arrived. Each village had a head man who would welcome the visitors and summon the people, who would sit around in the shade. The register would be called and amended as necessary if there had been deaths or the onset of disabilities. Many men were away in the mines and the common reply when a name was called would be "Ku Kabwe". This was the Lenje name for Broken Hill and it has now reverted to the local usage, one of the more sensible changes of name since decolonisation.

Then a discussion would follow and there would be a particular topic chosen, such as the need for children, particularly girls, to be sent to school, the desirability of making pit latrines and not just using the bush outside the huts, or conservation issues such as not ploughing within five yards of a stream bank. The gardens and grain bins in season would be inspected to try to forecast whether there would be any hunger that year. People could raise any questions they had, such as the destruction of crops by wild animals, the need for a school, a well or a road and so forth. Sometimes one could manage eight or ten villages in a long day.

It was the aim to visit every village every year, but staff changes meant that this did not always happen. It was closer administration than in the Sudan, where administrative officers were much thinner on the ground.

Meanwhile, the porters and servants had been making their way direct to the next camp and one arrived there to find the tent already erected and tea ready. The villagers had made a grass screen, a grass latrine and bathing area and a sort of gazebo of poles and a thatched roof called a "chitenje". The Union Jack was flying and the village women had brought water as well as chickens and eggs for sale. Except in the hottest months of September and October, there was a fire with plenty of firewood. A traditional campsite was usually under an especially large tree, and it was pleasant to sit beside the fire on a crisp evening after a long day cycling and talking. People would sometimes come to talk to the DO in his camp, making their approach known in the night by gentle clapping. This routine was continued for some 12 or 15 days. On return a tour report had to be completed in a fixed format.

This could become rather stereotyped and tedious, but it did mean that the Provincial Commissioner in each Province and the Secretariat in Lusaka had a picture of the condition of the people. It was said that Sir Gilbert Rennie, the Governor just before I arrived, read every tour report, but it cannot have left him much time for governing.

I have a vivid memory of touring in the most remote part of the district, west of the Kafue River. The people there had the habit, when they wanted to show particular affection or respect, of taking your hand, turning it over and spraying the palm gently with saliva. As I sat reading by the fire one night an old lady came and sat nearby until I noticed her. She wanted my help in tracing her son who had gone to the Copperbelt. Naturally I wrote to the DC concerned, who would send a district messenger to enquire. It was probably without result but her trust that the DO would help was moving.

There were about eight chiefs in Broken Hill Rural, each with his traditional title – Chipepo, Liteta, Mungule and the like. When a Chief died, or more rarely retired or was dismissed, his successor took the same title, not even distinguishing it as our monarchs do by using "the first", "the second" etc. All were members of the Lenje Native Authority which had its offices about 30 miles south of Broken Hill. They had a share of the tax revenue and a budget with a few educated African staff. A very necessary job was supervising the finances of the Native Authority.

Each chief had his own court with two assessors. A simple record, usually in English, was kept of every case. It was not always easy to get the chief to understand that an unhappy litigant had a perfect right to appeal, and that to do so was not an act of disloyalty in itself. In the Magistrate's court the Magistrate would end each record by writing IRA to show that the person sentenced had been informed of the right of appeal. In the chief's court it often happened that the court would say "six months' imprisonment, no appeal."

It was in many ways a fortunate district, although the Lenje did not have the enterprise to take full advantage of it. On the whole the soil was good, the rains adequate and the communications excellent, with the railway line and new tarmac road going right through the district. In addition, Broken Hill Rural contained three European farming areas from which the intelligent could learn. There was a programme of establishing peasant farms at Keembe, in the centre of the district, to introduce the Lenje to commercial farming. Of particular note was the introduction of ox carts for transport and a system of loans for fertiliser, seed etc. The traditional method of transport was by crude wooden sledges, but the wheeled carts caused much less erosion. When I returned in 2000 I found that Keembe had developed and an agricultural institute had been established, provided by Lord Samuel in the early years of independence to run courses for farmers.

By then a market had developed in dried peppers as well as the staple, maize, and some cotton. In Mumbwa district, to the west, a considerable amount of cotton seemed to be produced. A prominent European farmer nearby was producing fresh vegetables in polytunnels for the European supermarkets.

An event of 1957 was the visit of Queen Elizabeth the Queen Mother to the district. A site for a formal reception for the chiefs and other notables was built, mostly from grass and poles, in Chief Chipepo's area north of Broken Hill. All went off perfectly. At this time there was among Africans considerable loyalty to the Queen, who was known as Queenie, and her mother.

With things seeming fairly stable in Broken Hill Rural my own mother came out for a lengthy stay, bringing her favourite comfortable portable chair. She enjoyed it all very much,

especially as she could help with Stella and Matthew. Stella
had a sweet nursemaid called Rosemary, the daughter of third
messenger Lazaro Mumba. After a while Mother got a
temporary job as a teacher at the Convent, which she said
was quite different from being a teacher in an industrial town
in England as she had been 30 years before. It gave her some
real financial independence as well.

David, my brother, 21 months younger than I, had decided
that he did not see a real future where he worked as a farming
assistant in New Zealand. I arranged for a very good local
farming friend, Bob Burton, to offer him a job as an assistant
farm manager with a small house about 20 miles outside
Broken Hill. He arrived with his beautiful wife Joan and their
small children, Jackie and Stephen.

They would all come in to Broken Hill once a week for
shopping and some social life. Then Michael, my other
brother, came on his way home after two or three years in
New Britain, north of Papua New Guinea. He had with him
a school friend, Ian Ledingham. So Mother had her three sons
together again.

At this time the Federation was riding high and seeking
ever more powers to lead to independence as the Dominion
of Central Africa. Colonial Service Officers knew that
African opinion was bitterly opposed to this. It seemed that
politically there was an impasse, with the British government
refusing to grant further powers so long as African opposition
existed.

Although independence did not seem an immediate
prospect, the development of the public services in the
Federation meant that there was pressure to split off many of
the DC's powers. I concluded that whatever happened most
of us in the Provincial Administration would have to specialise,
and I chose law. I therefore began to take a correspondence
course in Part One of the Bar Examinations. I would get up
early and spend an hour or more each morning in the rondavel
which counted as our second spare room. I managed to pass
the exams in Criminal Law and Contract.

Figure 23 Broken Hill (now Kabwe) Rurul District, 1957. About to leave on tour, seen off by Mother, Rosemary the nanny, Stella and Matthew. On the lorry are the District Messengers (the DC's men), bicycles and the cook.

Every cadet joining the Colonial Administrative Service undertook a years' course, usually at Oxford or Cambridge. Sudan did not have a similar scheme, although I had been very lucky in being sent to MECAS in the Lebanon. There was also provision for selected Colonial Service officers to take what was called the Second Devonshire course, which was a form of sabbatical at the end of the second or third tour. I applied to go on this and we travelled home in July 1958 after a tour of three years and four months.

It had been a very satisfactory time, during which two healthy children had been born and my family reunited, with pleasant amenities and an interesting job in a good climate. Both my District Commissioners in Broken Hill Rural, John Blunden and then Hugh Haile, had been good men to work for. So we took the train for Cape Town and a Union Castle boat back to England, collecting a green Ford Consul with a front bench seat on arrival in Tilbury.

15

OXFORD AGAIN

We were able to stay at the Commonwealth Services Club in South Parks Road, Oxford. This was in a large Victorian house, which has now disappeared, opposite the laboratories.

We had decided to buy a house, if at all possible, as a base when we returned to England, which could be let in the interim. After looking at a number of unpromising places in the city we found an end-of-terrace, three-storey stone house in Woodstock. It was set back from the road on a separate higher terrace, which was just as well as the road was the A44 main road from Oxford to Stratford. The other disadvantage was that it had only a tiny garden at the side, through which there was a right of way for two rather unpredictable old ladies who lived at the rear in what had formerly been part of our house. The price, however, was very cheap, being only £1650. The entrance hall doubled as the dining room and there were two bedrooms on the first floor and another two, with one approached via the other, on the second. It had the accommodation we needed and we soon had the kitchen brought up to date.

We then engaged a French au pair girl called Monique. Her family had a grocery shop in Juan Les Pins on the French Riviera. She was quite unlike what one would expect from a daughter of the French Riviera, being very stolid and unadventurous. However, having accepted that our efforts to brighten and improve her life would never be successful, the arrangement worked well. The house was quite near to Blenheim Park and Monique could be relied on to take the children there safely. It also allowed Brenda to pursue her interests, including unofficially attending some literature lectures at the university, and lessons in harmony.

On the Second Devonshire course one could more or less choose one's subject for study, subject to the agreement of the Director of the course who was a genial District Officer from Nigeria. I elected to concentrate on the making of constitutions for multi-racial communities, a very live matter at the time. I was assigned to Dr David Yardley, the Law tutor of St Edmund Hall, a man of about the same age as I was who became a good friend.

There were some fascinating seminars to attend. One was with Marjorie Perham of Nuffield College, who of course had a tremendous reputation in colonial studies. We got on well and I remember fondly a tea and croquet party at her house high on the Berkshire Downs. I always regret not taking up her suggestion of corresponding with her on my return to Northern Rhodesia.

Then there was Sir Kenneth Wheare, the Rector of Exeter College, a very direct and witty Australian who was extremely knowledgeable on the different constitutions of the Commonwealth and how they came into being. A generation later my son Oliver was to live in a house belonging to his widow; she wisely would not let the house to an undergraduate until she had made sure that he understood how a plumbing ball-cock worked. Also very interesting were the seminars conducted by a white South African, Kenneth Kirkwood, the Rhodes Professor of Race Relations at St Anthony's College.

Meanwhile, in my spare time I was eating my dinners at the Inner Temple and taking the remaining Bar Examinations. I had chosen to do Roman Dutch Law instead of Conveyancing since it was the law of Southern Rhodesia, which had been brought up from the Cape where it had been established by the Dutch settlers. I went to lectures at All Souls by the principal authority on Roman Dutch Law and managed to get a Law Society second class, which meant rather more than it does in universities these days. I already had a second in Criminal Law. By mid-1959 I had completed Part One of the Bar Examinations.

In December there was a pleasant excursion. The French Government invited a number of British and Belgian Colonial Service officers to a conference in Paris. The French had recently put into effect a policy of self-government for French Dependent Territories. These territories could choose either independence or remaining within a union with France which would be very much to their financial advantage. All, I think, except Mali, had chosen the union. The French compared it to the British Commonwealth, but it meant so much subsidy from France to the newly independent countries that the UK Treasury would never have agreed to such an arrangement for British dependent territories. Paul and Ruth Bourne were part of the British delegation and we had a marvellous time. There were lots of receptions, visits to places of interest and an evening at the Folies Bergère. All this, I might say, was at the expense of the French taxpayer.

I was naturally attached to St John's College, which at this time did not have a middle common room for graduate students. My old tutor, Conrad Costin, had become President, and perhaps through his intervention, as well as that of Edwin Slade, the law tutor, I was invited to become a member of the Senior Common Room. It was a great pleasure to be able to lunch and dine there as I wished and meet so many interesting people. The privilege was not limited to my year there and I have continued to be able to take advantage of it subsequently, for which I am very grateful.

Before we left Broken Hill my mother had taken a job with the Federal European Education Service at Mazabuka, a farming area south-west of Lusaka. She had a small semi-detached house with a servant. She was enjoying life to the full when Michael, who had returned to England, announced that he was going to marry Anne Prendergast. Mother was not willing to miss this and so she returned to England, where she took a flat in Wimborne, Dorset, near where her sister Kathleen Kinnison lived after her retirement from teaching in south-west Shropshire, just below the rock outcrops known as the Stiperstones.

Mother and Kath came to stay and look after the children at Easter while we accepted an invitation to visit the Hicksons, whom we had known in the Upper Nile, in the Irish Republic. Gordon and Daphne had bought a farm about 30 miles west of Dublin, with a fine Georgian house, stables and other buildings. From there we went off to the west to see something of those beautiful but socially then very primitive places. In one dark pub it was clear that Brenda, the only woman present, was very unwelcome. The contrast with the Ireland of today could not be greater. Gordon said that Africa was a very good training for farming in Ireland. When he rang urgently for the vet at ten in the morning, the housekeeper said she would just see if he was up.

Less agreeable was the news that Brenda's bilharzia infestation, a legacy from the Sudan, was confirmed. She went into the Hospital for Tropical Diseases in London and suffered, with her customary courage, a course of antimony injections. These were given daily, each larger than the one before. When the dose reached 17 milligrams the poison caused her heart to collapse and she could not take any more. Fortunately the treatment proved to be enough, although the recommended final dose was 25 milligrams, and she could put the experience behind her. This was just as well in view of what was to come.

At the end of a very fruitful and enjoyable year we said goodbye to Monique and returned to Cape Town on a Union Castle ship, then drove to Northern Rhodesia in our Ford Consul.

16

MUNGWI DEVELOPMENT CENTRE

I had hopes of being posted to my own district after over four years in Northern Rhodesia and five in the Sudan, but this did not happen. The importance of the copper mines to the Empire's war effort meant that the country had developed economically at a fast pace along the line of the railway, and the administrative structures needed to respond. Accordingly there was a great bulge in the promotion structure because many men had been recruited from the forces after the war, some of them of high quality. So I did not get my district, but I did obtain the next best thing, which was to be District Officer in charge of a new development centre about 15 miles east of Kasama, the capital of the Northern Province. The Governor, Sir Arthur Benson, had been leaning heavily on the two great mining companies, Anglo American and the Rhodesian Selection Trust. He pointed out that the success and profitability of the mines had caused considerable social problems, especially in the Northern and Luapula Provinces from which a large proportion of their labour came. Men went to the mines and sometimes returned home only rarely. As a result there were many villages with few adult males living in them.

The consequence was that there was neither the motivation nor the labour to improve the conditions or the lives of the people, for example by building schools and improving communications. The two mining groups agreed to give a million pounds each, a lot of money at the time, for the development, both social and economic, of the two provinces. A Development Commissioner who was a senior officer in the agricultural department was appointed to lead the project, since it was recognised that the basis of future development would have to be in agriculture. There were few other natural resources, but the task was considerable since the soils are generally poor in these two northern provinces.

It had been decided that the main centre of development would be at Mungwi. It was planned that a major secondary school for boys would be established, and that there would be demonstration farms as well as a Development Area Training Centre (DATC). This was already operating under a Principal and ran courses in rural development, both for women and for men. The Principal was about to go on leave and we occupied his house which, like everything else, had been recently built. This gave an opportunity for the District Officer's house to be built, and we were able to move into it when the DATC Principal returned from leave.

The Mungwi Township and Development Area were contained within a triangle roughly three miles by five. The water supply came from a dam already constructed on a stream at the apex of the triangle. Water was pumped through the area by a ram which was extremely successful, using only the energy from the water pressure.

Electricity was planned and arrived a few months later. It was an extension of the Kasama town scheme which came from a beautiful waterfall a few miles west of the town. The aim was to provide some of the amenities which were attracting so many to the Copperbelt. In the centre of the Development Area was to be a township with shops, housing, a bottle store, the secondary school, a primary school and so forth. Shortly a telephone service arrived, again an extension from Kasama. I had a small temporary office in a prefabricated structure and was on the telephone one day during a thunderstorm. There was a sudden crash in my ear and I found myself on the floor. It seems that there have been no ill effects.

The main emphasis of the scheme of development was to be on agriculture and conservation. The Agricultural Department had a most energetic, enthusiastic and eccentric conservationist called Bill Verboom. He was a Dutchman who had worked in Indonesia and had great experience, as well as a fund of horrifying stories of the battle against Soekarno and the nationalists when the Dutch tried to return to Indonesia after the war

The need to protect the fragile soil of Africa had already penetrated the Federal Department of European or Commercial Agriculture, which was called the "Ministry of Conservation". In Mungwi an area cleared of trees and scrub would always be limited in area with strips of natural vegetation left all round. Where there was a slope there would be ridges constructed at intervals, often planted with chick peas. All earth roads would be cambered with frequent drains running off into the bush. Road grader operators, often mixed-race Afrikaners, were given detailed training and supervision. The farmers were taught rotation of crops. Initially about a dozen 40-acre farms were cleared and simple houses built for the farmers. There was an agricultural supervisor who had worked in Tanganyika. It was his responsibility to advise these farmers, and he and I had the job of recruiting and selecting them. He also operated a dairy using superior imported cattle in order to teach livestock management and better diet.

The soils of the Northern Province are very easily exhausted. The Bemba, the dominant local tribe, have evolved a system of agriculture known as chitimene. They would cut down the trees in a circle which they planned to cultivate, and would also cut off branches from trees around which were dragged into the circle. In the hot season, just before the rains, all this wood would be burnt and the seeds of maize or millet planted in the ashes. This provided reasonable crops for three years, after which another area would be burnt and cultivated. This system meant that villages would be abandoned and moved after a few years, making it very difficult to plan social services such as schools and clinics. There was no incentive to build more healthy and stable homes, and the aim was that if long-term sustainable agriculture could develop, the condition of the people would improve and the unemployed from the Copperbelt would be attracted back home to become commercial farmers.

The question then arose as to where cash could be obtained, since all agriculture had hitherto been restricted to subsistence. In addition to cereals, the people, the women in particular, grew sweet potatoes and cassava – a root vegetable known elsewhere as manioc. It is a starchy food of low nutritional value but it does provide a hunger reserve, and the women had the sense to make sure that there was always some to be harvested from mounds built around the village. Unless soaked for a considerable period in the stream, cassava was poisonous. It smelt terribly and one was always aware of it when giving a lift to a Bemba village woman. On revisiting Zambia in 2000 I was told that chitimene had been forbidden by law, but this seems to have had no effect since on flying from Kasama to the Luangwa valley one could see a great number of burnt circles below.

The problem remained to find ways of putting cash into the hands of farmers. The best possibility seemed to be the encouragement of Turkish tobacco. Kasama is about 500 miles from the line of rail (although some 20 years later it did acquire a rail connection through the Chinese-built Tanzam, or Tazara, railway). The product selected had to have a high ratio of value to weight to justify the long haul. Sir Stuart Gore Brown, at Shiwa Ngandu, had tried hard to produce essential oils but eventually he had to admit failure. Virginia tobacco, which could be very profitable to a skilled farmer in the European farming areas on the line of rail, was too complicated and required too much capital for barns and other equipment. Turkish tobacco, on the other hand, is a peasant crop in which the whole family can assist. The leaves are cured by being removed from the stalks and hung out to dry on strings. It was thus a suitable crop and normally could provide a reasonable reward. The trouble was that the market was very small, and usually there was only one trader to buy the crop. So although there was some success it never took off.

In 2000 I met a British man, the Deputy Head of the Mungwi Secondary School, who had retired to Kasama and taken up land given to him by the Bemba Local Authority. He was having success with coffee and perhaps that will be the future for the Northern Province.

Mungwi was something of a showpiece, so everyone who visited Kasama would be wheeled out to see it. Brenda had to undertake a great deal of entertainment, but usually only for coffee or tea and at most for lunch. Among the visits was one by the whole of the Monckton Commission, which was later to advise that the experiment of the Central African Federation with the capital in Salisbury, Southern Rhodesia was not sustainable in the long run against the wishes of the majority of the African populations.

Mungwi was intentionally placed in a Native Authority area, being within the jurisdiction of Paramount Chief Chitimukulu. The liaison with him was through the Bemba Native Authority representative called Barnabas Mwamba, with whom I had a good relationship. The paramount chief himself was a tiresome and rather drunken old fellow whose residence was about 10 miles east of Mungwi. The Bemba is the biggest tribe in Zambia, extending over four districts. They are intelligent and rather slippery people, providing the most active and successful politicians in the country.

Although we were so far from the line of rail it was a good time for the family. Stella began school in Kasama, although there was one very worrying incident when an overbearing district messenger demanded to drive the Land Rover she was in and crashed it into a tree. Fortunately the real driver, Lemon Shula, who was also in the vehicle, saw the crash coming and protected Stella with his body.

Figure 24 Model Farm in Mungwi Development Area, Kasama,
Northern Province, designed on conservation principle of crop
rotation to provide an alternative to shifting cultivation based on
burning trees to plant maize and millet in the ash.

The time at Mungwi began sadly. In September 1959, shortly
after arriving, I had a telegram to say that Mother had died at
the age of only 60. Spring Cottage in Abbots Bromley had
been sold by us a few months before, at her request, and until
we could see whether it would be practical for her to return to
Northern Rhodesia she had remained in her flat near her
sister Kathleen in Wimborne, Dorset. She fell seriously ill one
night and the people in the flat below, a vet and his wife, had
telephoned repeatedly to the doctor for help. All that he did
was to tell her to take an aspirin. The following morning he
came and immediately ordered her to hospital, but she died
from a ruptured aorta. Later her cousin Hilda made a formal
complaint and the doctor was reprimanded. As the years have
gone by I have realised more and more what a splendid
mother she was and what sacrifices she made for her children.
She was the personification of love, humour and duty.

Some 14 months later, in November 1960, we took all our
local leave to visit East Africa. We drove north through

Tanganika, stopping first at the Ngorongoro crater which at that time we had almost to ourselves. We stayed at a small lodge on the rim of the crater and went down into it in the Ford Consul, seeing all kinds of wildlife in great profusion. Matthew was nearly four, and spent much of his time under the dashboard in front of Brenda. When invited to get up and see the lions resting only a few yards away he replied, "I like it here."

We went right across Tanganyika into Kenya to stay with the Waughs, previously colleagues in Khartoum, who were then in Nairobi. By this time they had five children; their intended fourth turned out to be twins, Giles and Juliet. Duncan was a Security Liaison Officer for MI5, although his employer could not be mentioned aloud then.

We continued north into the highlands to stay at the magnificent Outspan Hotel, with its fine garden and wonderful view of snow-capped Mount Kenya. Then we turned southeast to the coast, stopping at the Tsavo Park on the way. This has glorious views of Mount Tanganyika and I have a memory of a line of elephants of all ages passing before us in the sunset with the mountain behind.

We were booked for a few days into a group of holiday cottages at Bamburi, about five miles north of Mombasa. The cottages were thatched with palm leaves, the usual roof covering on the coast, and situated in a grove of coconut palms on the edge of the Indian Ocean. One day we went for a day's surfing at Malindi, about 100 miles north. On another day there was a real adventure. We hired a local white youth to take us big game fishing in his boat. A man at another cottage came with us and we shared the expense. Brenda was with me and so was Matthew, but Stella stayed behind to play with the man's daughter. We were equipped with the harness necessary for big game fishing. After an hour without success the youth said that he would take us along the reef where we would be sure to catch something. As he went alongside it a wave knocked us right over and we all found ourselves in the sea. Matthew had been in the cabin but he had just come back to talk to us. I grabbed him, but was hampered by the harness. The owner managed to unbuckle it from both of us and we all tried to cling to the upturned boat while I was also holding onto Matthew, but the waves were too large and we were repeatedly swept off the boat. A worry was that there was an African deck hand trapped in the cabin; he would not dive down to escape but remained alive in a pocket of air there. Eventually the owner managed to wrench off the tilting window, taken from an old Austin A40 car I suspected, and the African shot up to the surface. That was not the end of the worry, though. He had been in a beer fight the night before (this was Sunday morning), and I was afraid, although I did not mention it to Brenda, that sharks would scent his blood. The other man and I were trying to keep Brenda and Matthew hoisted up onto the boat, but the waves continued to push them along it or away. For weeks afterwards Brenda, who was three months pregnant then, had parallel marks across her abdomen from the friction of the ribs on the upturned boat.

Eventually Brenda said that she did not think she could hold on for much longer and the owner revealed that he did have life belts, but they were inside in the upturned boat. I said that if he could manage to get one for Brenda and Matthew, I thought that the men could manage for some time. On his second attempt, by diving down into the cabin he managed to bring up a life belt. Brenda and Matthew got into it and we were fairly sure they would then be safe.

Fortunately, all this time we had been drifting towards a gap in the reef. There were a number of Sunday holiday boats in the calm water between the reef and the shore, who had seen what was happening but could not get near to us. However, as we drifted away from the reef rescue became possible. An African canoe came and took aboard the owner and his deckhand while a local European, a bank manager I think, took the rest of us in his boat.

We had taken Absent, our cook, with us on this holiday. He of course had never seen the sea before, and he watched us as we arrived in our bedraggled condition, pitying our foolishness. That night we went to the Anglican cathedral in Mombasa to give thanks for our safety. The disaster was due, I think, to the fact that the boat was largely homemade. It had no keel and could be turned over easily by a large wave. We were also grateful that we only had one child with us. Had Stella come with us too, it would have been nearly impossible to hold onto both children in the waves.

The next major family event was the birth of our third child, Oliver, in Kasama European Hospital on 22 May 1961. The hospital was really a large house which we located on our trip to Zambia with Oliver in 2000, when it was about to be bought from the Government by the middle aged African woman school teacher who occupied it. The birth went well, but afterwards Brenda developed a complaint which was diagnosed as amoebic dysentery. She undertook a course of treatment, at the end of which she was notified that the laboratory assistant had made a mistake. Meanwhile, Oliver had not been putting on weight because he had been absorbing the treatment with his mother's milk. Mother and baby came happily home to Mungwi, but some six weeks later Brenda woke up unable to move. It was only with the greatest difficulty that she could get into the car to be taken to Kasama. As we later discovered, this was the first onset of the rheumatoid arthritis which, with greater or lesser remissions from time to time, was to be her unwelcome companion for the rest of her life. For some three years or so there was a reluctance by every doctor to say clearly what the problem was. Not until we were in Choma in 1964 did a blunt doctor there say definitely that she had rheumatoid arthritis. Brenda, however, had always suspected it since she had nursed her father at the end of his life and he had suffered from the same disease.

When we first arrived in Mungwi I was the Acting Community Development Officer at the DATC with the support of an excellent deputy, Edward Musonda, as well as being the DO In Charge. Brenda was the Acting Assistant Community Development Officer, since the quite sensible policy of the Department of Rural Development was that husband and wife teams should be appointed if possible, as women's development was an essential part of the policy. The Commissioner for Rural Development wanted Brenda to continue with her work with the local women, which she did on a part-time basis. I continued to have close contact with the DATC after the Community Development Officer's return, since I was given the responsibility of training the chief's police, known as Kapasus in Northern Province. They came in relays for courses of about three weeks and I had a senior district messenger who had been in the army as a kind of sergeant major, and also an African police officer. The Kapasus wore khaki uniforms with red trimmings. They were given basic instruction in the principles of policing, drill, law and so forth. Some District Officers in the Province felt that this was becoming rather military, and indeed the motivation was partly to help the chiefs deal with political unrest and enforce the law. At the end of each course there would be a passing-out parade and awards made, usually by the Provincial Commissioner. I had the impression that the courses instilled some pride and confidence in men who had traditionally been little more than personal retainers of the chief.

There was one incident worth recording. There was much building going on throughout the Mungwi area, for which I was responsible. We had good supplies of stone and a rather attractive brown slate which could be used for flooring and cladding. Good concrete plinths were absolutely necessary to prevent white ants from climbing up walls and causing the eventual disintegration of a building. For concrete, stone of the right size was required and a stone crusher invaluable. I managed to borrow one and we moved it from place to place on the back of a five-ton lorry. This meant that it had to be pushed up a ramp, since there was no winch. On one occasion the pushers were having some difficulty and I lent a hand. The pit-sawn planks of the ramp were not strong enough. They bent and the crusher fell over; it caught my left wrist and there was rather a lot of blood. I was taken to the house. Brenda kept the children out of the way and bound me up temporarily. She then took me into Kasama Hospital with my arm held up and attached to the frame of the Land Rover canopy. On arrival the surgeon (one of only two doctors in Kasama) was waiting and operated under local anaesthetic. I heard him say at one point that the airport could be told that the plane need not wait any longer. I later learnt that my junior clerk, Gervase Chikopela, had realised that the scheduled flight had just arrived in Kasama. He telephoned to say that the injured District Officer was on his way and the plane should be kept in case it was necessary to take him to the Copperbelt. I always think that this was a remarkable exercise of initiative and self-confidence by a very junior clerk.

The arm had to be kept in a sling for a few weeks, but there were no lasting ill effects except a sensitive area on the left wrist where a nerve was somehow relocated close to the skin. As a result I have since then worn my wristwatch on the right wrist.

There was one unexpected interlude while at Mungwi. I was posted for what I expected would be a six-month spell as Acting District Commissioner at Isoka. This district is in the extreme north-east of the country adjoining Tanganyika to the north and Nyasaland to the east, with its boma on the Great North Road. It is fairly hilly and has some beautiful country. I was to take over from Philip Large, who was expecting to return after leave. As he took me around the District I remember him saying that he would give up the job if he did not get a really good laugh every day. One of the features of the district was a very good senior clerk who was literally a lunatic; at the new moon he would strip off and climb the district flag pole. Otherwise all was well. I must confess that I never saw this spectacle and rely on Philip's information.

The DC's house was in a fine position with a distant view and the small township below. Brenda went to the butcher to get meat and he took her through, behind the shop, to where there was a dead cow lying covered in flies. He invited Brenda to select the cut that she would like. Soon, however, there was a change of plan and in the end the permanent DC, Ian

MacDonald, arrived to take over. So after three weeks we returned to Mungwi.

Politically an enormous change took place during the Mungwi period between 1959 and 1962. Until then most African political activity had been directed towards opposition to the Federation with Rhodesia and Nyasaland. Many officials were unsympathetic to it as well, since its policies were biased towards Southern Rhodesia where the majority of the (mostly white) voters lived. The wealth of Northern Rhodesia's copper was diverted to Salisbury and Nyasaland. At a meeting in Broken Hill I heard Sir Godfrey Huggins, the Prime Minister of the Federation (and later Lord Malvern), defend the federal principle on the basis that "we (i.e. Southern Rhodesia) had to agree to it because we hadn't a bean". The British Treasury supported the Federation for a similar reason: it took the burden of poor Nyasaland off its back. So the other two territories took a share of Northern Rhodesia's copper wealth.

The Monckton Commission, after its visit, reported that the Federation had no viable future against the opposition of the majority of Africans in the two northern territories, which would in consequence be expected to make their own way towards independence. In 1960 Harold Macmillan, the British Prime Minister, made a widely reported speech in Cape Town declaring that the "wind of change is blowing through Africa". The nationalist parties scented power and stepped up their agitation both against each other and the government. The fact that the country was woefully unready by almost any measure was brushed aside.

The change of policies which took place between 1954 and 1960 was astounding and I have not yet seen it fully analysed. In 1954 the United Nations Committee on Colonialism, a body devoted to ending any arrangement which it would describe, however bizarrely, as imperialism, recommended that Britain should work toward independence for Tanganyika, a former League of Nations Trust Territory, in 1979 – i.e. 25 years away. Britain rejected this recommendation as being too soon! How very different the fate of Africa would have been if the recommendations had been accepted as a basis for a joint policy, with the United Nations and Britain working towards an agreed programme of deliberate decolonisation, with the interests of the native populations as the guiding principle.

So the politicians in Northern Rhodesia and Nyasaland correctly concluded that he who shook the tree most vigorously would gather up the fruits of power. Two main parties had emerged in Northern Rhodesia; the African National Congress (ANC) was led by a comfortable man called Harry Nkumbula who loved drink and women. His main support was among the Tonga of the Southern Province. The other party, the United National Independence Party (UNIP), had as its leader the more ascetic, though rather unstable, Kenneth Kaunda. He was not actually a Northern Rhodesian, being the son of a Malawian from the Church of Scotland Mission at Livingstone who had been transferred to the Chinsali Mission, the most easterly Bemba district. It was said that as a teacher, young Kenneth had been dismissed for fathering a child by one of his schoolgirls. Whatever the truth, it illustrates one of the main problems of politics in Central Africa at the time: the leading actors were often failures, misfits or even criminals. The range of employers for a man educated to secondary level was very narrow, extending only to the government, teaching, or the mining companies. If an employee was unsatisfactory no one else would have him, so the only career left was politics.

UNIP became the dominant party among the Bemba in the north and Luanpula Provinces and also in the Copperbelt. In August 1961 Kaunda toured the Northern Province, and although he did not actually incite violence he declared that the angry people would fill the prisons. In fact in the front of his audience there was a claque of wild youths chanting Bemba war songs. Widespread sabotage occurred: schools were burned, trees felled across roads and bridges destroyed. Attacks were made on Native Authority buildings and many people were beaten up for the offence of not possessing a party membership card. In the towns where there were both UNIP and ANC supporters, simple people would be tricked into producing the "wrong" card and so beaten up. Others had their houses burned while they slept, a very easy matter since all that was needed was a match to the thatch. In one case, which reached the High Court, the door was secured from the outside while the house and its occupants burned.

In Kasama my DC was Ian Wethey whom I very much admired. As a former officer in the Indian Army he was experienced in dealing with such a situation, and he quickly brought his district under control. This was important because the Federal Army was believed to be more than ready to come to the aid of the civil power, and we could have been faced with a lengthy insurgency. As it was, very few lives were lost and order was soon restored. I undertook touring in the district round Mungwi, visiting the villages and talking to the people in the ordinary way. They responded with their traditional courtesy as though the troubles had never occurred.

In Mungwi there was one night when fires were lit round the periphery of the development area, but we were not attacked. The government and native authority staff assembled in my office and we patrolled constantly. Brenda was given a gun for self-defence. The following day a fearsome collection of confiscated clubs, axes and spears was brought in.

Peter Clark, my friend from Broken Hill, came as Provincial Commissioner and it became clear that there had been a revolution in Lusaka. His view was that the DCs in Northern Province had been too tough and we should not have offended UNIP, which was the coming power. The splendid Ian Wethey was chosen as the sacrifice, and he was transferred to the Labour Department. Later, when I was DC of Sesheke, the head of the Provincial Administration, Len Bean, visited on a tour to assess staff morale. I said that morale in the Provincial Adminstration would not improve unless Wethey were rehabilitated. Bean said he was sure that his sterling qualities would be recognised. In the event, Ian and his charming family left the country before independence. I suspect that Wethey's head had been demanded by Kaunda.

Many admired Kaunda, particularly some churchmen such as Colin Morris and Labour politicians, but I was not one of them. I do concede that he was the best of a bad bunch at the top of UNIP. He managed tribal rivalries well, helped by not being part of a local tribe, as we British were not either. However, his economic policies were disastrous and the country's standard of living plunged. The adoption of a one-party state led to serious oppression, inefficiency and corruption. In 1964 the gross domestic product per person in Zambia was twice that of South Korea; in 1999 South Korea's was 27 times that of Zambia.

We made good friends in Mungwi with Edward Robinson who had come from Mapanza Secondary School in Southern Province to be Deputy Head of the new Mungwi Secondary School, working for the then Universities Mission to Central Africa (now merged into the United Society for the Propagation of the Gospel) at a salary of £48 per year plus keep. He was then still a bachelor. He taught me the delights of chess and talked art and music with Brenda, giving her useful advice. In our year in Oxford she had concentrated on music more than art; Edward said that she would never be more than ordinary in music, but in art she might achieve something unusual. She wisely took that advice and the results are around me as I write.

Edward gave the best explanation of Kaunda's behaviour in the Northern Province, which was quite out of character with the picture he presented to the outside world. In a letter to Christina Lamb, the author of *The Africa House* about Sir Stuart Gore-Brown, Edward quotes from the last few lines of Richard II: Exton brings the coffin containing the body of the murdered king, only to be upbraided by Bolingbroke who was to become Henry IV:

Exton: "From your own mouth, my lord, did I this deed."
Bolingbroke: "They love not poison that do poison need, nor do I thee …"

191

Kaunda ran his poor country down until 1991 when, possibly under the influence of events in Russia and Eastern Europe following the disintegration of the Soviet empire, he agreed to hold elections in which the Movement for Multi-Party Democracy could take part. The result was a rout for Kaunda and UNIP. It is believed that Ex-President Jimmy Carter, whose invaluable organisation had been monitoring the election, was instrumental in persuading Kaunda to retire with dignity.

To return to Mungwi, the Nyanja language was of no use at all in Bembaland, so I had to set about learning Bemba, as did Brenda. Bemba is a far more difficult language than Nyanja and bears little relation to it. The Nyanja-speaking people of the Eastern Province and Nyasaland probably came from the south while the Bemba group were from Central Africa, most likely the Congo area. The Bemba language has a grammatical feature which I have not found elsewhere, known as concords. Words vary according to their position in the sentence. This gives an impression of an absence of definition which seemed to me to reflect the character of the people. After a few months' concentration I passed the higher exam and Brenda the lower, collecting the respective bonuses. Once that was done we felt much more at ease in our jobs.

After a little over two-and-a-half years, leave was due. Being so near to East Africa we decided to return home by the east coast route in March 1962. I drove the Ford Consul to Abercorn and handed it to Barnabas Mwamba, who had bought it with an official loan, to drive back to Mungwi. We then took a plane to Dar es Salaam, which really felt like the tropics again after being on the high plateau of Zambia at over 4000 feet in Mungwi. We took a Lloyd Triestino ship which had come from Cape Town on its way to Trieste. The cabins were rather small and far down, but the food and the ship were fine.

At Aden we were able to spend a day with Mary Charles who had been Brenda's great friend at the London Hospital and who had later encouraged her to come to the Sudan, so she was responsible for our meeting. Aden was appallingly hot and we sat for tea on what Mary said was the only lawn in Aden, a patch of grass about ten foot square. Unfortunately her husband, Charlie, who was the Speaker of the Legislative Assembly in Aden, was busy with work all day so we did not see him. In 1965 he was assassinated by terrorists. His Arabic was of course good, being ex-Sudan Political Service, and he had a regular tennis four with three Arab friends at their club. The terrorists knew this and simply shot him as he came away in his tennis clothes. By then he had already been knighted.

Aden was at that time still exceedingly busy and prosperous, quite unlike the distressed and abandoned place it was to become after Britain withdrew. I think it was the only British territory in which we were unable to leave behind a legitimate, constitutional government with some claim to popular support. It is no accident that its people have had a truly miserable life since independence. It is encouraging that a united Yemen did express a desire to join the Commonwealth, but this is delayed by fanatical Muslim terrorism.

We woke up one morning on the ship to find ourselves moored at the Zattere in Venice, where Brenda and I had spent part of our honeymoon. We went on the vaporetto across to the Doge's Palace. It was the first of April, and we had not foreseen how cold it would be on the water. Oliver, 10 months old, was without socks and the Italian matrons were very disapproving. We went immediately to get some warm clothing for everyone.

During the next night the boat moved to its final destination in Trieste. We had to wait the whole day for a train to Stuttgart. It was raining very heavily and we camped in the first class waiting room. I went out to get some food and the dozen people in the waiting room complained to a railway inspector that we were turning the place into an albergo, a tavern. The inspector's first action was to ask to look at their tickets, and at ours, of course. It turned out that we were the only ones present with first class tickets, so all the others were swept out, leaving us to our privacy. The train travelled through the night to Stuttgart; I put my wet trousers on the heating pipes below the seat and in the morning they were burnt through. The Mercedes car we had ordered was not ready, and we had to spend three days in a hotel waiting for it to be delivered. We took the children to the zoo, and one evening managed to get a babysitter so that we could go to the St John Passion in Stuttgart's largest church. The seriousness of the German audience and their attention to the music, as well as the message, was impressive.

On getting the car at last, we drove through the Black Forest and the children saw snow for the first time. They immediately wanted to build a snowman, but the cold soon overcame their excitement. Earlier we had seen some of the German baroque churches, overwhelming in white and gold. In Armentières in northern France we stayed with Madame Guermonprez, one of the many French war widows from World War I. Brenda and her son Michel had reciprocated in a school exchange when they were about 14. Michel took us on to Deauville, where we went riding before crossing the Channel and back to our little house in Woodstock. Later, Michel and his family came to visit us there and we were able to show them round Oxford.

It was strange being in England again without Mother, but we were able to take up all our Oxford and Woodstock friendships again. Brenda needed her left elbow attended to as she had suffered a riding accident when nursing at a Butlin's Holiday Camp in her early twenties. The elbow was becoming increasingly painful and she returned to the London Hospital for the operation. All went well, although the standards of nursing were not as they had been 20 years before, she thought.

The main distraction of that leave was Oman. I was worried that because of the large wartime seniority group mentioned earlier I might still not get a District, although I was now 35. I therefore went to the Foreign Office to ask if there were any posts available for an Arabic speaker who was an experienced administrator. My contact said that he thought I would be very suitable for the post of Development Secretary in the Sultanate of Oman, as indeed I was with my recent experience of development work. I spent considerable time researching this and visited Neil Innes and his wife in Dorset, who had recently returned from Oman. Neil had been in the Sudan Political Service, ending up as Director of Prisons, and I had known him in Khartoum. The job of Development Secretary seemed very suitable, but it had always previously been filled by a retired man, either a bachelor or with grown-up children. It seemed that the cost of air conditioning might be a problem, and I insisted that the appointment would be on secondment with my pension rights preserved. The Foreign Office thought that there should be no problem, and all that was necessary was to get the formal approval of the Sultan Said bin Taimur. This proved not to be so easy, and word came that the Sultan did not agree to the appointment. When speaking to Ralph Daly many years later in Muscat he said that this was typical; the Sultan would only take British Officers who came on contract towards the end of their careers, who could be got rid of more easily than young men with families who were still part of a career service. Although the job sounded extremely interesting and worthwhile, being, so to speak, the third minister in the Sultan's Government, it would have turned out to be disappointing. Sir Hugh Boustead writes in his memoirs that his period as Development Secretary in Muscat and Oman was the most frustrating of his career, so perhaps I had a lucky escape.

Shortly afterwards, with the expulsion of Said bin Taimur and the accession of his son, who had been at Sandhurst, the atmosphere changed completely. Oman strikes the visitor now as the best administered and happiest of all the Arab countries.

17

SESHEKE, BAROTSELAND

As things turned out I was given what at the time seemed the perfect posting – Sesheke, which is the first station reached when travelling up the Zambesi from Livingstone and the Victoria Falls. It is in what is now the Western Province of Zambia, but was then called Barotseland. The Barotse people were in a direct treaty agreement with the British Crown and always regarded themselves as separate and different from the rest of Northern Rhodesia – and perhaps even superior. The dominant tribe was the Lozi and their language was related to the Zulu of Natal, South Africa and the Matabele of south-western Southern Rhodesia (Zimbabwe). Most of the other Northern Rhodesian tribes were believed, rather vaguely, to have come from the north of the Congo basin. There were four districts in Barotseland, each of them with a representative of the Paramount Chief who had his court at Lealui, a few miles from Mongu and further upstream from Sesheke. The Zambezi flowed through the Barotse territory and dominated its life, with the exception of Mankoya District to the east which lies astride the road to Lusaka. Geographically the area was an extension northwards of the Kalahari desert and the soil was very sandy. As a result, road construction was difficult and bicycles often had to be pushed through the sand. The people depended mainly on their cattle, which usually did well, and on millet and fish.

Sesheke was in the extreme south-east of Barotseland. North-west of it was Senanga District, where the Queen Mother of the Barotse traditionally lived, and Mongu with the Resident (not Provincial) Commissioner. The different title indicated the greater independence of Barotseland. West of that was Kalabo, which had a network of canals. Witchcraft was rife and some years earlier a number of witchcraft-inspired murders had been uncovered. Sesheke, Senanga and Kalabo Districts all bordered Angola, then still under somewhat corrupt and rickety Portuguese administration.

There was a vast amount of tradition and protocol surrounding the Barotse royal family. The counsellors were called Indunas and many had traditional titles. Every subject, when approaching the Paramount Chief, had to drop to the knees before being given the sign to advance further. This did not apply to Government Officers, but there was still considerable formality in a call on the Paramount Chief. His representative in Sesheke was Chief Lubinda, a charming gentleman who lived in a large compound in Mwandi about 30 miles downstream from Sesheke. There he headed the Native Authority. The DC's rest house was built on a bluff overlooking a lagoon with large trees all round. There was a great deal of wildlife and it was the place where Livingstone first crossed the Zambezi. He was said to have preached his first sermon in Northern Rhodesia under a large fig tree which fell down shortly after I arrived. The Director of the Rhodes-Livingstone Museum in Livingstone, a former Resident Commissioner named Gervase Clay, wrote and asked for the timber to be sent to the museum. His idea was that local carvers would be able to sell objects made from Livingstone's tree, but unfortunately the wood was too rotten. Figs are rather short-lived trees.

Mwandi was the site of a station of the Paris Mission. These French Protestant missionaries were an early influence in Barotseland. On re-visiting Mwandi in 2000 I found the dispensary enlarged into a full hospital receiving annual visits from a medical team sent by a Protestant church in the United States. It is one of the best ways, I believe, of helping the Third World, another being economic development resulting from the much reviled globalisation.

Sesheke was a beautiful station with most houses strung along high ground looking over the Zambezi. The drawback was that Barotseland was hotter than most of Northern Rhodesia. We usually slept on the verandah and it was a joy to wake in the morning and see the great river going by with its bird life and snorting hippos.

Almost opposite Sesheke across the river was the South-West African administrative post of Katima Mulilo. Here dwelt the Magistrate, who was also the administrator, and his wife, Mr and Mrs Boshoff. They were very pleasant, cooperative people and we often crossed the river in our small boat at night to play bridge. Behind the Magistrate's office was a huge baobab tree. The previous Magistrate, a well known figure, Major Trolloppe, had cut away a door and made his private lavatory inside. There was a medical officer, Dr Jameson, who made no distinction between patients from Northern Rhodesia or South-West Africa.[1] The store was run by an Irish trader called Finnerty, who had a tennis court where Sesheke and Katima Mulilo residents would play on Saturday afternoons. His wife, who was Afrikaans, made marvellous boerewors, the traditional sausage.

Katima Mulilo was the administrative centre for the Caprivi strip which juts out from South-West Africa to meet the Zambezi, west of Livingstone.[2] There is one point where Southern Rhodesia, Bechuanaland, South-West Africa and Northern Rhodesia meet, commonly known as criminal corner since evaders from justice and smugglers could easily hop between countries. All those territories have now changed their names to, respectively, Zimbabwe, Botswana, Namibia and Zambia.

Just north of Sesheke Barotseland extended across the Zambezi to the south and west of the river, and there was a

Figure 25 View of the Zambezi from the garden at Sesheke. There were always hippos in the river.

powered metal ferry. The bush men of the Kalahari, further south, sometimes came up to the Zambezi here and I once visited a small community of about 20 who were living in temporary grass shelters. They are a short and slight people with wrinkled faces, their skin colour more yellow than black.

The Provincial Forest Officer of Barotseland lived not in Mongu, the administrative headquarters, but in Sesheke. This was because one of the principal natural resources of the province was the extensive teak forests lying some 100 miles north-east of the boma and north-west of Livingstone. The tree is called *baikiaea plurijuga*, and is attractive with a pink leguminous flower in season. It was marketed as Rhodesian teak, and at the time was much used for parquet flooring. There was a privately owned sawmill with two or three European staff. The mechanic, Bob, had been in the Sudan previously. When we were having tea a Rhode Island Red hen pecked at the window. This was Jenny, and she was let in to have tea with us. A snake had infiltrated the hen run, and when Bob went to the scene he noticed that one egg was about to hatch. He took it to bed and incubated it. The chick safely hatched and grew up treating Bob as her mother.

There was a light railway from near Livingstone to the sawmill at Machili, used for the export of the timber. This has been much written about by railway enthusiasts and David Shepherd, the wildlife artist, organised the transport of an abandoned engine to Britain. The management of the sawmill had a Ford Prefect car fitted with iron wheels to run on the railway and on one occasion I travelled on this, being met at Machili by boma transport.

Sesheke was virtually cut off from Livingstone by road because of flooding on the north side of the river. We did manage to get through by Land Rover on our first arrival, but the children in the back were covered in black dust. Transport to Livingstone was mainly by boat but it could not get further than Kazungula, about 20 miles upstream from Livingstone, so there had to be some arrangement for onward road transport there. At Katima Mulilo there was a detachment of the Witwatersrand Native Labour Association, known as Wenala, a recruiting organisation for the South African gold mines. They had a barge on the Zambezi which would sometimes bring supplies for Sesheke. There was an agreement with the Barotse Native Government for the treatment and welfare of the workers who were engaged by the mine. The workers had to be given transport home after the period of engagement, usually one year, and remittances sent regularly to their families. There were theoretical political objections but the system worked quite well. Its abolition after independence has resulted in further problems of illegal immigration to South Africa, unemployment, vagrancy, families left at home without support and so forth.

I had two good District Officers, Ian Hart and David Taylor, and we worked well as a team. The main domestic problem was that Stella and Matthew had to be educated, and Brenda undertook this by a correspondence course from the Federal Ministry of Education in Salisbury. It was the early days of distance learning and the teachers did not appreciate the effect of a critical comment upon a mother struggling in an outstation. Brenda became so upset by what she saw as her failure to do the job correctly that I began holding the mail back until I could take it myself at lunchtime and we could look at the comments together. I think that Matthew was a particular trial; so cheerful and good-tempered, but difficult to get him to concentrate. Another problem for Matthew was that he was bitten by a dog when we were playing tennis at Katima Mulilo. Dr Jameson said that we could not risk rabies, but as it took time to get a laboratory analysis from Salisbury it was essential to begin the inoculations. This was a terrible experience with poor little Matthew hiding away or climbing a tree when he knew that his daily inoculation, given by Brenda, was due. It was not until the end of the course that we heard that rabies was not identified and his suffering had been unnecessary.

Rapid communication was always difficult. Mail came by a small Beaver aircraft which arrived at our primitive airfield three times a week. The maintenance of landing grounds was another responsibility of the DC.

I had a vivid experience of the failure of minds to meet across cultures. A man was accused of pointing out another as a witch, which was an offence under the Witchcraft Ordinance. I was the Magistrate and David Taylor the Prosecutor. The accused elected to give evidence and explained that his brother had been fishing and had been bitten by a snake, as a result of which he died. David asked him why he had pointed out a man as a witch when he knew that the cause of his brother's death was being bitten by a snake. The accused replied, "Yes, he was bitten by the snake, but there must have been a witch to cause the snake to kill my brother, and this man, the accused, I believe, was that witch."

The Witchcraft Ordinance had been instituted as a result of widespread deaths in Mkushi Distrrict in Central Province in 1924. It eventually came out that a man called Mwanalesa had been travelling round the villages claiming to be able to point out witches who were causing harm. He used a method

Figure 26 The Boma (DC's office) at Sesheke with the Court House on the left.

of trial by water, and over 400 are believed to have been drowned. While at Sesheke I heard reports of a witch finder operating about 80 miles away. A district messenger went to investigate and reported that he had seen a ceremony in which a boy of eight was accused of being a witch. Each of the villagers had to mount a dais and the witch finder put a snake skin round their chest. So long as he could move the skin round the body all was well, but if the skin stopped then that showed that this person was a witch. The poor child was chased off into the bush to fend for himself until more messengers arrived to rescue him and arrest the witch finder.

Although the traditional life seemed well entrenched there were political stirrings, and a small United National Independence Party group was operating locally. After imprisoning the man who pointed out the witch who inspired the snake to bite his brother, I received an angry letter accusing the oppressive DC of punishing a man who performed the essential function of pointing out witches. The letter asked who would now rid the people of witches. The traditional chiefs of the Barotse were uncertain as to how to deal with this new phenomenon of disobedience, since they had always been used to unquestioning loyalty.

I expected to do a full tour in Sesheke, but then a circular came to say that the Judiciary was expanding so as to be able to deal with all the cases previously heard by District Officers and thus complete the planned separation of the Judiciary from the Executive before independence. They therefore wanted a number of District Officers to transfer to the Judiciary. The opportunity to obtain more judicial experience, as well as the prospect of a school for the children, induced us to decide reluctantly to leave Sesheke. Jeanne and Murray Armor came to take over, full of stories of their honeymoon in the United States where they had won lots of prizes in a radio chat show. The Wenala took us all, piled into a boat with a high speed outboard motor, down the Zambezi to be met by transport at Kasungula. It was a beautiful day and a most exhilarating ride, with great monitor lizards sliding into the water from the sand banks as we passed and thousands of weaver bird nests dangling from the trees at the river side. Our Jack Russell terrier Bessie and fluffy white cat Alice came with us in the open boat. The car and luggage came on by a Wenala barge. In Livingstone we stayed with James and Joan Wright (now in their nineties and living in Queensland). Joan had been Stella's first teacher in Kasama, and James had been Brenda's doctor. Eventually we were back on a tarmac road again, and travelled up to Choma in the red and cream diesel Mercedes.

18

CHOMA AND THE JUDICIARY

Strung along the 300 miles or so of road from Livingstone to Lusaka there are three main centres of commercial agriculture. These are: first, Kalomo, which is on higher land out of the Zambezi valley and was the original capital of North-Western Rhodesia; then Choma, about half way between the two towns; and finally Mazabuka, the largest of the three centres.

The jurisdiction of the Magistrate at Choma covered Choma itself, a smaller centre at Monze, and Mazabuka, which contained the headquarters of the Veterinary Department. This is where Mother had taught for a while in 1958. Commercial agriculture mostly meant European agriculture in those days, and was based primarily on Virginia flue-cured tobacco. The soil was also suitable for maize and the climate was good, as the area was mostly around 3500 to 4000 feet above sea level. The local people are the Tonga, some of whom had advanced into commercial farming. To the south of Choma is an escarpment which descends to the valley where the Valley Tonga live. In the late 1950s much of their land was flooded by the massive Kariba Dam, efficiently built by Italian contractors. Great efforts were made, with some success, to train the Valley Tonga in the alternative pursuit of fishing. Two small resorts had been developed, Sinazongwe and Siavonga. The Valley Tonga had been very cut off from the world before the dam was constructed and wore few or no clothes. Sadly, a number continued to resist re-settlement even when the water was rising, and eight men were killed by government forces.

Courts were held once a week in Monze and in Mazabuka with occasional special journeys to the valley. To the north was the Kafue River, a tributary of the Zambesi, Namwala District and the Kafue Game Reserve. With all this travelling along reasonable to good roads the Mercedes really came into its own, after being almost unused in Barotseland.

The court was newly built and well appointed, with a carved royal coat of arms behind the Magistrate's chair on a dais worthy of a High Court. There was a European Clerk of the Court and comfortable chambers. It was strange to be able to concentrate upon just one aspect of work rather than be the "jack of all trades" which was the District Officer's lot.

Though I was kept fairly busy there were occasional quiet spells when I was able to get on with study for Part II of the Bar Examinations, which had been necessarily put aside in Sesheke.

Dress changed, in that a magistrate wore dark lightweight trousers and a black jacket and tie. Prosecution was done by the police, who I always found to act properly, sometimes withdrawing a case of their own motion if the evidence seemed insufficient. The circuit allowed an agreeable routine made all the better because of the hospitality of friends. Thursday was Mazabuka 100 miles away, and accommodation in the guest house of the DC Reg Thompson and his wife Mary. Sometimes there was a stay in Monze with the District Officer Julian Crozier and his wife Maurna. We had known both the Thompsons and the Croziers in Kasama. Brenda was able to lead a more private life, which I think she enjoyed, and she had a wider range of women with whom to make friends. However, she was rapidly recruited by Betty Clay, a daughter of Lord Baden Powell and the wife of a retired Resident Commissioner of Barotseland (mentioned earlier as Director of the Rhodes-Livingstone Museum) to be the local Commissioner of the Girl

Guides. I think they were all African girls there, and they were delightful.

In spite of the growth of political feeling the people were mostly agreeable, although there was one instance when little Matthew, coming home on his bicycle, had some grit thrown at him. However, one does have to bear in mind that similar things happened to my grandchildren at independent schools in Sevenoaks and Tonbridge. Matthew continued to cycle to school with Stella.

There was a European farming area in a circle around Choma, rather like Broken Hill. We made some good friends and would visit a farm most weekends. A valuable amenity was the Tennis Club, at which Brenda won a competition in spite of her increasing disability. She had such height and reach that she was effective at the net in spite of not being able to run well.

We took one local leave from Choma to eastern Southern Rhodesia and Mozambique. We drove to Umtali in the east of Southern Rhodesia and then north to Inyanga, which is a high region of rolling heathland. The rivers are well stocked with trout and it is a great place for riding and walking. Our cook, Absent, was with us and we stayed in a log cabin looking onto a lake. After a few days we went on to Beira, driving through Mozambique to the coast. There the atmosphere was completely Portuguese with typical food and wine. We stayed in a self-catering apartment and spent the days mostly on the beach with good sand and gentle waves, ideal for the children. The principal concern was to see that they kept themselves covered and did not get burnt, not entirely successfully.

An early UMCA Mission (Universities Mission to Central Africa) was at Mapanza, a few miles north of Choma, where Edward Robinson had served originally on arrival in NR. There was a leading secondary school there and they had some good staff, including two who had taught at Shrewsbury who gave us good advice on English independent schools. The local Federal Government Department of European Education establisment, the Beit School, which Stella and Matthew attended, was very satisfactory, but we were reaching a stage of thinking about secondary schools. Stella was now nine and Matthew seven and a half. Indeed, so rapid was the political change that preparatory schools were also under consideration, as we had to consider the possibility that we would return to Britain before secondary education was reached,

Father Twell would come in from Mapanza each weekend to stay a night and take the services in the small inter-denominational church. The DC was John Robb and it was rather odd being out of the swim of things, but he kept me in touch and invited us to his farewell dinner for the Governor, Sir Evelyn Hone, and his wife. The dinner table looked beautiful as we went in and I remember Lady Hone saying, "Well, Mr Robb, you will probably never seat your guests at a dinner table like this again."

Mother's sister, Aunt Kathleen, came to us for an extended stay and thoroughly enjoyed her time. In the usage of her age she always referred to the Africans as "darkies", as in "I really do like your darkies here." We took her round, of course, and managed to visit Wankie (now Hwange), a game park in Southern Rhodesia, with its huge herds of elephants – indeed, rather too many.

We went several times to the Victoria Falls for long weekends, taking Absent with us and hiring two rondavels with a barbecue for ten shillings (50p) a night each. They were less than 100 yards from the river with the Falls within hearing distance.

I enjoyed the intellectual challenge of applying the law and arriving at the appropriate sentence, but had it been a career, I think the incessant procession of criminals would have become tedious and depressing. The records had to be kept meticulously, with full notes of what each witness said and then a reasoned written judgement quoting all appropriate authorities at the end of every trial. A Magistrate had powers of imprisonment for up to three years, and in civil matters the powers of a County Court Judge in England. When District Officers were invited to transfer the prospect was held out for promotion from Second Class Magistrate to First Class. I was gazetted as a First Class Magistrate some months before leaving. I thought this would be of some help in obtaining future employment, since I would then be able to show that in the Sudan, then in the Provincial Administration of Northern Rhodesia and finally in the judiciary, I had been promoted in every case.

Independence came in October 1964. Ironically it was very much a British show, with the Administration organising all the celebrations and even, I have since heard, writing the new national anthem to replace "God Save the Queen".

Clearly the good little school at Choma would not survive in the same form. Although most staff could stay on if they wished, we decided that it was time to bring the African period of our lives to an end.

The Tennis Club gave us a good send-off, but we were aware that many friends had to stay to face an uncertain future, made all the worse because the political party favoured by the Tonga of the Southern Province had been roundly defeated by UNIP, who were strong in the more populated Copperbelt and northern provinces. Absent brought all his family, dressed in their best clothes, to bid us farewell at our house. The heavy luggage had gone ahead and we drove the loaded car to the motel outside Choma. We were up at six the following day ready to drive south, and found that once more Absent and his family were there. It was not easy to drive away from them, but we had found a job for Absent with friends who were moving to Lusaka and he was given a good gratuity.

We reached Bulawayo that night and stayed at a beautiful campsite with cabins among the granite boulders of the Matopo Hills outside Bulawayo. We climbed to see Rhodes's simple grave the following morning before we left. Then it was over the Beit Bridge, crossing the Limpopo into South Africa, leaving, as I thought, the Rhodesias for the last time.

The Federation had completely broken up, with Northern Rhodesia and Nyasaland becoming independent under the

Figure 27 November 1964. Leaving Zambia soon after independence, with Absent, Joyce and family.

respective names of Zambia and Malawi. The future of Southern Rhodesia was still uncertain, but it did not need to be as painful as it turned out.

We had planned a fairly ambitious tour round South Africa, since always before we had taken the direct route through the interior via Johannesburg. We turned south-east through the beautiful north-east Transvaal, staying at an Afrikaner bed and breakfast farm. When the farmer asked if we would like wine I asked what we were likely to eat, and he said, "I don't know myself, but anyway you will get a plate of food." We settled for red wine. Then we travelled through Swaziland, which seemed mostly to consist of sugar fields, staying in the capital Mbanane. From there it was down to the northern Natal coast to a huge seaside hotel called the Cutty Sark. Next, after a night in Durban we struck south-west into the Drakensberg Mountains to a resort below the mountain called Champagne Castle. This was a delightful place for a family holiday. The encounter with a family whom they saw as refugees from the Black North discomforted some of the guests. However, most did not think it conceivable that South Africa would follow the same course, at least not in their lifetime.

We had intended to follow the coast through the Transkei and the Garden Route to Cape Town. Unfortunately, however, Stella fell ill, and a doctor who was staying at the hotel diagnosed the trouble as jaundice. He said, "She has only got one liver, and you must get her as quickly as possible to a specialist in Cape Town as you are going in that direction." Unfortunately there were no planes available so we decided to drive non-stop to Cape Town, keeping Stella as comfortable as possible.

We telephoned the hotel where we had booked and they agreed to accommodate us early and give Stella an isolated room. We drove through Bloemfontein and across the Karoo, changing drivers every hour or so. On arrival Stella soon got good attention. She had her own eating utensils and did not leave her room, but the few guests were able to talk to her through her window onto the verandah.

The hotel, which had looked so romantic in the brochure with its Dutch gables among the vineyards, turned out to be rather run down. The problem, we discovered, was a drunken owner, while his wife and mixed-race, or "coloured", staff were doing their best. There was a swimming pool which we used, but it was so green that when little Oliver, aged about three, plunged in, he would disappear until his head bobbed up again. The bowling green promised for the Christmas guests was far too late in being ready, but in spite of it everything it suited us well because Stella was in the best possible place. We went daily down to a beautiful beach near Somerset West, beside a small Malay fishing village with a tiny mosque. Afterwards when we told people where we had been they said that it was actually a beach for coloureds and not for whites. Since the coloureds, who I expect included Malays, did not seem to use it, we had it to ourselves and no-one worried.

At Christmas we went for midnight communion to the small Anglican church on the green in Stellenbosch, surrounded by ancient oak trees. The large congregation and the priest were coloured and we were the only whites.

Shortly after Christmas we drove to the Cape Town docks and boarded a Holland Afrika passenger ship, the "Randfontein". This was for Brenda and me a most luxurious passage. We were travelling first class and there were only eighty passengers instead of the more than three hundred who could have been accommodated. We were at the table of the Purser, a genial Dutchman who said that we were virtually on a private yacht. Surprisingly, though, for the Dutch are said to like the young, the conditions for children were most authoritarian. All ages were confined to a small nursery with two tough child carers. The children were only allowed on the passenger decks for half an hour each in the mid-morning and the mid-afternoon.

As was the custom, people stocked up on drink and tobacco before arriving in England. As we sailed up Southampton Water Brenda took her hundreds of cigarettes to the stern of the boat and threw them all into the Solent. So we were all to start a new life – I with a different job, Brenda as a non-smoker, Stella about to go to a boarding prep school and the boys also to new schools in a country they knew little of. However, after driving up the A34 from Southampton, we were returning to our own home in Woodstock.

19

THE HOME CIVIL SERVICE
AND THE LAW

So, for the second time I had returned home from Africa uncertain as to what the future would hold. This time we had three children to consider. Fortunately we had a home which we loved in Woodstock, small as it was, and a second sum of compensation, all of which could be invested in stocks and shares and the childrens' education.

The first objective was to get the children into schools. We had already corresponded with St Mary's in Wantage, which admitted Stella to the junior school at Great Oaks, near Pangbourne in Berkshire, which was run largely by Anglican nuns. We had about three days to buy Stella's uniform and install her. Matthew was to attend the primary school in Woodstock until he was eight and could go to King's Canterbury Junior School at Milner Court.

The choices for me seemed to be the Civil Service or the law with my uncle's practice in Leek. The Home Civil Service had a few places for late entry Principals and had already run a preliminary written examination. I had taken this a few months before leaving Choma, having been coached a little by a relative of Reg Thompson from the Commonwealth Relations Office who was staying with him. I think four men from Northern Rhodesia got over this hurdle.

I was not fully prepared for the next stage comprising two days of tests and interviews, which, I realised afterwards, were designed to see how one could work under pressure. There was a constant succession of statistical questions, analysis of problems, reports, interviews by psychiatrists and others – all very exhausting. Some days later there was the final interview before the Civil Service Commissioners which, though intimidating, must have gone satisfactorily because I was offered an appointment.

During the interval between the two-day tests and the final interview, I was invited to talk again to MI5 (having done so 10 years previously on leaving the Sudan). When I said that I was due to go to the final interview for the Home Civil Service I was very fairly advised to choose that if I were appointed, since the promotion prospects were very much better than in MI5. This was quite correct, since at that time in what was then the Administrative Class of the Civil Service, everyone would be expected to reach the rank of Assistant Secretary, with of course the opportunity to go higher. In MI5 the promotion pyramid was much flatter.

We did not consider a job abroad again, since we wanted the children to have stability in their education and Brenda was anxious to take advantage of the cultural life of England. Two years later a circular came round the Home Civil Service asking for six people to transfer to take the place of Diplomatic Service staff who could not go abroad again. John Stewart, who had followed me a year later from Northern Rhodesia into my very job with the Home Civil, said that he would definitely apply. I took the circular to Brenda who said that it should not be considered. She thought a move then would not be fair to the children, and I would be used only to fill the unwanted posts in horrid countries over which we had no influence. John's later career proved this to be only partly correct. He had postings to Laos and to Mozambique, which must have been rather disagreeable at the time, but he did finish with some compensation as High Commissioner to Sri Lanka and a good retirement job deciding on senior police appointments.

I was posted to the Ministry of Technology. The Labour Government under Harold Wilson had come to power with a small majority in 1964, which he greatly increased the following year. One of his promises was to create "a new Britain in the white heat of the technological revolution", and he set up the Ministry of Technology to give expression to this.

We found a tall, well-built, semi-detached Edwardian house in Kingston Hill, only a hundred yards outside the Kingston Gate of Richmond Park. Between the park and the A3 there are three roads of largely Victorian family houses, which made a very pleasant community. We had been told that people who had never been abroad could be unfriendly to those returning, but this was not our experience at all. Our house was almost opposite the enormous Victorian St. Paul's Church and through it we made many friends, some of whom are still friends today.

The Ministry had been cobbled together from a number of different departments or agencies so there was an atmosphere of everyone feeling their way. In internal minutes individuals were addressed by their names and not by departmental numbers, although that was brought in later by the second permanent secretary Sir "Otto" Clarke, who came from the Treasury.

At that time several leading countries had a space programme, and this was, as would be expected, accelerating technological advance. Naturally, therefore, the Ministry (or Min. Tech. as it came to be known) was interested in what was going on. I was given responsibility for developing that interest and helping British industry get a share of the contracts that were going. It was all very absorbing, but the Department of Education and Science had a firm grip on the British Government's involvement in international ventures and were not going to let it go. Also, of course, the Treasury was very concerned to limit Britain's commitment, and while I was doing that job it persuaded the Government to withdraw from the collaborative European Launcher Development Organisation (ELDO). Seeing all the papers at the time made me understand how often major decisions are reached in a hurry because a Minister has to be briefed one way or the other before an international meeting. The French decided to go it alone and are still providing a launching facility, for a price, with Ariane rockets in Guiana. A site on or near the equator was necessary to put a satellite in orbit.

After a year I handed over the desk to John Stewart, just arrived from Zambia, and moved to head the small unit devoted to the use of public purchasing to increase industrial efficiency. This had been part of the Labour Party's manifesto, the idea being that the superior knowledge and skill available to government could be used to improve industry's performance. A White Paper was planned, the lead being with the Department of Economic Affairs which had been split from the Treasury. (Neither Min. Tech nor the DEA survived the later change of government.) It was interesting to see how a White Paper is put together and government policy evolves. I can still recognise a few phrases of my own in the finished product. Marks and Spencer was then riding high, and a government team which examined their purchasing practices reported very favourably. M&S at that time proudly claimed that their products were sourced almost entirely in Britain, so they were able, through their specifications and inspection, to improve the performance of their suppliers. Unsurprisingly, some of the suppliers thought that they were overbearing.

Labour ministers believed in interference in industry and trying to pick winners to be backed with money. The more officials looked into the matter, the more they concluded that positive interference would be of dubious value. I concluded, and I think most officials agreed, that the best way a government could help was by examining and improving its procurement policies. This meant, for example, buying what is already in production rather than specifying something different, arranging long production runs, collaboration between departments to buy the same product and so forth. I attended the press conference arranged to launch the White Paper on behalf of Min. Tech. It was regarded by the press as being very uninspiring, and as failing to offer an exciting story. This was exactly what I thought was best. I did not and do not think that civil servants are competent generally to tell commercial firms how best to run their businesses.

My first minister had been the left-wing Trade Union leader Frank Cousins, who actually turned out to be rather good, albeit out of his depth in the House of Commons. He was succeeded by Anthony Wedgwood Benn who had come from the Ministry of Posts, a bright and charming young man who had overlapped with me at Oxford after serving in the RAF. He was at the time enamoured of the excitement of industry and technology, spending much time with industrial leaders. As part of the policy of intervention, Min. Tech. was encouraging mergers between leading companies in the belief that larger units were better able to undertake research and development and to export. One of the favourite sons was Arnold Weinstock of GEC, who was encouraged to take over Amalgamated Engineering Industries. He moved rapidly to rationalise the many factories in his new empire, including one at Woolwich, almost on Parliament's doorstep. A long strike there made Benn realise where these policies were leading, I think. He sent a circular round the department saying we were too involved with management and should develop more contact with the unions. His progress to the far left and his new persona as the plebeian Tony Benn had begun.

There were other ways in which the policies of Min. Tech. had not been thoroughly thought through. Many were inherently protective. For instance, International Computers and Tabulators was selected as the Government's preferred agent for the promotion of the new computer industry, which was of course at the heart of what Min. Tech. stood for. All government agencies were instructed to buy ICT (later ICL) products. On the other hand, much good work was done in internationalising standards, for instance in metrication. Our present paper sizes A3, A4 etc. are a result. Rather surprisingly the building industry took the lead in metrication, and Min. Tech. (i.e. myself) collaborated with the Ministry of Works in adopting the French system of approval for the quality of house building.

I had some interesting special assignments. One was a proposal to absorb the Atomic Energy Authority into Min Tech, which had to be kept a close secret at the time. It was fascinating to collaborate with the Treasury Solicitor's office on the proposed legislation. In the end the scheme fell by the wayside, which was probably just as well in view of subsequent privatisations. Another assignment was to produce the first assessment of how the policies of the European Economic Community, as it then was, would affect the policies of Min. Tech. if we entered.

Harold Macmillan had some years before applied to enter the EEC and had been rebuffed by de Gaulle. There was much feeling that we had been rejected by the very people whom we had saved in the war. Harold Wilson renewed the application saying he would not take "no" for an answer, but in the end he had to. It was not until Ted Heath was Prime Minister in the early 1970s that we entered what became the European Union. My very amateur study therefore was the first time that Min. Tech. had begun to understand that entry into Europe could have a fundamental effect on the way we conducted our affairs. I began by obtaining a copy of the Treaty of Rome from the excellent departmental library and went through it section by section. It soon became clear that many of Min. Tech's policies would have to be set aside, or at best greatly modified. Any actions which were discriminatory between one firm and another, or which favoured this country over other EEC members, would be forbidden, with fines to follow for infringement.

I enjoyed the atmosphere of the Home Civil Service. Most people were intelligent, conscientious and cooperative. I made friends who continued long after I left. There was great professionalism and the desire to follow the truth wherever it led, although often the political reality could not accept the truth. This could be very frustrating. Industrial relations were such that new systems and economies such as container ships could not be introduced. We were well into a generation of industrial strife which held up the country's progress and seriously impoverished it. The senior ranks worked hard and long, but there was still not the dedication to the job and the people that there had been in the overseas services. This was perhaps to be expected, since colleagues rarely met out of work and there was not the same "esprit de corps". Home and office were two entirely different worlds; in Africa they had merged. Further, one's actions in the dependent territories affected people directly, whereas in Whitehall the immediate contact was with ministers. Another feature was that usually the higher one rose the harder one worked. I believe that I did my fair share, but the Under Secretaries and above regularly took bulging briefcases on the train to their homes in the suburbs.

At that time there was a somewhat old-fashioned donnish culture in the administrative class of the Civil Service. Senior and junior wrote to each other using only surnames, except in the case of a female colleague. If anyone was referred to as Mr, that would indicate that he was of the executive or clerical class.

Brenda's rheumatoid arthritis waxed and waned. She found the house difficult to manage with its three residential floors and the garage in the basement. Fortunately we had a delightful plump Italian lady called Maria from southern Italy to help once or twice a week, and Brenda was thoroughly enjoying what London had to offer, such as the Richmond College of Art, an active church, the National Theatre at the Old Vic and later the new South Bank building. She would drive up from Kingston Hill and collect me at Millbank Tower in our large red diesel Mercedes, formerly used in Barotseland and Choma, to go on to the theatre.

Civil Service leave was quite generous – six weeks annually at my level as a Principal. Summer holidays were spent in a rented former coastguard's cottage at Hallsands on the south Devon coast, a few miles south of Dartmouth. The cottage stood on a cliff with the derelict Trouts' Hotel nearby (since renovated). Below the cliff is a shingle beach and the remains of a fishermen's village, destroyed by a high sea years ago. The lighthouse at Start Point lit up the windows of the cottage as it revolved. Beyond Start Point was Matchcombe Beach, which Brenda used to bring to mind as the most beautiful place she could concentrate on when in the dentist's chair.

Brenda had been careful to keep open her relationship with my father, writing to tell him whenever a grandchild had been born, and Mother's death in 1959 had removed a source of embarrassment. He had the children to stay at Willoughbridge and they had a wonderful time on the farm while the lambs were being born, although we did find out later that they did not wash for a week. He came to stay with us in London and took us to lunch at Sheekeys fish restaurant.

Father was then aged 66 and he developed cancer, having always been a heavy smoker. He died in 1967 after being in hospital for about a week. I visited him, staying at Willoughbridge for the first time in many years. The well attended funeral was at Mucklestone Church, where Mother had worshipped weekly and where I was confirmed. Father's grave is there. His will opened up new possibilities as he had left everything between his three sons. David came home from Southern Rhodesia while Michael and Ann moved to Willoughbridge, where he worked hard on very necessary repairs to the buildings.

We agreed that sale of the farm was the only practicable course since, if one of us took it over, it would not have the earning capacity to pay out to the other two, even over a period of years.

I enjoyed the Civil Service and its intellectual challenges but did not really welcome the prospect of commuting for another 20 years and climbing to perhaps half way up the tree at the end. The thought of having more independence and working for myself was attractive. I think that I have always preferred to be a large fish in a small pond, if possible, rather than a small fish in a large pond.

My father's younger brother, Philip, was senior partner in a solicitors' practice in Leek, in North Staffordshire, and he agreed to pay me much more than the usual Articled Clerk, about half of what I was getting in the Civil Service. I applied to the Law Society for exemptions on the basis of the Bar Examinations which I had passed. They were very generous and gave me exemption from the whole of Part I, even though I had studied Roman Dutch Law instead of English Property Law.

I resigned from the Civil Service and in a farewell party my colleagues presented me with a technologically advanced, i.e. stainless steel, garden spade. I then enrolled on a six-month course with the College of Law which was run by the Law Society at Lancaster Gate, London. This was a real crammer. There were lectures either morning or afternoon with written homework, and it was very intense with no relief. Brenda and the family allowed me to concentrate almost entirely on study. I used to get up at in the morning and work all day, the only breaks being the journey to and from Lancaster Gate. I remember only two days off with the family, but I passed all the exams, even Conveyancing, in spite of the absence of real property preparation, leaving only Accounts to be done later after some practical experience. We had a farewell party for all our friends in Kingston and moved to Manor Farm at Endon in North Staffordshire in the autumn of 1968.

The office of Bowcock and Pursaill, Solicitors, is in a fine eighteenth-century listed house in one of the main streets in Leek. Of course, I was something of an anomaly coming in as an Articled Clerk at the age of 41. The period of articles was two years. It is now called a Solicitor Traineeship, which is probably a better description. The practice covered all aspects of the law – except Admiralty, it was said. It was run very much as a public service, open at reasonable hours and without extra closed days after public holidays, or at least with a skeleton staff to deal with emergencies. A good deal of legal aid work was undertaken. The principal speciality was

Figure 28 54 St Edward Street, Leek, head office of Bowcock and Pursaill, Solicitors.

in agricultural law, in which my uncle had built up a reputation extending over several counties. It seemed fitting to keep in touch with agricultural affairs since they had preoccupied me during the first 21 years of my life.

I passed the Accounts exam without difficulty and was admitted as a solicitor in November 1970 at the age of 43, and was immediately made a partner.

The law practice expanded steadily, although changes in client circumstances could result in loss of work. Adams Foods, a big client which had greatly expanded, was bought by the Irish Dairy Board which took their business to Dublin and London solicitors. For many years we had done all of the Staffordshire Moorlands District Council legal work until they set up their own legal department at vastly greater expense to the ratepayer, but the agricultural work was growing and I joined the Agricultural Law Association on its formation. I was appointed as a part-time Chairman of the

Agricultural Land Tribunal for the south-east of England and was glad to have a judicial function again. There were two other Chairmen and we took cases in rotation. The other two were barristers who later became High Court judges. The work was often difficult but always interesting in its agricultural, legal and human aspects.

20

ZIMBABWE INDEPENDENCE ELECTIONS

At the end of 1979 there came a completely unexpected interruption to life at Manor Farm. The dismemberment of the Federation of Rhodesia and Nyasaland had, in my view, been badly managed, even though the responsibility had been given to the usually wise old R.A. Butler. Southern Rhodesia had a very large measure of self-government and was almost independent in reality if not in theory. It was obviously going to be extremely difficult to negotiate a constitution which would satisfy both the 300,000 whites who were in control of almost every aspect of national life, and the 6 million or so blacks who were educationally far in advance of those in the northern territories. In spite of vociferous outside criticism of the Rhodesian settler government, their education services were much better than any further north in the continent. In my view the British government should have aimed to bring all three territories towards independence at the same time. In this way the northern nationalists could probably have been induced to support the principle of a gradual extension of the franchise to blacks in Southern Rhodesia, instead of a slogan of "one man one vote now". The northern nationalists would have put pressure on those in the south to agree to a gradual policy so as to allow the north to move more quickly.

Anyway, this did not happen. Zambia and Malawi reached independence in 1964 under Kaunda and Banda respectively, as executive presidents aiming for one-party control. This left Southern Rhodesia in limbo with both sides taking up extreme positions. The Rhodesian Front came into power in Salisbury and in the autumn of 1965 made the Unilateral Declaration of Independence (UDI), thus throwing down the gauntlet not only to Britain but also to the rest of the world except South Africa. I was at a meeting of the Royal Commonwealth Society being addressed by Barbara Castle when the news of UDI came through. Sanctions were imposed and Harold Wilson, the Prime Minister, promised that they would be effective within weeks, not months. It was not to be. The Rhodesians were extremely inventive in avoiding sanctions and could have held out indefinitely if the South Africans had not decided eventually to withdraw their support. This demonstrates that the later African National Congress government in South Africa could have easily brought down Robert Mugabe if they had so chosen. Various attempts at mediation failed, and a commission led by Lord Pearce found that African opinion was now not prepared for a gradual extension of the vote, instead demanding the franchise immediately.

Rhodesia could have probably continued much longer with the whites united under Smith, so long as the only hostile frontier was with Zambia where Joshua Nkomo's ZAPU was supported by Kaunda. Zambia itself was suffering greatly because most of its supplies came over the railway crossing of the Zambezi at the Victoria Falls. This was the motivation for the Chinese to offer to build a railway from Dar es Salaam, the capital of Tanganika, to join the existing railway north of Broken Hill. They imported Chinese labour and got the job done.

The critical moment for the Rhodesian rebels came when Salazar, the dictator of Portugal, died and his regime was replaced by a Communist-dominated army. The Portugese completely changed their African policy overnight. They had always been proud of their long history in Africa and had planted many peasant settlers there. Abandoning all this they left almost overnight, taking all they could with them and leaving the inhabitants to fight it out among themselves. This they duly did for a number of years.

Mugabe had broken away from Nkomo, the established nationalist leader, and settled into his base in Mozambique. Here he had a much easier military task than Nkomo who had to cross the Zambezi, an excellent defensive feature. Along their frontier between Rhodesia and Mozambique the Mugabe faction was in mountainous territory, easy to infiltrate. As the Rhodesians found it more and more difficult to control their territory they did a deal with the only possible black politician living inside the country, Abel Muzarewa, who was an African Methodist Episcopal Bishop and part of an American church. Smith and Muzarewa concocted a scheme for joint sharing of power and the renaming of the country to Rhodesia/Zimbabwe. Zimbabwe, like Zambia, was a fanciful name to distance the country from its colonial predecessor which carried the name of Rhodes, who for all his great achievements, was not popular with African nationalists. Great Zimbabwe is the name of the stone fortress near Fort Victoria, now Masvingo, built in the Middle Ages.

The Smith/Muzarewa deal did not satisfy anyone, either the two nationalist leaders or world opinion generally. For 15 years the UDI and the future of Southern Rhodesia had been poisoning international relations. This applied particularly within the Commonwealth, where Britain was always in the dock being baited by the newly independent former colonies who thought it was easier to do this than deal with their own problems. The Conservatives returned to power under Margaret Thatcher in 1979 and Lord Carrington took a rapid initiative to lance the boil. A gruesome civil war had been going on for seven years and many whites were leaving to escape conscription. A conference at Lancaster House resulted in an agreement whereby there would be elections on a universal adult franchise. These elections would be run by the Rhodesian Civil Service but supervised by British representatives. There would also be observers from the British government and from the Commonwealth.

The governor, Sir Humphrey Gibbs, had bravely continued for some years, though with a hostile prime minister, but he had given up when he considered he could no longer do anything useful. Lord Soames was appointed Governor with full executive powers. It was no disadvantage that his wife was Sir Winston Churchill's daughter, Mary.

The Rhodesian army was efficient and well disciplined, but it was a different story with the guerrillas who now occupied many of the rural areas, terrorising the villagers even more than the army did. Eventually a plan was agreed whereby Commonwealth troops would set up collection areas throughout the country, to which the guerrillas would be instructed to come and hand over their weapons.

As soon as I learned that experienced former colonial service officers would be needed to supervise the elections, I sent in my name and was rapidly summoned to an interview at the Foreign Office. On hearing of my selection my partners agreed to a three-month absence. Although it could not be denied that there was an element of danger, Brenda knew that I wanted the challenge and bravely agreed that I should go.

This was to be probably the most supervised and observed election in history. The mutual suspicion of the parties at Lancaster House had been so intense that layer upon layer of oversight was imposed. The Rhodesian Civil Service was charged with actually running the elections. They had managed one successfully quite recently when Bishop Abel Muzarewa was elected Prime Minister. The civil administration of the country now largely matched that which previously operated in Zambia and Malawi. The native commissioners, regarded by the whites as being responsible for the African population alone, had now been replaced by provincial and district commissioners along the British Colonial Service model.

At all levels the administration of the election was to be supervised by British officers responsible to the new British

Governor. Thus the Rhodesian Chief Electoral Officer was supervised by the British Chief Election Supervisor, Sir John Boynton, who had previously been a Chief Executive Officer of Cheshire. At the provincial level there were two British Election Supervisors in each Province and one or two District Election Supervisors in each district. The purpose of having two supervisors at each level was that one would be an experienced electoral officer from Britain while the other would be an administrative officer with experience of Africa. In practice, many of the districts only had the colonial retread. The police in the provinces had a British police supervisor and the Army had a liaison officer at the level of lieutenant colonel. Thus the whole exercise would be under British responsibility with the job on the ground being done by the Rhodesian Civil Service, which was entirely competent.

There was a plethora of observers who had no executive responsibility. The Commonwealth had quite a high-level team, led by an Indian. There was also a group of former Governors, soldiers and the like appointed by the British government, known generally as the "Old and Bold". I think that the United Nations put their oar in somewhere, and of course there were hordes of journalists. I formed a good opinion of most of the official appointees, but the journalists were a rather miserable lot. Most had arrived with pre-formed views of what they wanted to happen, namely the victory of Mugabe, and made no pretence of impartiality. One notable exception was John Ashworth of *The Times*, and his later death was a great loss.

The Provincial Supervisors formed the first wave of supervision to leave and we travelled from Brize Norton in an RAF Viscount after being interviewed by Kate Adie for the BBC. This was the occasion, related earlier, when I asked the Captain where we were after passing over Khartoum. When he showed me his cockpit maps, not only was I able to find Malakal, where Brenda and I had been married almost exactly 27 years before, but I also managed to pick out where Stella was at that time, in Ler to the west of the White Nile during her medical elective term.

It was by now nearly 15 years since the unilateral declaration of independence and the imposition of sanctions, and some seven years since the serious civil war began. The Rhodesian Government had been able to evade the serious impact of sanctions by the exercise of their people's ingenuity and the support of South Africa. Smith had an understanding with Salazar, the quasi-dictator of Portugal, but when his regime collapsed after Salazar's death the Portuguese did a dreadful disservice to the people of Angola and Mozambique when they withdrew immediately without installing a legitimate successor government. Mozambique collapsed into chaos and the civil war went on for many years. Since then, with the attainment of stability, it has joined the Commonwealth. Angola had an equally miserable time with a civil war drawing in South Africa on one side and Russia with Cuban satellite troops on the other.

The eastern frontier, between Southern Rhodesia and Mozambique, is mountainous and was virtually impossible to defend with the Rhodesian forces. From his base in Mozambique Mugabe sent in his guerrillas, so that they were able to establish themselves throughout the eastern part of the country which was occupied by Mugabe's Shona tribe. Roads were mined night after night and transport could only travel in convoy. When South Africa decided at last to comply with sanctions Ian Smith had to sue for peace, resulting eventually in the Lancaster House Agreement.

There was little sign of all this on arrival in sunny Salisbury in January 1980. The Monomotapa Hotel had become multiracial and looking down from my room there were black as well as white bodies in the swimming pool, something which would never have been seen when I was last in Southern Rhodesia. The city looked clean and fresh, with beautiful trees and flowers everywhere. I heard one of the British local authority chief executives say to the other, "Why can't we have cities like this in Britain?" However, there was a reminder of the war in the number of young white men who had been mutilated or wounded.

The Governor was legislating prolifically for the election, so extensive briefings had to take place. I was posted to Fort Victoria, now called Masvingo, almost due south of Salisbury and halfway to the main crossing to South Africa over the Limpopo River at the Beit Bridge. It is the capital of the South Western Province in the country. As Rhodes's Pioneer Column pushed north in 1890 they build a fort here and named it after the Queen Empress. It is a pleasant little town, not far from the famous Zimbabwe ruins and Lake Kyle, with a well-stocked wildlife park. We were put up in a rather horrid hotel in the town but soon moved out to the Flamboyant Motel about two miles south. This proved to be a very comfortable and suitable base, with good food and a place to meet anyone who wanted to see us. Many people did, since all the parties were now gearing up for the election.

My fellow provincial supervisor was John Barratt, Chief Executive of Cambridgeshire County Council. He was a steady and capable Mancunian and we got on well. We had a small hired car and the Provincial Commissioner allotted us an office for our own use where we could see whom we wished. We considered it important to show that we were quite independent of the local civil service, although we had every assistance from them including a competent Rhodesian District Commissioner, posted as liaison between the Provincial Commissioner and us.

Also in the town there was a retired British senior police officer who liaised with the Rhodesian police and two army liaison officers. One of these was the contact with the local army and the other with the rebel force, which in that area was ZANLA, the Zimbabwe African National Liberation Army. This was an extremely tricky and potentially dangerous job which he carried out with great diplomacy. The Commonwealth observers were represented by one of their staff, an agreeable Australian diplomat called Hugh Craft.

A few days later the district supervisors arrived. One was a younger former DO in Northern Rhodesia called Lawrence Taylor, whose father, I think, was in charge of a church establishment in Birmingham and who was rather pro Mugabe – as was, incidentally, the Bishop of Lichfield, who had previously been the Bishop of Bulawayo. Another arrival was Colin Baker, who had been a DO in Nyasaland and has become a prolific author with a Chair in history at a Welsh university. In Fort Victoria District itself the supervisor was the Town Clerk of Wigan. They were a good and cheerful bunch who got down to work and coped with the discomforts in spite of their age.

The area was dominated by the Karanga, the principal sub-tribe of the Shona. One frequently saw rocky hills crowned by primitive forts of stones rolled together to make a wall. These were refuges for the Karanga against the raiding parties of the Matabele from the east; such raids occurred frequently before the British occupation. The Matabele, centred on Bulawayo, are an offshoot of the Zulu of Natal and have a warlike tradition. Modern democracy, with its "one man one vote" principle, will now always put them at a disadvantage, since they only numbered about one fifth of the whole population, the other four fifths being largely Shona. Joshua Nkomo, the original nationalist leader, was supported by the Russians, while the breakaway Shona party led by Mugabe was backed by the Chinese. There seems to have been a great failure of Russian intelligence in their choice of Nkomo, since once he lost Shona support he could never win, so great was the disparity in numbers between the tribes.

There was a great deal of talk and propaganda about the privacy of the ballot and the right of every voter to make up his or her own mind, but I think that the real truth was told to me by some Swiss Roman Catholics at a mission about 30 miles south of Victoria. They had been in Mozambique and had been thrown out when the Portuguese left; they were clearly determined that they would not be on the losing side again. They were very definite that talk of individual choices was unrealistic and said that the Shona had made a collective tribal decision that Mugabe was their man. This was proved right when the poll on 29 February showed that his support was over 87 per cent. Interestingly enough this view was supplemented by that of the Provincial Commissioner, Menzies, who held that tribal loyalty means that a collective decision will nearly always outweigh an individual opinion in the matter of deciding how to vote. This corresponds with my own experience in the Sudan and Zambia.

There was constant low-level insecurity throughout the period leading up to the election, due to a number of factors. Assembly points had been established, mostly at the periphery of the country, for the rebels to come in with their weapons and wait while the election was being held. Of course, they would have the right to vote along with everyone else. These assembly points were administered (guarded is hardly the word) by Commonwealth troops. The rebels were suspicious and volatile, leaving the assembly points when it so pleased them. The Commonwealth troops had a number of very dangerous situations to deal with. The assembly points were supplied mostly by Hercules aircraft and we went on one of these trips. The interior of a Hercules is a large noisy shed and as the dropping zone is approached the rear door is opened. The operators are attached by wires to rails along the top of the plane and they push the bales forward and out over the dropping zone. The wires prevent the operators from dropping as well. Unexpectedly, a large number of women soldiers came into the assembly points and womens' toiletries had to be bought and supplied.

If not otherwise occupied we usually went to the morning security briefing run by the army. There would be reports of incidents during the previous 24 hours, including such matters as caches of arms being found, mujibas (young thugs) intimidating old people or extorting food, girls etc., the occasional shot fired at a vehicle or a mine exploded. Ranald Patterson, also a former NR DO, was shot at in his vehicle. One brave Nkomo supporter stood as a candidate in the district adjoining Matabele land. He was strangled with wire and thrown onto a fire. The overt ZANU (PF) line was, "We have fought for this area and no-one else is going to come into it". Joan Lester, a prominent left-wing Labour MP, spent some time with me and tried rather feebly to support that case.

As a further assurance that the election would be entirely above board, some hundreds of British police officers were flown in with the intention that there should be one in each polling station. This was a somewhat bizarre event, but they were a good crowd and their presence was appreciated, particularly by the inexperienced polling officers.

For the three days of polling John and I had the use of a Bell helicopter. We were able to use this "magic carpet" to drop in on any polling station in the province where we thought that there might be trouble or which the district supervisor was not able to reach by road. There was still the worry that someone might take a shot at us and the pilots had become very practised in flying low so that if the chopper were a target it would appear and disappear very quickly. The pilots of the RAF Hercules delivering supplies to the assembly points operated in the same way; it was sometimes quite frightening flying through twisting gorges in mountainous areas, of which there are plenty in Zimbabwe.

Some three weeks before the election a letter smuggled out from Mozambique reached the Governor. It was from some of Mugabe's prisoners. They asked that they could return home and take part in the election. It turned out that they had opposed Mugabe on some issue and had been imprisoned by him in underground pits. Soames took a strong line and told Mugabe that if they did not return he would be forbidden from standing in the election. The governor had extremely wide powers which enabled him to do this. Mugabe obeyed and the released men tried to form a party from the Karanga, an affiliated tribe, but there was insufficient time in the face of the Mugabe band wagon. Mugabe had returned to a tremendous welcome in Salisbury from what was said to have been the biggest crowd ever to be have assembled there.

We had to deal with a constant stream of complaints about the security forces and the auxiliaries, a kind of home guard, who were supposed to provide protection in the tribal trust lands. On the whole the political leaders were articulate and courteous, all of them speaking good English, but their complaints were almost always untrue or exaggerated. There was throughout an atmosphere of apprehension and suspicion which was not surprising in the aftermath of seven years of civil war. When John and I were having lunch one day in the garden outside our rooms at the Flamboyant Motel, we saw an explosion on the road to the airport about a mile and a half away. We knew that Mugabe was in town, and sure enough explosives hidden in a culvert had damaged one of the vehicles in his convoy, but he escaped. We never found out who had been responsible for this. The Rhodesian army was battle-hardy and efficient. It was not unrealistic for African politicians to fear a possible military takeover in the event of an election result which was unpopular with the army leaders. General Wall, the head of the army, was a very powerful figure and Mugabe was wise to recruit him as an ally after his election success.

Immediately after the election the Provincial Supervisors had to report to the Governor on its conduct. It was agreed that I would go and use the helicopter for this purpose. With me was Peter Snelson, whom I had known as an education officer in Northern Rhodesia and who was now one of the senior staff of the Commonwealth observers. I saw the Governor, Sir Christopher Soames, and his deputy, Sir Anthony Duff, to present my report. This was based upon the Election Supervisors' final report, which forms Appendix 7 of this book. It seemed that Victoria Province gave more cause for concern than any other and the possibility of annulling the results was discussed. However, it was concluded, rightly in my view, that in spite of all the defects the results did broadly reflect the wishes of the majority of the people. Mugabe emerged as the clear victor and took the advice of the Governor to adopt a conciliatory approach to the whites, making use of the existing military and civil structures.

Zimbabwe seemed to be a success for a decade or more until Mugabe's ruthlessness and ambition for unfettered power took control. He has now become a touchstone for the standing of African governments. Any which support him must be regarded as being without principle or compassion.

So it was time to say goodbye to kind friends made in Fort Victoria, especially through the Anglican Church. There were a few days spent in Salisbury (now Harare, of course, which was the name of the African suburb). I stayed at the very comfortable Rhodesian Club, meeting lots of old Northern Rhodesian friends and Harry and Durban Davis, to whom I had an introduction. Harry was a High Court judge, and like most of the white Rhodesians he was very shaken by the result of the election. Mugabe made a very statesman-like speech which went some way to reassuring many whites. It was not to last.

Finally there was another RAF Viscount back to Brize Norton where Brenda and the Robinson family met me in the middle of the night, and so home after an extraordinary and unexpected episode. When we left Africa 15 years before, I had not expected to return. What affected me most (apart from the task, of course) was the experience once again of Africa in the early rains – the fresh growth, the smell of the moist earth, the lush vegetation and the sound of bird song.

21

FAMILY AND RETIREMENT

It is natural that as I reach the latter stage of these memoirs they should concentrate more upon the personal and family affairs than on the wider world. By the 1980s the course of the remainder of Brenda's and my life was more or less set and changes came about through decisions made by our children.

While I had been away in Zimbabwe Brenda had been thinking about her future, particularly in the light of her rheumatoid arthritis. The children were all living away and she felt the need of a house that was smaller and easier to run, so we converted a large farm building at our home, Manor Farm, into a comfortable house. Brenda said that we had lived in 14 houses since our marriage and this was quite the best.

Our children were all moving on into successful adult careers, our daughter Stella as a doctor, Matthew joining a computer company as a graduate trainee and Oliver as a teacher, first in Japan and later in New York.

In addition to work in the law practice I thought it right to undertake a proper amount of charitable work. These were first of all the Beth Johnson Foundation for the Elderly, where I became Chairman of its Housing Association. After two years I was obliged to give this up as I was asked by the Bishop of Lichfield to Chair the Diocesan Pastoral Committee. Every

Diocese is obliged by law to have a Pastoral Committee which oversees the pastoral provision throughout the area. Much of the work is taken up with decisions on the merging of parishes, the redundancy of churches, the establishment of new pastoral schemes such as team ministries, ecumenical schemes and the like. I found the work worthwhile and interesting.

Another charitable responsibility arose when I was invited to chair a steering committee to set up a Citizens Advice Bureau in Leek. It all went swimmingly and I think that we held the record for the shortest period between examining feasibility and opening the bureau. It was opened by the Minister Linda Chalker and I subsequently became Chairman for a five-year term.

Matthew married in 1981 and he and his wife Helen took up a post in Australia in 1982, eventually staying there for 14 years. This provided us with opportunities to visit them on average every two or three years, always planning an interesting stopover on the way out and back. It was a revelation and a great delight to make acquaintance with the Far East for the first time, including China, as well as Australia.

In September 1984 Stella was married to Charles Shee, who had been spending a year doing research at McGill University, Montreal after qualifying at St. Thomas's some four years before Stella. After the usual houseman jobs at several hospitals Stella became consultant haematologist at Queen Mary's Hospital, Sidcup and her future life in west Kent was laid down. Eventually Charles obtained a post at the same hospital as Stella in chest medicine, general medicine and the new speciality of palliative care.

By this time Matthew had set up on his own company to provide computer security using chip cards, starting in a spare room in his house, and Helen soon joined him in the business. Within a few years the company, Security Domain, was employing over 50 people and had found markets throughout south-east Asia.

Oliver decided that he would like to stay in New York, and after a brief change from teaching he took up a post at

St Bernard's School, on East 98th Street. He joined up with James Sparks and they eventually settled in a handsome building in West End Avenue. When the legislation in New York State permitted it they married in November 2013.

Our first grandchild, Harriet, arrived in January 1987 while Stella and Charles were living in a four-storey house in Pimlico, a pleasant area of London between Victoria Station and the river. The house had also been home to Matthew, who had renovated the basement flat prior to leaving for Australia, and Oliver, who renovated the ground floor. Harriet was followed by Edmund in 1989 and Justin in 1991. Their youngest, Amelia, was born in 1999.

By then Stella and Charles were searching for a house in Kent. They asked us if we would like them to look for a place which had or could have a flat for us as well in the future. Stella pointed out that she was now our only child in England; she would always look after us as necessary, but it would be difficult if we lived 200 miles away at the end of an increasingly crowded motorway. We fell in gratefully with this idea and in 1992 they finally settled on a fine Victorian farmhouse in Otford.

Brenda and I engaged a young architect to prepare plans for our proposed flat but became embroiled in a protracted planning dispute, which we eventually won hands down on appeal. The local planning department were appalling to deal with, quite unlike those I had encountered professionally in the Midlands.

Finally we could make detailed plans for our retirement. In 1992 I had negotiated terms for my retirement from being senior partner when I was 65. I was to continue as a consultant for five years, undertaking tribunal work on my own account. I had been made a Director of the Leek United Building Society some years before and this was also a personal commitment.

In about 1989 Brenda had been accepted on a part-time introductory year towards a full-time degree course in Fine Art at the North Staffordshire Polytechnic. She had tried this some years before but her health did not hold up. This time she managed to keep going with the benefit of a special parking space. She found the degree very challenging but rewarding. The teachers were of very mixed quality, some of them much more interested in their own work and left-wing politics than the interests of the students. She felt to some extent discriminated against because she was a middle-class elderly woman with a southern accent. This did not by any means apply to all the staff, nor to her fellow students, with some of whom she made very good friends although they were 40 years younger. She would not have been confident of fair treatment if the degree had been awarded by some of the staff, but there were outside examiners and she obtained a good upper second degree. There was a rather pleasing little article about her success, despite her disability, in the local newspaper. The degree gave her more confidence in her work which she continued to pursue actively for the rest of her life.

Matthew and Helen's son Dominic arrived in November, 1994 in Sydney. Brenda saw a video of him, but as things turned out she never got to meet him in person.

Brenda was becoming rather distressed by the delay in moving to Otford, wondering whether she would ever go to live next door to her grandchildren. By early 1995, however, all the necessary planning and building regulation approvals had been obtained for the flat and we were ready to go out to tender. At about the same time her gynaecologist advised her to have a hysterectomy and she was admitted to the Nuffield Hospital in Newcastle-under-Lyme in good heart. The operation was reported to have gone satisfactorily, but she did not recover as she should have done after a serious but routine operation. For several days she failed to improve and eventually I sent for Stella, after advice that a second exploratory operation was recommended. I collected Stella from Stoke station and we found Brenda weak but in good spirits. She had suffered a distressing night and was grateful for the medical insurance which provided private accommodation. She said how fortunate she was, because she had, that morning, received in her bed a call from her son in Australia and another from her son in the United States. Now here were her husband and daughter. The following day I arrived to see Brenda before the operation but discovered that she had already gone to the operating theatre.

On investigation the surgeon had found that peritonitis had set in and Brenda was transferred to the intensive care unit at the North Stafford Royal Infirmary. She was on a respirator and never recovered consciousness after that second operation. Matthew and Oliver came over from Australia and the United States respectively; we took it in turns to be with Brenda and hopes would rise whenever there was a slight improvement in test results.

Stella considered that Brenda was lucky to be in that intensive care unit. It has four consultants attached to it with excellent nursing staff. It was comforting to see how respectfully they spoke to Brenda and nursed her, even though it seemed that she was quite unconscious.

At the end of 17 days a consultant spoke to us all and admitted that they were not winning. We all agreed that Brenda would not have wanted support to be continued longer, to no purpose. Jonathan Eades, our priest at All Saints Church, Leek, anointed her and said prayers. So she passed on to another place on 8 April 1995.

The funeral service was arranged for Easter Saturday, 21 April, and the large church was full, even though many people would have arranged to be away from home on Easter Saturday. The undertakers said there were at least 400 people present. The coffin was covered by a pall which is one of the treasures of Leek, sewn by ladies of the Embroidery Society. Brenda had planned her funeral and wanted a communion service, but there were no complaints at its length. Matthew read a lesson and Oliver and I spoke briefly about her life. After the service many people came to Smith House where we had arranged an exhibition of Brenda's paintings in the barn. Later I had a transcript made of the service, together with some quotations and thoughts which Brenda had recorded. It was so popular that I had to have a second printing done.

Since we had been intending to move to Otford it was decided that the memorial to Brenda should be there. Matthew and Helen had previously made plans to come to England in May and to have their son Dominic baptised. Brenda's ashes were interred on a Thursday in the presence of all the family at St Bartholomew's Church in Otford. There is a small memorial tablet to her at the Garden of Remembrance, which is all that she would have wanted. In the years since then I have tried to take fresh flowers from my garden weekly throughout the year, and when Harriet, my eldest grandchild, was married to Richard Bell in 2011 they stood beside the tablet to be photographed.

On Brenda's death I immediately told the builders to cancel any tenders while I reconsidered my position. After some time I decided to proceed with the move but reduced the size of the building.

I had put out feelers about joining the Athenaeum Club in London and was elected with the support of good friends. This has been the source of great pleasure in my retirement, which became almost complete on my move from Endon, although I still had some trusteeships, including that of a large estate, the Llysdulas Estate in Anglesey. I joined the University of the Third Age (U3A) and took advanced French classes as well as European studies. U3A tutors are not paid, but offer their services for the love of their subject. Frequently, therefore, they are very good indeed. A major interest has been a Workers Educational Association literature class in Otford which has compelled me to read some good authors and not fritter away my time on ephemeral magazines.

Before moving south I was telephoned by my old Sudan chief, Sir Gawain Bell, who had succeeded Sir James Robertson as Civil Secretary on the latter's appointment as Governor General of Nigeria. He was President of the Sudan Studies Society of the United Kingdom and invited me to join the committee. This I have been pleased to do for the last 15 years or so. It is a non-political organisation which has kept me in touch with the Sudan and its people, and I have written the occasional article for its twice-yearly publication *Sudan Studies*. An article on the return to Khartoum published in January 2006, the fiftieth anniversary of independence, is included in the Appendices. I also wrote one on rinderpest that was published in January 2011.

All these activities, together with making the garden and planting an orchard at Park Farm Cottage, have kept me active and occupied, but there has also been time for more travelling than Brenda could have managed, much as she would have wanted to do it – she always said she would like to be a nomad.

In 1990 Brenda and I, in partnership with Stella and Oliver, bought a small farmhouse in northern Provence, close to the foot of Mont Ventoux, which I continue to visit regularly. It has also been possible to see more of the Far East than could be visited on stopovers to Australia. There have been guided visits to Sri Lanka, where the civil war between the Singhalese and Tamils has mercifully ended, to Rajastan, Delhi and Agra in India, and a cruise with lectures in the Indian Ocean, calling at various ports on the west coast of India, the Maldives and the Seychelles. It has been possible to recover something of my Arabic in Oman, Syria, Tunisia and the Sudan. In spite of the horrifying hatred for non-Muslims in some corners of the Islamic world, I have never come across any hostility to a Westerner in these countries. The traditions of politeness (idaba) and hospitality (diafa) I have found everywhere. However, we must not forget that there is a tradition of jihad as a reason for slaughtering infidels, probably stemming originally from the Wahabi movement of the eighteenth-century in what is now Saudi Arabia. Doughty's "Arabia Deserta" gives the flavour of it as it was in the nineteenth-century.

It has been particularly interesting to study the condition of the countries which have emerged from Communist rule since 1990. The Baltic countries have recovered well on the whole and have joined the European Union – in spite of Russian hostility. Estonia, the most enterprising, was the first to join the Euro currency. Romania and Bulgaria were probably allowed into the European Union too soon, but that does not lessen the beauty of Romania's painted churches in the north of the country, many fortified against the Turks. Four river cruises have been very rewarding; the first took me from Moscow to St Petersburg starting with Stalin's canal which was so costly in human life, and the second from Prague to Potsdam and Berlin with a passage down the Elbe, through Dresden where I met my nephew and his family. The third river cruise was from Budapest to Nuremburg, mostly on the Danube, and the fourth on the Rhine, passing many centres of civilisation and beauty.

The remaining travels, apart from Europe, the Black Sea and the Mediterranean, have been on the American continent. At the time of my seventieth birthday Matthew and his family were living in the area of Silicon Valley, south of San Francisco in California. Oliver was (and still is) teaching in New York, so to celebrate the occasion I flew to stay with Matthew and then drove eastwards, taking a big loop south through the Yosemite National Park, Death Valley, the Grand Canyon, Arizona, New Mexico, the Texas Panhandle, Arkansas, Tennessee and North Carolina, Jefferson's estate at Montebello, finally to be welcomed by Oliver and James in their elegant apartment on the Upper West Side of Manhattan. A journey like this brings home some realities of the States. For instance, for hundreds of miles there were almost no national newspapers. The only one available was the Wall Street Journal which could be read at no cost on the sofa of a bank, with coffee available. No wonder most of Middle America is not well informed about affairs on other continents.

Other visits on the American continent have been to British Columbia in Canada, to Mexico, a cruise of the circuit of the Caribbean islands and a cruise with lectures of the west coast of South America, ending in the Galapagos Islands. February in Florida one year was followed by a drive via Savannah and Charleston to New York to visit Oliver and James.

The next generation have been making their contribution. Stella uses her experience to propose new ways of treating certain types of cancer; Matthew, having sold his business and returned to England, works voluntarily for a number of charities, for which he has been awarded the CBE; and Oliver continues to teach at St Bernard's School in New York and to support the Episcopal Church of St Michael, Amsterdam Avenue. My grandchildren have also thrived, now at various stages of careers, university or school.

My contemporaries usually agree with me that this is the best time in history to be old, at least if living in a democracy with a market economy and under the rule of law. Advances in medicine have meant that the "thousand natural shocks that flesh is heir to" have become less painful and less onerous.

It has been a good life. Deo gratias.

22

SOME REFLECTIONS

ATTITUDES TO EMPIRE

During my youth the British Commonwealth and Empire were regarded by the majority in Britain as beneficial to all parties, the ruled as well as the rulers. Peace and trade on favourable terms brought a rising standard of living to all its peoples, while defence arrangements under the Chief of the Imperial General Staff gave a sense of security.

There was a feeling of belonging to a family of many skin colours. Robert Baden-Powell, the founder of the Boy Scout and Girl Guide movements, was a confident imperialist but he could lay down in the Scout Law that "[...] a Scout is a friend to all and a brother to every other Scout". The vociferous anti-racists of today might be surprised that this unequivocal message came from the hero of an imperial war in South Africa over 100 years ago. The King's broadcast to the peoples of the Empire fostered the idea of a family. People from all parts of the Empire came to academic institutions in Britain and most had a favourable experience. In my first term at Oxford in 1944 the President of the Union was a suave black gentleman from Jamaica, Mr Kenneth Tudor.

There was a huge sense of gratitude for the support and sacrifices of imperial troops during World War I from 1914 to 1918, and this was continued in World War II of 1939 to 1945. The Dominions were independent but most regarded themselves as being at war as soon as Britain was. Even South Africa, where there was a pro-Nazi faction among the Afrikaners (who were a majority among the whites) came into World War II under Smuts, who had fought against the Empire in the Boer War.

Then there occurred the dreadful humiliation of the surrender of Empire troops at Singapore in 1941. Hong Kong, Malaya, Singapore, Burma and part of Papua New Guinea, as well as other islands, fell rapidly to the Japanese. India was seriously threatened. The promise of mutual security had been broken and nationalist leaders could argue that their countries might as well be on their own. In 1947 the Indian Empire became independent and divided itself into India and Pakistan amid scenes of appalling slaughter. In spite of strenuous efforts, Britain had been unable to keep India united under one democratic government. Burma, Malaya, British Borneo and Singapore followed to become independent within the next decade, and Britain withdrew from 'East of Suez', as the expression went.

The Movement for Colonial Freedom led by Labour MP Fenner Brockway then tried to rush the pace in Africa, giving support to every self-styled nationalist leader or agitator. Two outside bodies joined in. One was our ally in a 'special relationship', the United States of America. Their policy was that any situation which could be labelled 'colonial' was wrong and should be brought to an end as soon as possible. (They showed no awareness or shame over the unprovoked war with Mexico and the annexation of Texas, New Mexico and Arizona during the previous century.)

In a rather incongruous, unspoken alliance with the United States, Communist Russia also conducted a vigorous anti-colonial campaign both in Britain and in the Colonies. It was an important weapon in the Cold War. This had a powerful effect in many British educational institutions, where anything 'colonial' was automatically declared wicked. After the fall of the Soviet Union and the Berlin Wall, evidence was found showing that at least one university teacher had been paid Russian money. At the same time the Russians insisted that their conquered territories in Asia and the Caucasus were not colonies but freely associated within the Union of Socialist Soviet Republics. This argument did not survive the fall of the Berlin Wall, since most Republics walked away as soon as they could.

Meanwhile the Cold War had a ruinous effect in Africa. There occurred what might be described as a second scramble for Africa, with the USA and the USSR each competing to acquire as many client dictators as possible without concern for how they treated their subjects. There was much disillusion with the state of newly independent Africa at this time, but the major blame often lay with Washington and Moscow.

In Britain the Cold War propaganda seemed to produce a mood of self-denigration, the idea that everything the country had done or stood for was shameful. For instance, for many years there were exhibitions or broadcast programmes about the slave trade, rightly reported as quite appalling, but without mention that British people had been the first to campaign against it, leading to the abolition of the trade in 1807 followed by banning the institution itself in 1832 in British Territories. This was a great commercial sacrifice as Spanish Cuba and the USA continued slavery for another generation, to the severe detriment of that part of the sugar trade controlled by Britain.

During the nineteenth-century the Royal Navy patrolled the oceans to stop the slave trade. When the European-run Atlantic trade was ended the Arab operations in the Indian Ocean still had to be dealt with. It is only in recent years, perhaps with the showing of "Amazing Grace", the film about Wilberforce, that a more balanced account has been presented. The sense of shame about the past brought with it a certain self-satisfied arrogance, a belief that here was a new generation that was morally superior to any that had gone before.

Perhaps our troubles in Afghanistan and Iraq will remove some of the smugness of the anti-imperialist generation. A particular irritation has been to hear BBC interviewers trying to goad speakers from countries formerly under British rule to say how much they suffered, when clearly the person being interviewed wants to say something quite different.

THE MORALITY MOVEMENT

Many commentators on the Empire portrayed it as a continuous story of greed and oppression. This is to make a serious mistake. There were two British Empires: broadly the two centuries from the seventeenth-century when Bermuda was discovered and settled and Cromwell conquered Jamaica, and then the second Empire from the mid-nineteenth-century to the end.

During the first two centuries examples of greed and oppression were numerous; after all, why should people go to dangerous, distant and unhealthy places if not to enrich themselves? Towards the latter part of the eighteenth-century a new spirit appeared. The Society for the Abolition of the Slave Trade was founded in 1787, arguably the first human rights organisation in the world. Captain Coram's hospital for foundling children and the London Hospital in Whitechapel were established by the middle of the century. Wesley's extensive preaching journeys, covering some 250,000 miles and delivering 40,000 sermons, mainly in the open air, had a great effect upon the conscience of the working people, many of whom had previously been untouched by the Church of England.

The Clapham Sect, a group of mostly rich and well-connected evangelical Christians, influenced society and government at the other end of the social scale in the first half of the nineteenth-century. They were at the heart of the campaign to abolish slavery and to establish a home for freed slaves in Sierra Leone. By the 1830s Roman Catholics had been emancipated and the first parliamentary reform bill had been passed. The Anglo-Catholic or Oxford Movement were not to be left behind; they responded to Livingstone's call to the University of Cambridge to end slavery and establish fair commerce with the Universities' Mission to Central Africa.

Public services had so far not been greatly affected by the moral movement, but in 1853 came the Trevelyan-Northcote Report on the civil services which proposed "full security for the public that none but qualified persons will be appointed and that they will afterwards have every practicable inducement to the creative discharge of their duties". The remedy was to be open public examination with appointment and promotion based on merit. The reform was successful, with the result that the British Civil Service is probably still the best in the world. Traditionally, most in the upper half of the Civil Service examination went into the Indian Civil Service; their record has withstood the efforts of Indian nationalists and British revisionist historians to denigrate them. The shock of the 1857 Indian Mutiny and the action of the British Government in taking over the government of India from the East India Company facilitated the reforms.

A generation later the sale of commissions in the armed forces was abolished. Recruitment for the Colonial Service, and later the Sudan Service, was not through written examination but according to record, recommendation and interview; the same principle of merit alone applied.

The effect of these reforms and the moral climate supporting them was to lead to a different kind of empire. It was recognised that with the advance of education the territories would eventually be self-governing, though it was thought by many that there would be an "infinity of time" before that could happen. And so the concept of trusteeship grew up. Officials believed that their authority was held in trust to benefit the people and lead them eventually to responsible self-government. In my 15 years in two African services I never met a colleague who abused his authority or helped himself to something he was not entitled to, though the salaries were low and there must have been temptations. I cannot think of any ruling caste in world history which did less to feather its own nest. The motive was always "what can I do to improve the conditions of the people for whom I am responsible?" When there was a conflict with immigrant claims, as in Kenya, the principle was that the interests of the native people were paramount.

By the time of the Trevelyan-Northcote reforms the judiciary had already established their independence in Britain and this fed through to the colonies. Admittedly the district administrators were usually also magistrates, but they passed a case to a visiting full-time resident magistrate if there was any danger of administrative factors affecting the decision. High Court judges had an independent status similar to Britain.

The police were trained on British lines and were tough on bribery, though it would be naïve to expect that police constables never took a reward for not reporting an illegal beer sale in a village. In dealing with civil unrest the principle was to use only the minimum force necessary to end the trouble, although it has to be recognised that sometimes things got out of hand. Nothing is perfect in this world, but British policing is the widely accepted standard.

The impression has been created, or taught as Marxist theory, that all private enterprise in the Empire was exploitative. I could never see this. Provided that an enterprise treated its employees fairly, obeyed the laws and paid its taxes, it should be welcomed as a creator of wealth. The great mining companies in the Northern Rhodesian Copperbelt were good employers and responsible citizens. They provided better housing, health and education facilities for their employees and families than the Government, on the whole. The international banks had a similarly good record. It is a sad irony that Barclays, which did its best to mitigate the hardships of apartheid, should have been the object of boycott by students and compelled to withdraw from South Africa.

Kaunda nationalised Zambia's mines and they were so mismanaged that the World Bank later found it very difficult to privatise them. Indian and Chinese interests have moved in, with mixed results, and there are numerous reports of discontent. The Chinese are now economically powerful in most of Africa, but seem not to be popular because they bring in fellow Chinese for much of the work which could be done by locals. Where they do employ indigenous people there are complaints that the hours are too long and the supervisors too exacting.

One must hope for more Western investment in those African countries that are developing a civil society, both in its own right and to provide an alternative to Chinese domination of their economies.

THE DECOLONISATION PROCESS

The withdrawal from Palestine has been criticised; however, it was not a colony but was held under a League of Nations Mandate. Outside factors, namely American, Russian and United Nations policies, forced the British withdrawal. The Sudan we left sooner than expected. The Gold Coast became independent as Ghana in 1956, but East and Central Africa were expected to follow much later. When I went to Northern Rhodesia in 1955, aged 28, it was conceivable that I would have a full career there. In 1954 the United Nations Committee on Decolonisation had recommended that Tanganyika, a League of Nations Mandate, should become independent within 25 years. The British Government rejected this as too soon.

Then, in 1960 Harold Macmillan spoke in Cape Town of the "wind of change blowing through Africa". This was like a reveille bugle call to the nascent nationalists. There subsequently occurred a complete change of policy; constitution making and Africanisation of British posts became urgent. In the end we somehow produced, as we had rather imperfectly in the Sudan, a largely agreed democratic constitution and a successor Government with a claim to popular consent. In Northern Rhodesia the cry at political rallies was "one man, one vote".

To this the cynics, myself included, would add "once". And so it proved for a generation, as the first independent rulers gathered all the fruits of power to themselves and brutally suppressed any opposition. However, by the end of the century there were some hopeful signs – Ghana and Zambia had held elections which led to a peaceful change of government according to law. There are promising developments in Tanzania and Sierra Leone, after a cruel civil war which was ended by British troops. The Congo and Somalia are still badly failed states and the previously successful Ivory Coast has suffered from the throes of civil war, as has Mali.

Britain can feel some satisfaction that her former African territories are providing better lives for their people than the territories of other colonial powers. Somalia provides a clear example of this. The smaller part which was British Somaliland has organised itself as a successful state within a state, providing refuge for many fleeing from the chaotic former Italian Somalia. If the self-styled Republic of Somaliland could be internationally recognised, it could provide the means to defeat the pirates infesting the Indian Ocean.

There are probably two main reasons for the comparative success of former British territories; the trouble taken to transfer power constitutionally, and the bequest of a functioning civil service with a full treasury and a tradition of conscientious and honest behaviour.

There was one very delicate factor in decolonisation. The great majority of civil servants and police were extremely loyal to and friendly with their British supervisors. We had to do all we could to ensure that this did not result in them or their families suffering after independence, as there had been some unpleasant attacks on them for being traitors and the like. The best way of dealing with this was to discourage them from being openly anti-nationalist, and at the same time to point out to the nationalists that reliable civil servants would be essential to running the country after independence. On the whole, this was achieved, I believe, although of course we were out of touch once we left.

THREE CIVIL SERVICES COMPARED

Queen Victoria and (until his early death) Prince Albert had personified the moral purpose of the Empire. The Sudan conquest occurred shortly before Queen Victoria's Diamond Jubilee, being regarded from its start as a field for Christian duty in fulfilment of Gordon's sacrifice. Almost one third of the members of the Political Services were sons of the vicarage or the manse. Colleagues and their wives were friendly, hospitable and proper. I cannot recollect a single case of divorce while in the Sudan.

The other side of this coin was a certain sense of superiority. After the demise of the Indian Civil and Political Services, the Sudan was top, they thought (but did not say out loud). They inherited from India the jibe of being the "cock angels" or the "heaven-born". However, they loved the people and their work in spite of all the hardships. They were hardworking, intelligent, good-humoured and benevolent. I regard it as a great honour to have been part of such a service.

The atmosphere in Her Majesty's Overseas Service (formerly the Colonial Service) in Northern Rhodesia was different. Circumstances meant that it existed on a more mundane plane. Along the line of rail, there was a mostly British or British South African white population who were running the towns through municipal councils, as in Britain. The DC would have a white female secretary. Away from the railway line, the situation was much more like the Sudan, though the districts and their populations were smaller. Procedures were more regularised and there was less room for individual initiative. Nevertheless this is not to criticise – all these differences were right and proper for the circumstances.

In Northern Rhodesia, with the first tour of three years, followed by tours of two and half years, everything felt much more settled than in the Sudan, where British staff enjoyed 80 days leave in Britain each year after the first tour. Wives had longer to become bored in out-stations and marriages were less stable, but the quality of administration was equally high.

There were a number of DOs who did not have a university degree, but this was due to the war. Procedure and etiquette were a little too important. John Hannah noted the differences; when he was in charge of a district in the Sudan while his DC was on leave, his Governor visited and asked, "How can I help you?" When the Provincial Commissioner of Northern Rhodesia came he would be on a formal inspection, almost looking for things to that might be found wanting.

The Home Civil Service Administrative Class that I joined in 1965 had some hints of an Oxbridge Senior Common Room. The top echelon had been described by R.A. Butler as "having Rolls Royce minds". They wrote to each other using surnames, though women colleagues were always addressed as Miss, Mrs or Dr (Ms had not arrived.) This mitigated the oppressiveness of rigid seniority and made use of expertise at whatever level it occurred. On the other hand, work was very Whitehall-centred and the ivory-tower image had some validity. Citizens who had business with the department were expected to come to London; officials were not encouraged to go out to the provinces. This would have cost money, but it would have been worth it. Generally the Service was careful with money. After attending a whole-day session at the Council for Scientific Policy where a sandwich lunch was provided, one would be asked the next day to pay the six shilling cost.

Corruption seemed as alien as in my previous two Services, although there was a serious case in Scotland after I left and there may have been some lavish entertainment by defence companies. The major difference from previous experiences was the attitude to the job. Being always subservient to "our political masters", there was a degree of cynical resignation. Overseas one *was* the Government; this brought a great sense of involvement or vocation. In Whitehall the minister got the glory, but he also took the rap.

My criticism of government in Britain is that it is very fragmented. There are so many local government bodies, agencies, quangos[1] and councils, all acting without reference to others it would seem. When I left government and observed from outside I could see money being wasted because of a lack of consultation between spending agencies. The Northern Rhodesian system of the DC chairing the District Team with a monthly meeting to share information on future plans would result in greater efficiency and economy, but there are now too many vested interests in Britain which will prevent it. The French have seen the need and have their Prefet de Departement.

THE MONARCHY

A tendency seems to have grown up for the typical *Guardian* reader to claim to be a republican. One can see the logic in this view; no-one should hold a position of power or status at the cost of the public purse unless they are elected or appointed by an elected officer.

In this matter, one may recall the probably apocryphal discussion between John Stuart Mill and his father James. Father advanced a proposition, to which son objected that it may be all very well in theory but would not work in practice. Father sternly replied that if it was valid in theory, it must be valid in practice. So let us observe the practice and ask which country one would most like to live in, if one had no other attachments. Most would choose the Scandinavian countries, Holland, Canada, Australia, New Zealand, and Britain. All these countries happen to be monarchies and are indubitably democratic, showing no wish to change their status. The last time Australians had a choice they voted against a "politician president". Spain and Belgium are divided nations, yet they too value their monarchs.

There is a further reason for a constitutional monarchy. In the United States, France and the new states of Africa, the President is both head of government and head of state. A large minority of the people will have voted against that person and may be strongly, sometimes bitterly, opposed to him or her. A civil servant or officer in the armed forces would find loyalties divided. In Britain we may dislike the current government intensely, but we give our loyalty to the monarch as personifying the whole nation, present, past and future.

Politicians tend to think in the present; they are less concerned about our children and future generations than they are with the current voters. Still less will they respect the past if there are votes to be gained from disowning it. The monarchy embodies the continuing nation as, in Burke's words, "a partnership not only between those who are living but between those who are living, those who are dead and those who are to be born".[2]

There is a practical point too. The President of the United States, for example, has too much to do in running the government, being Commander-in-Chief of the armed forces and still having to carry out the ceremonial functions of head of state. Because he wants to have around him only civil servants who are on his side and who did not vote for his opponent, there is a wholesale change-over at the top of government when a new president assumes office; it is not by coincidence that this practice also occurred in eighteenth-century Britain. The system in Britain today is infinitely superior; a non-political civil service welcomes the new Prime Minister with extensive briefings and serves as loyally as it did the old, for the new leader is both elected by the people and appointed by the head of state.

The British weakness for self-denigration and guilt blinds us to our achievements. This country has achieved much for the benefit of the world in literature, learning, engineering and other fields. However, it has been most pre-eminent, over the course of many centuries as far back as the creation of the Anglo-Saxon jury system, in working out how people can live together in peace and co-operation to their mutual benefit.

To take one simple example, most of the games played internationally follow rules worked out and applied in Britain. On a larger scale, the system we have developed over the centuries of an elected parliament, a constitutional monarchy, a non-political civil service and armed forces and an independent judiciary was our gift to the Empire and will now be to the world.

How long will these gifts last? The Roman Empire left an astonishingly long and respected memory. In AD 800 Charlemagne revived the ideal in Western Europe in the form of the Holy Roman Empire. Although by the time of the eighteenth-century enlightenment Voltaire could say that it was neither holy, nor Roman, nor an Empire, it was not until 1805 that it was abolished by Napoleon. The defeated Francis II was forced to abdicate and was never replaced in the west.

However, this was not the end. When the Eastern Roman Empire came virtually to an end with the Turkish capture of Constantinople (henceforth to be Istanbul) in 1453, the Russian ruler claimed to continue the Roman Empire and called himself Caesar or Tsar. So in terms of title the Roman Empire endured until the murder of the Tsar and his family in 1918, or the abdication of Kaiser (Caesar) Wilhelm II of Germany later the same year. Thus the desire to be the inheritor of Julius Caesar lasted for nearly 2000 years.

There are still two remaining relics of the Roman Empire. One is Latin, still used in the Vatican and the Roman Catholic Church. The other is Roman Law, which forms the basis of a number of jurisdictions throughout the world. The great codification of Justinian (527–565), the Eastern Emperor, is still relevant.

How will the British imperial legacy fare against this record? The Roman influence was largely felt in Europe and parts of the Near East and North Africa. However, the legacy of the British Empire is worldwide, manifested chiefly through the English language. French, Spanish and Arabic, all tongues of learning and culture, have given up the struggle and conceded that English is to be the world language. Almost everywhere English is compulsory in schools. Esperanto was a brave enterprise but is now almost forgotten. George Bernard Shaw tried to correct the irregularities of spelling, pronunciation and grammar in English but failed, so it seems that the English of the Oxford English Dictionary, entailing so much learning of irregularities, is to prevail. The whole world will enjoy the inestimable benefit of access to Shakespeare, Johnson, Wordsworth, Eliot, Dickens and their successors.

The critical moment that settled the future of the English language was the Seven Years War of 1756 to 1763. Britain and France struggled for supremacy mainly in North America and India. It has been said that one of the critical facts in world history was that the United States of America grew up to speak English and not French. It could turn out to be equally important that India was united by the English language, as it now makes huge progress in computer technology.

The Commonwealth is a bequest to the various countries that were formerly part of the Empire. It seems from the outside to be a purposeless biennial gathering attended by the Queen. However, half a century after the end of Empire it still continues and there are new members applying to join. The professional links and the exchange of teachers, agriculturalists, lawyers and the like are clearly valued; democratic standards are largely upheld. There can be no way of forecasting how long the Commonwealth will last, but the likelihood seems to be for an indefinite future.

Finally, there is the English Common Law and the judicial system developed to apply it. There are some members of the Commonwealth, Sri Lanka and South Africa, who apply the Roman-Dutch law of the early Dutch settlers. The rest of the Commonwealth, and of course the United States, apply English Common Law, which they mostly find suits them well.

I think that my grandchildren will say in coming years that the Empire is a legacy to be grateful for. If my words are discounted because of the my nationality and experience, here is a letter to *The Times* of 11 May 2012, from Mr R.P. Fernando who describes himself as a former colonial subject:

Sir. Ben Macintyre (Opinion, 8 May) should not assume that all former colonial subjects are antagonistic towards the British Empire. In many ways, those of us from the colonies are better placed to appreciate the benefits of British rule. These extend further than the rule of law, English language and cricket, as mentioned in his article.

Concepts of parliamentary democracy, independent judiciary, equality under law and a free press were all introduced by the British. Tens of thousands of miles of railways and modern roads were constructed. The founding of thousands of hospitals, dispensaries and schools and hundreds of universities and colleges improved health and education services. The British irrigated millions of acres of land and the introduction of new crops, such as tea and rubber continue to be an asset to former colonies. The provision of telegraphic services, modern banking and detailed maps should be noted. The cities of Calcutta, Bombay, Madras, Singapore and Hong Kong were established during this period.

The first systematic study in the modern age of Eastern cultures was initiated by the British following the founding of the Royal Asiatic Society and departments of Oriental Studies in universities in the UK and elsewhere. The contribution the Archaeological Survey of India made to further the understanding of Indian history was immense. It is regrettable that these achievements are now so seldom acknowledged.

APPENDICES

Appendix 1

WESTERN NUER DISTRICT: MONTHLY DIARY, JUNE 1953

I wrote this while the DC was on leave and happened to keep a copy. All the district monthly diaries were collated by the Secretariat in Khartoum and gave a useful picture of the state of the whole country. Paragraphs were numbered consecutively for reference.

80. GENERAL

June has been on the whole a quiet month. With the roads closed, no visitors and no trekking, work has consisted of supervising the running of the station more closely than is possible during the dry season, and in getting all office work up to date.

The Nuer are busy in the fields, encouraged by the favourable rains. There is little hunger and most people appear well and contented.

It seems that at last Government propaganda to persuade people not to sell grain they will later need has produced some results, as merchants report their sales of dura are far below normal for this time of the year.

81. PERSONALIA

The DC was on leave during the month and the A/DC and Mrs Bowcock left on the 26th. They returned from trek on the 2nd and spent the whole of the intervening time in Bentiu.

82. LOCAL GOVERNMENT

On reports reaching the merkaz that all was not well with the Awet Dinka, two policemen were sent and found that the H/Chief Jiel de

Koic had taken all the fines cattle to his own luak, or distributed them to his relatives. The policemen succeeded in recovering all the cattle and Jiel is to be brought to Bentiu to explain himself.

Otherwise local authorities functioned satisfactorily except for a few signs of friction between the Head Chief of Leik and the new Court President, Deng Jak. Their respective duties have again been explained to them but it is inevitable that some misunderstandings should arise when the idea is still new in the northern part of the district.

83. LOCAL NEWS OF INTEREST

As the A/DC did not return from trek until midday on 2 June, it was not possible to make elaborate preparations for the celebration of the Coronation. However, in the evening officials were invited to the A/DC's house to hear Her Majesty's speech on the radio.

84. PUBLIC SECURITY

The two fights mentioned in para 65 of last month's diary have now been dealt with.

The Leik fight illustrates again the importance of quick payment of blood money. Three men were killed in January and the blood money of two was rapidly paid, but that of the third dragged on owing first of all to Gardat Kwac's visits to Malakal (politics to blame) and secondly to disease. The brother of the uncompensated man took the law into his own hands and attempted revenge, unsuccessfully, only wounding his victim. The relatives of the wounded man immediately set off in anger and killed a relative of the would-be murderer. The latter was given six years for attempted murder, and six of the killing party got four years.

The Jikany fight resulted from their tribal propensity for singing rude songs and was a straight inter-cieng spearing match. One man was killed and suitable sentences awarded, ranging from five years to six months.

Two merkaz ostas were found brewing araki. The owner of the still was given one year and his assistant (our chief builder) six months. This is the first case of araki in Bentiu for over a year. Increased vigilance by the police and heavier sentences would seem to have had the desired effect.

During the past two months, three gardeners and three ostas have found their way into prison, and the wages bill is much reduced.

The police post in Ganglil has now been established with a strength of one corporal and three men. Police houses, a lock-up and store and a well have been built. The presence of police in this hitherto semi-administered area has had a reassuring effect on the Nyuong, and greatly assisted in the preservation of public security and administration generally.

85. LABOUR

Scarce, rates 5 p.t. or 6 p.t. per day.

86. AGRICULTURE AND FORESTS

Work has started on clearing two feddans for a bamboo plantation. The bamboos should grow away during the rains, and the Forests have lent a 2" pump to keep them going during their first two dry seasons.

Prisoners have also started clearing two feddans in the toic for a small rice experiment. Fellata rice will be sown, and seed has arrived from SIA.

The oranges are in flower and scent the garden strongly.

87. MIGRATION

Nothing to report.

88. CLIMATE

The early part of June was quite dry, but since about the 15th there have been regular and heavy showers. These came in time to save the crops which on the lighter land had shown signs of drying. The soil will not now absorb more water and there is a good deal of mud about.

The temperature was variable, usually pleasant but sometimes very hot and sticky.

89. PUBLIC HEALTH

Jadwals in Bentiu were dug out and cleaned. The mosquito men were kept busy dealing with the pools of water left by the rains.

May figures for Riangnom dispensary were:

Out Patients 530
In Patients 5

These comparatively low figures show that many of the Kwil were still in their cattle camps.

Bentiu figures for half June were:
Out Patients 685
In Patients 16

The MA Bentiu went on trek through Jikany to Kwernyang. He found all well.

90. EDUCATION

Bentiu School closed prematurely on the 8th when the headmaster went on leave.

The Bul have failed in their promise to build the village school at Wangkai for use this year. They built two classrooms and four tukls, but did not roof them properly and as a result they are already dilapidated. It seems that it will not be possible to install a teacher until after the rains, when the DC will be able to get at the Bul and stimulate them once again to self help.

Riang Nhom School has 60 children in three classes. Building is going on there and proposals have gone forward for upgrading to a four-year EV school.

91. VETERINARY

One of the bloodslides sent from the Nyoung cattle (para 71 of May diary) has proved positive for tryps. The usual measures are being taken but it seems odd that neither the stockman not the Nuer associated the disease with tryps which they know very well. Perhaps it is an unusual form of the disease.

92. NATURAL HISTORY

The Game Scout has gone to the Kwil Dinka to deal with the lions which are such a nuisance there during the rains.

June is the best month for the job as later the grass grows too high.

93. COMMUNICATIONS

Roads: Preparations have been made to start ramping the Jikany road at Kwac where it crossed the toic which constitutes the course of the Khor Thiak at this point. Seven culverts will be needed, and fortunately a supply of old bitumen barrels has just arrived.

RT: Reception has much improved and the set is working well.

94. WATER SUPPLY

The well at Kwac has been half lined and left for the rains as it is impossible to get more materials to the site. The water is slightly salty but apparently very welcome to the local people nonetheless. The Kwac site is probably more useful as it serves a more populous area.

95. BUILDINGS

Work seemed to go on very slowly. The Scale J house now awaits the thatcher.

A deck tennis court was begun. Most of the ostas were still working outside Bentiu and could not be visited.

96. LANDS AND TOWN PLANNING

Nothing to report.

97. TRADE

Grain demands were everywhere (except in Nyuong) less than expected. As a result, there were less cattle brought for auction and all other trade was quieter than is usual in June.

98. FINANCE

Accounts were brought up to date and dura stock taking completed.

99. MISCELLANEOUS

The total correspondence for the month of June is as follows:

Total In Letters – 92
Total Out Letters – 95
Total Out Telegrams – 30
Total in Telegrams – 28

Signed P.P. Bowcock
A/District Commissioner
Western Nuer District
PPB/GBA

Bentiu, 25 June 1953

Addressed: Governor UNP (2)
DC CND Fagak
DC END Nasir

Appendix 2

JOURNEY TO NYALOK

Account by Brenda Bowcock of a trek to a cattle camp in Zeraf District in the dry season.

Nyalok is nothing more than a few simple dwellings of the Nuer tribe in Upper Nile Province of the Southern Sudan. This remote centre in the middle of a flat, hot and windy plain had sufficient water during the dry season to sustain a large gathering of tribal chiefs and litigants. In order to inspect the native courts my husband, the District Commissioner, had arranged this isolated rendezvous. From our home in the district headquarters of Fanjak we were to travel inland from a tributary of the Nile and then to take a footpath through the flat plain left by the retreating river.

As dawn broke we drove from the small resthouse where we had stayed the previous night. Three Nuer servants, an interpreter, two tribal policemen, boxes of court records and all our trek equipment made a very loaded lorry. We drove twelve miles to Gart, a small village where the road to Nyalok diminished into a rough track. Awaiting us we found our groom with two horses. Two tribal policemen and forty prisoner porters had been employed to carry our baggage. They were all merry young Nuers who had been involved in one of the tribal fights which had, as happened so frequently, ended in bloodshed. Despite the six-month term of imprisonment that they were serving, their spirits were not subdued.

The distribution of our luggage was an amusing scene. Amidst great shouts and laughter everything was unloaded from the lorry to the ground. As each man was none too anxious to exert himself there was a rush for the smallest box. The swiftest, however, had a slight shock, for he discovered that instead of having the lightest load, he was carrying the car battery. Eventually the policeman in charge subdued the laughter and each man was organised with a load. The tall men swung these onto their heads with ease. Then they set off. The long line of naked porters with intent expressions on their faces striding out across the deeply cracked cotton soil indeed made an impressive sight.

The rest of us set off at an easier pace, guided through the sparse thorn forest by two tribal policemen carrying spears. Perched skilfully on their heads one carried the water bottle and the other my shopping bag, looking strangely incongruous here. After an hour of walking we reached a small group of apparently deserted huts and cattle byres. On hearing our voices some bent old women followed by fly-covered children came out to greet us. These old people, the children and the sick are left behind each year in the dry season whilst the young men and girls take the herds to permanent water where there is good grazing.

The sun was rising fast and we soon became tired. The distant landscape shimmered before us and the sun seemed to burn through our clothing as we moved slowly on. The sweat dripped from our faces, the flies settled on us and the saddles became hot and uncomfortable but we journeyed on, determined to get the worst of the journey over before the sun reached its height. Though the heat was hard to bear the journey was far from miserable. We would often pass a solitary young man singing, happy as a king, as he drove his much-loved bull to the grazing ground. Occasionally a youth would greet us and then tag on to the wake of our retinue.

At 11 a.m. we halted by a group of trees and a muddy stream. In a short time Deng, our cook had produced a delicious breakfast of paw-paw, eggs, sausages, coffee, toast and even our homemade marmalade. We then tried to rest during the heat of the day on our camp beds protected from the tormenting flies by mosquito nets [...] even reading seemed an effort.

At three o'clock we set off on the last stage of the journey. The terrain became greener and more attractive as we left the scrub and thorn trees and approached the cattle camps. Tall, graceful young men and girls wearing nothing but coloured beads and ivory bracelets, their slim bodies shining in the sun, ran out to meet us. The girls stared hard at me and burst into fits of laughter when I spoke in halting Nuer. These young people were a pleasant contrast from the sad creatures we had passed earlier. We picked our way across the fresh green grass and passed large herds of grazing cattle. Nyalok was pointed out to us as a group of trees on the horizon. We looked back from our horses and saw a straggling line of prisoners behind us. They had obviously not been able to resist the temptation of a rest from their loads and a bathe in the first large pool.

We reached our destination as the sun began to set and found that the leaders of the people had arrived the previous day. They came to greet us as we sat about on boxes drinking tea and wearily waiting for the chairs to arrive. The chiefs wore red and white sashes over any bush jacket or brilliantly coloured shirt that they kept for special occasions. Their hats, great tokens of dignity, varied in style from smart trilbys to cheap, brightly-coloured peaked caps. Two of them had visited the local merchant's shop and wore striped football socks on their heads, giving them a look of friendly pirates.

The provincial police, who had been sent in advance, had prepared two small grass huts which were to be our home for the next five days. Soon after the last porter arrived we were sitting in canvas chairs drinking tepid drinks and listening to the world news from London. At times like this our servants were invaluable. They were also tired, yet without stopping to rest they bustled about, cheerfully preparing a fire, producing tea or bringing minute amounts of bath water and setting up our beds. Doubtless they greatly enjoyed giving orders to the many prisoners. A bull was killed and pieces of the raw meat distributed to the men. We listened to the murmur of their good-humoured voices and watched their shadowy figures squatting around the great communal fire as they roasted their beef on the end of spears. Meat was a great luxury to them. Once we had all eaten I conducted a small out-patient department outside our hut: none of the prisoners had serious injuries, but they enjoyed showing off their bandages and sticking plasters to their friends.

The next day brought a great amount of work for my husband at the court meetings held nearby, under the trees. I found a large number of chiefs' wives, their children and villagers waiting outside the hut for medical attention. The news of my simple out-patient department had spread rapidly. Unfortunately I had only a small supply of drugs and bandages and could only treat serious ailments temporarily. I was saddened to see many neglected, unhealed wounds. One young boy had deep, old puncture wounds in the back of his neck. He had been dragged, half asleep, from his hut by a leopard and then released as the beast, on being disturbed, fled into the night. I insisted that relations should take some of the sick to the nearest dispensary 16 miles away: not a great distance by Nuer standards. If the patient was seriously ill we kept him in the camp until we and the relations could transport him back to the nearest hospital.

A number of pretty girls aged between 12 and 15 came to see me later in the day. Each one wore beads, bracelets and small jangling cow bells. Some had shaved their heads to leave a circle of hair which they had dyed yellow. This process involved the application of cow's urine and wood ash for a number of days. The group came into my hut with cheerful greetings, sat on the wooden boxes or ground sheets and smiled at me as if we were old friends. Running out of conversation I would ask them in turn to pose whilst I tried to make quick sketches of these lovely nubile creatures. But they soon grew tired and would curiously examine everything in the hut, gazing into the mirror, patting their hair and adjusting their earrings as any English girl might do.

Every day visitors would come either for treatment or merely to greet me. Very few had seen a white woman before and their curiosity compelled them to make sure for themselves that my skin was really white and my hair not black and curly. My husband's predecessor, whilst trying to wash in a canvas bath, had heard giggles outside the rest house. The girls who were peeping through the cracks were not amused by his nakedness at all, but simply by the fact that he was white all over. We were in fact never without visitors, so that it became necessary to post a tribal policeman on the door of our hut when we wanted to rest. This we did always when the heat of the day became unbearably oppressive. Once when we were lying on our camp beds trying to keep cool, covered only by a towel, a young woman walked in, greeted us and settled down to pass the time of day, not in the least concerned that we were undressed. The head chief, Garwec, a dignified old man who was always accompanied by two loyal policemen, would come to visit us each evening when the lamps had been lit. He claimed that there were problems to discuss which could not be expressed in the courts. It was strange that he and his followers always seemed to arrive when dance music was to be heard on the radio.

Five days passed quickly enough. Soon we were retracing our footsteps through the cattle camps in the early morning light, past large flocks of pelicans that looked strangely pink and undignified out of water. At the group of trees where we stopped for breakfast a swarm of bees were too thirsty to touch us or the marmalade, mercifully for us, and only settled on the water bottles hung on a nearby branch. Once more we tried to sleep whilst the sun was at its highest, but we were glad to get back on the road after a few hours of restlessness. At sunset we reached Gart and found the police had lit fires and cleaned out a large cattle byre for us to spend the night. Within an hour of arrival we had bathed, dined and were fast asleep.

The following day we drove back to our home in the district headquarters at Fanjak. There we had such splendid luxuries as ice, a bath in clean water and our gramophone player. We had greatly enjoyed our journey to Nyalok and knew that soon we would have forgotten the heat, the flies and the exhaustion and would remember only the unspoiled, happy Nuers who seemed so pleased to see us.

269

Appendix 3

ZERAF DISTRICT ANNUAL REPORT, 1953–4

This had to be in a fixed format but I see that in the introduction I could not resist the temptation to offer some reflections based on the study of political science at Oxford. It had no effect on the political parties, now headstrong and determined to resist the attempts of the British Southern Governors to bring in a federal constitution.

1. GENERAL

This has certainly been the most fateful year for the people of this district since the Nuer settlement began. It became clear that the British DCs would have to go very quickly; this report is written by the last in the line.

It is doubtful whether the change will be for the good of the Nuer, but in these strange days, the old liberal Utilitarian axiom that the purpose of a government is to secure the greatest happiness for the greatest number of its people has given way to the more revolutionary doctrines of Rousseau and Marx. It is a pitiable irony that in the Age of the Common Man his interests are least regarded. What the future holds for the Nuer people none can yet foretell, but in probability it will be neither so bloody and insecure as the chiefs and headmen prophesy, nor so happy and prosperous as the politicians promise.

There is a sensation of exasperated bewilderment abroad caused by the fact that no notice is taken of what the chiefs have been saying for the last two years. Changes are made against their wishes and they feel impotent. To the ordinary Nuer, the hard fact behind all the fine words is that he will change a British DC for a Northern Sudanese one. Great political tact will be required during the next two years if the delicate framework of mutual confidence between chiefs and DC, on which public security depends, is to be handed on unimpaired.

However, in spite of all the difficulties caused by constitutional changes and shortages of staff, the administration of the district continued successfully. Some material progress was made and the authority of the Government's representative was virtually as great at the end of the year as at the beginning. In the circumstances it may be considered satisfactory merely to maintain the prestige of the administration, especially after the Southern Minister of State had in February sought to give the impression that the elected Government was at variance with the Civil Service.

A major administrative reorganisation took place on 11 February on the departure of Mr D.C. Carden. After eight years of administration from Fangak, the Lou Nuer were formed into a separate district with headquarters at Akobo. Fangak became the headquarters of Zeraf District only, as it was before 1946. The district thus recreated covers approximately 10,000 square miles and has an estimated population of 120,000 persons.

In May the 18,000 Dinka were informed that the project for joining them to Malakal had been dropped, for some years at any rate. There was some discontent at this, but it is hoped that they will soon realise that administratively they will probably get a better deal from Fangak than Malakal, since they are much more accessible from Fangak, being on the lines of communication. However, the Luaic will continue to be a problem, far away as they are on the Khor Felus.

The condition of the people generally was satisfactory. There was a severe shortage of grain but the merchants played their part well and imported over 2,000 tons. There were no cattle epidemics and a CSM outbreak among the Dinkas was controlled. Throughout the year the people remained healthy, happy and smiling.

2. PERSONALIA

Mr D.C. Carden left Central Nuer District on 11 February on appointment to a post as Second Secretary in Her Britannic Majesty's Foreign Service. During his four years of careful and conscientious administration he had consolidated and advanced the innovations of his predecessors. It is a testimony to his methods that his successor was able to take over all the multifarious activities of the district without finding a single loose end. Many chiefs and headmen protested at the departure of "Pernyang" and sent a petition to the Governor to persuade him to stay.

Upon the split of CND Mr Roussel became DC of Lou Nuer, the area in which he had chiefly worked as A/DC of CND.

271

After 11 February, staff of Zeraf District was as follows:

DC – Mr P.P. Bowcock, formerly A/DC Western Nuer
Sub-Mamur – John Eff Warabek, succeeded in June by Manasseh Eff Pac
Bookkeeper – Saraf Aziz Eff Yusif Abdalla
Clerk – Gabriel Eff Abuong

Other staff attached to the district were:

EO ZIQDC – Titus Eff Tipo, who left in February and was succeeded in June by Joel Eff Abbathur
MA – Joshua Eff Nyal
Head Stockman – Abdel Rahman el Sir, succeeded in May by Loh Wyal, a Garweir Nuer
Sanitary Overseer – Abdel Rahman Daw el Beit, a new appointment made in March

The Governor visited the district several times and so did both D/ Govs and almost the whole of the Province staff. The only non-official visitors were a party from the World Health Organisation wishing to gain information for a tuberculosis immunisation campaign.

3. FRONTIERS

Relations with other districts were very good on the whole. Frontiers are treated separately below.

Bor District – Peaceful. The inter district meeting took place at Dul Faiwil in February. In all matters discussed, it was agreed to uphold the status quo. There was a warning in March that trouble might occur over fishing rights, but this was averted by the dispatch of mounted police.

Western Nuer – No trouble, although people seeking to escape arrest or the execution of court judgements tend to cross the Nile. Cooperation between chiefs on either side is quite good.

Shilluk – The most difficult frontier. Eighteen Nuer crossed again without permission and were brought back to be imprisoned or fined. Perhaps this measure prevented a fight occurring once again.

Lou Nuer – Possible trouble between the Lou Nuer and Luaic Dinka was averted by sending a party of police from Malakal and holding a chiefs' meeting. Many Lou brought their cattle to the Duk ridge but caused no trouble.

Malakal – One Luaic chief tried to anticipate the possible transfer and joined the Nuok with many of his people. He was returned and stripped of his sash of office.

4. LOCAL GOVERNMENT

During the first seven months of the year the Zeraf Island Rural District Council made promising advances, but the change of chairman and the transfer of the executive officer in February meant a slowing down of the pace of advance. The DC and Sub-Mamur were fully occupied with public security and tribal problems, and in consequence it was not until June that some thought could be given to the future of the Council. Then Manasseh Eff Pac who had been Chairman of Bor RDC arrived to take over as Executive Officer. Proposals were submitted to the Governor with a view to bringing the whole of the Zeraf District under the control of the Council, and transferring the budget, safe and bookkeeper to the Council's charge. This would give the whole district a unified and one hopes effective deliberative body, and at the same time reduce the administrative and financial work involved in having the district split up into the Council area (Zeraf Island) and the directly administered area (the Mainland).

The Council started the year well by doing good road work. Maintenance of buildings was satisfactory but dilatory. A well was dug at Ful Lita and the lining almost completed by the end of June. In January the budget for the following year was fully and intelligently debated.

In February, Mr P.P. Bowcock succeeded Mr D.C. Carden as Chairman and Sayed Buth Din remained as Vice-Chairman throughout the year. As the Council representative, he attended the Local Government conference in Khartoum during March.

5. LOCAL POLITICS

The Nuer area of the district formed the Zeraf Valley constituency. During the elections the Dinka joined the Lou to make a constituency called Central Nuer East.

In Zeraf Valley the candidates were Buth Diu standing for the Southern Political Association and Paul Riak, formerly Storekeeper, who was supported by the NUP. An unfortunate campaign followed which rather puzzled the Nuer. The NUP brought various charges of threats and corrupt practices against Buth Diu, none of which were substantiated at the magisterial enquiry. They also accused the DC of interference with the elections until he offered to allow representatives of the party to observe him and trek with him on foot throughout the period of the election.

The elections were indirect. There was a contretemps in Thiang where the tribal sections began to sing songs and run for their spears. To prevent this from happening again the primary elections were postponed and held in the various Cieng areas.

The proportion of the electorate which voted was everywhere small; e.g. at Fagwic, 100 voted out of over 4,000 eligible. The secondary election was held at Let on 21 November.

The main issues were two:

a) Do you want British or Egyptian officials.
b) The personal merits of the candidates.

Buth Diu was returned with a comfortable majority.

The Dinka contributed to the return of Dak Dei unopposed as an independent candidate; on the announcement of the results he joined the NUP and was appointed as minister of state without portfolio.

During February two Southern ministers without portfolio, the same Sayed Dak Dei and Santino Deng, with Sayed James Gatluak Kuny, Deputy Speaker of the Senate, toured the district and held some meetings. Speeches were made in Fangak to the effect that the British officials now resembled a snake with the head cut off, which writhed in agony and yet had no power to harm. Officials and employees were encouraged to submit any complaints they might have against the DC to the Minister, who would immediately dismiss him if the case warranted it. To the more educated, this gave the unfortunate impression that the Government was at variance with its Civil Service; to the Nuer tribesman, among whom the DC occupies a position as a tribal institution personifying the government, is seemed little less than an incitement to civil disobedience. Events in Lou, where one chief had defied the DC and a Minister had imprisoned the Sub-Mamur, were accordingly watched with the closest anxiety by all chiefs. It took some months of careful explanation to restore the prestige of the Local Authority.

6. PUBLIC SECURITY AND JUSTICE

Public Security

There were two very large fights during the year. Both could have been prevented if the chiefs had acted properly. It may be that there is abroad a general feeling that the Government is not what it was, and in consequence native authorities are less ready to take firm action against the young warriors.

The first of these fights took place in Radh Garwier on 10 December; six men were killed and over 20 wounded. The cause was the beating up of a Cieng Jitheib man by three from Cieng Joak at night. Garwec Diet and Jal Loh, the executive chiefs, failed to bring the accused to trial and so Cieng Jitheib sought revenge.

Around 400 men were imprisoned and built a road from Goet to Gwadhgol. The two chiefs also got three months each.

The other large fight took place between the Jueny and Anieka sections of the Ruweng Dinka on 31 January. It was a most serious affair with over 500 men involved. Some 21 were killed and 42 wounded. The cause was the singing of rude songs connived at by the rival ambitious chiefs, Gajang Mareang and Macar Baduot. The Executive Chief and the court failed to take action against the song leaders and the final explosion was the result of 10 months of rising temper. The Fangak main court saw the case, convicted all the killers and sentenced 536 men to various terms of imprisonment.

A smaller fight took place in Bar Garwein in December which resulted in two deaths; there were also a number of lesser, and fortunately not fatal, affrays in Thiang and Lak. Needless to say, all the above incidents kept the district staff busy from December until March, and custody of prisoners will remain a problem until the end of 1955.

Apart from the fights reported above, there were six homicides during the year and one attempted homicide. The culprit in the latter case seems to have been mad and has probably escaped to Ethiopia.

One case in which elements of 'dhom' and 'biem' were involved went to a Major Court and resulted in a sentence of 10 years. In a similar case, the accused was a boy of 15 and the case was dealt with by the Fangak Main Court. The other four homicides were really small fights and were seen by the Regional Courts, on receiving the DC's sanction to proceed.

Justice

The criminal work of the native courts is usually good. Rarely do prisoners wish to appeal except when convicted of 'stealing' a girl or a cow, in which case there are usually two sides to the question.

Nor is it often necessary, except when offences by chiefs are involved, to refer back a case for alteration of the sentence. Offences by chiefs, of which there have been a number, are often difficult as a "chiefs' trade union" is growing up. It would really be more satisfactory if such cases could be referred to a Resident Magistrate.

Court work in civil cases is not nearly so good and to raise it to the same standard as the criminal work, in which of course the DC must take a closer personal interest, requires a great deal more time than he can spare. The "disc" procedure works well on the whole, except when the clerk makes a mistake with the numbers, which results in chaos. (The "disc" procedure was devised by J.S.R. Duncan, Mr Carden's predecessor, to witness the execution of judgement – vital to prevent litigants from taking the law into their own hands.)

The chief failings are:

a) tardiness in bringing the defendant to court, after the plaintiff has registered his case. It is often difficult to find where responsibility lies for this as the defendant's headman will say, "But I brought D to court and plaintiff was away." More regular court meetings should reduce this.
b) failure to execute court judgements. Mr Carden's rules have brought about a great improvement here, but vigilance is necessary to see that they are applied.

An attempt has been made during the year to enforce the old system of courts meeting automatically at either the full or the new moon. The idea is a good one and appreciated by the chiefs and people but it requires a great deal of attention to make it work unfailingly, especially if it is linked to the payment of salaries, with the penalty of no pay for a chief who does not turn up.

The appeal system is not entirely satisfactory. It takes up too much of the DC's time and many people do not succeed in getting their appeals heard. Proposals have been submitted for putting the system onto a more regular basis.

Details of magistrates' cases can be found in the appendices.

Notes on Individual Courts with which are included tribal notes

No.1. Kwemerony – 4,072 tax payers. This is the new permanent centre for the Jonyang Lak. It is a pleasant place and good buildings were put up in December. In the dry season, the court will continue to meet at Wathkec where the cattle camps are situated.

Numbers of tax payers have topped 4,000 and it is a busy court ably presided over by Po Mier. The other chiefs are a poor lot, particularly in Nyapir. In their jealousy of Po, they deliberately delay executions and some injustices are done. Oth Deng, the Executive Chief, was imprisoned for abusing his authority and flogging a Nuer merchant. Unfortunately, there is no one to replace him.

No. 2. Fagwir – 4,180 tax payers. The Kwagbor Lak run themselves satisfactorily. Kic Wur, though getting old, is still by far the most respected chief in the district and has prestige enough to keep the Executive Chief, Buom Wur, in his place. Cases are sometimes rather slow in coming to trial.

No. 3. Mareang – 2,842 tax payers. The Thuang court works well. Both of the senior chiefs are good at their job.

No.4. Nyod, formerly Jumbiel – 1,656 tax payers. The work of this court has been seriously hampered by the big Radh fight of December in which the Executive Chief of Falagh and the Court

President of Nyod, being both from C. Jitheib, joined to oppose their respective colleagues who were from C. Nyadakwon. Chiefly for this reason, it was decided to amalgamate the two courts into a combined Radh Court on the Famir. Much work has already been done towards this goal and the idea has been popularly accepted. There is a widespread feeling that something is badly wrong with the present arrangement which involves an artificial split in one tribe.

No. 5. Awoi – 4,867 tax payers. The Bar Garweir court works under great difficulties set by size, distance and the untamed character of the people. Clan feuds are a constant threat to the peace while the Bor Dinka border has to be watched carefully. In the circumstances, Mateat Kan and Cuol Kur manage very well. If occasional lapses come to light, the fault is chiefly the lack of sufficient administrative staff to give them regular backing.

No 6. Atat – 3,324 tax payers. This court was badly smitten by the terrible fight of 31 January.

Abednego Awer Agwer, the Court President, is a good judge but lacks a strong personality, and in any case he lives too far away to control the court effectively. It is probably desirable to give the Luaic a sub-court of their own. The Executive Chief, Deng Pakak, can be good but sometimes tends to mark time: perhaps his appointment as the district's representative in the Provincial Council will bring him up to his old standard. The sub-chiefs are not bright and this court needs a good deal of alteration, especially in view of the resentment of some at not joining Malakal.

No. 7. Falagh – 3,012 tax payers. Not good. Gatcang Jal, the Court President, is well-meaning but overshadowed by the powerful personality of his Executive Chief, Garwec Diet. Control of the people living on the Duk Ridge, who tend to be a law unto themselves, is difficult. It may be desirable to have a sub-court there, particular after the move to Wilori. See also notes on the Nyod Court above.

Fangoli Main Court – This court meets whenever summoned to try fights and major criminal cases. It now has a clerk and book of its own. The elasticity of its constitution is particularly valuable under Zeraf conditions.

Fangoli Branch Court – This court for Fangoli township functions satisfactorily under the presidency of Jok Dong and relieves the DC and Sub-Mamur of many tiresome petty cases.

Police

The district establishment is 1 shawish, 4 ombashia and 18 anfar, one of whom is a police clerk. Of these, 1 ombashi and 3 anfar are based at Ayod post, the rest in Fangak. The two fights, which entailed standing patrols and the custody of about 800 prisoners, meant that reinforcements were sent from Malakal consisting of 7 mounted and 12 foot police. The establishment of 23 is manifestly far too small and allows no slack for emergencies. The situation would be even more difficult were it not for the energy and devotion to duty of the shawish, Biliu Kuny.

Prisoners

A prison population varying from 800 to 350 was a constant problem and it is a testimony to the prestige of the police that there was only one big attempt to escape.

The Inspector of Prisons, Southern Provinces visited Fangak in March. From his report, it appears that accommodation needs to be doubled. A latrine was begun in June.

Witchcraft and Kujurs

A Garwei man was imprisoned in Western Nuer for peddling a bad medicine called "murjok" which comes from the Ruweng and is quite common in this district.

After crossing over from Western Nuer without permission in April 1953 Dwal Diu quickly established a big following in Garwei. He produced good crops, made barren women fertile and, so they say, wrought miracles. In March he was taken on a visit to Fangak and Malakal where he was interviewed by the Governor and warned against anti-government activity. In May Kerbeil, being very old and blind, was allowed to return to his home. Macar Teny and Tut Me Bor were quiet.

These Kujurs are probably still real leaders of the Nuer and could easily remove support from the government chiefs. At the moment they could not lead the people against the government, but they might be able to do so if, for any reason, such a move should in the future become popular. Correct treatment of these men may well be the key to public security during the coming years of transition.

7. LABOUR

The shortage of grain, combined with a rising ambition to better the standard of living, meant that there was always available more labour than was required at 6 PT per day.

The elections and the Minister's visit caused some upset among employees and affected the standard of their work. By the end of the year morale had been restored and output was satisfactory by local standards.

The introduction of merissa (local beer) regulations caused some confusion and discontent. Eventually it was necessary to hold a public meeting, place each householder on an official roster and warn former holders of a vested interest against causing further confusion. The resulting general content was worth all the trouble taken.

8. MIGRATION

After the Radh fight, it was ruled that the Famir belonged to the C. Jitheib and that C. Joak had no rights there. Otherwise, migration of the cattle camps followed the traditional pattern.

9. CLIMATE

December was colder than any could remember. Otherwise the climate was much as usual. Rainfall figures can be supplied from Fangak if required.

10. AGRICULTURE AND FORESTS

In July it appeared that the grain crop would be excellent but the heavy rains of August drowned it. Garwei had better crops than usual owing, they said, to the return of Dwal Diu (the holy man). The Dinka got by but Lak and Thiang were very hungry.

By the end of June, the crops were promising well.

The Department of Forests have decided to move back to Wathkec since the Berboi area is for the time denuded, and are putting up buildings there.

The wood cut was quite popular since the people needed the money to buy grain. About 12,000 metres were cut in all.

Fangak bamboo garden was extended; planting of neems was continued and it was possible to cut some useful timber out of the plantation of neem and sunt begun by Mr Howell.

Talh gum was very profitable this year. The merchants paid 11 PT per ruba for it and over 8,000 ruba were exported. (These are Arabic measures of weight.)

The installation of the "Cyprus" bull sagia proved a great success. One can believe the maker's claim that it will irrigate 20 feddan. It was possible to open a large area south of the DC's home, just about doubling the size of the garden.

11. PUBLIC HEALTH

There are dispensaries at Fangak, Wathkec, Let and Awoi.

During the year a new one was built at Wunulam on the Khor Felus where it was badly needed. Joshur Eff Nyal, the MA in Fangak is keen and there are fully-trained dressers at all of the other dispensaries: The benefits of their training course are manifest. Much very good work is done in the dispensaries, but they are very scattered and do not reach many of the people who need them. There is much progress still to be made in the field; nevertheless the year's advances were satisfactory as far as they went. It would be wrong for official anonymity to prevent mention of the work of Mrs Bowcock in saving a number of lives and encouraging the medical staff to attain higher standards.

Fangak dispensary was always busy, especially with in-patients who averaged 200. An attempt is being made by the council to set up a collecting post at Fagwir in order to reduce the number of in-patients, many of whom are in for trivial complaints but have to be fed since they are too far from their homes to return each day.

There was a limited CSM outbreak among the Dinka during February, March and April which appears to be an annual event. The PMI sent dressers and transport: out of 127 patients brought to the quarantines, only 5 died, a worthy achievement. As usual the first rains ended the epidemic.

Public health work in Fangak got under way in March with the appointment of the first sanitary overseer, Ramada Eff Daw el Beit. He took over conservancy work and organised the burning of refuse. Fangak now looks much cleaner and latrines are being built in a number of places. The PHI visited Fangak several times and as a result of discussions with him, comprehensive sanitary proposals have been submitted.

The World Health Organisation team inoculated Nuer in Fangak, Wanglel and Wathkec. They reported that 80 per cent reacted, which showed that the proportion had either had tuberculosis or had been in contact with it. This result was a shock, showing that the Nuer are probably the most prone to TB of all of the peoples of the Sudan.

12. EDUCATION

In April the American supervisor was withdrawn from Wanglel School, leaving the Nuer headmaster, Berbam Buth, in charge between the monthly visits of Mr Webb. There are about 150 boys in four classes: the PEO seemed satisfied on his visit in April.

The supply of boys wishing to enter school just exceeds the number of places. There is still no general acknowledgment of the value of education – not surprising when one sees the unhappiness to parents and to themselves caused by the behaviour of the semi-educated rejects. The emergence of this class may be inevitable, but is nonetheless a problem.

13. VETERINARY

Mr A.W. Polden remained posted as Fangak Veterinary Inspector of the Nuer Districts but was unable to spend much time in the Zeraf area. Owing to this and to three changes of head stockman, there was not much progress made during the year. However, the health of the cattle was good on the whole and two moderately successful AGV immunisation campaigns were undertaken. There is some opposition to this as to other veterinary work among the more conservative chiefs and headmen, but a policy of "direct attack" on the Zeraf by steamer proved more successful than expected. The young men with their cattle were glad to have the vaccine brought to them.

There is a good deal of CBPP in the district and not much to be done about it since the vaccine has not proved very effective.

Haemorrhagic septacaemia and trypanosomiasis were present but not serious. The district was mercifully spared anthrax, probably as a direct result of the energetic efforts of the SVS in Bar.

The cattle trade was brisk during May and June, the months of the famine, and a full-grown bull was fetching between £8 and £12. This was after the holding of government supervised auctions in Fangak and Fagwik, which resulted in the price of cattle rising by over 50 per cent.

The price of females at government auctions went down to the extent that a reasonable cow would fetch £7 instead of about £10 formerly.

The hides trade continued moribund, awaiting the new legislation.

The Bar were so obstructive over the rinderpest vaccine in December that the stockmen in Awoi were withdrawn. To balance this, the Dinka were rewarded for their enthusiasm by the building of a red-brick home at Atar to accommodate a literate stockman shortly to be posted there.

14. NATURAL HISTORY

Corporal Tiptip Pec continued to perform the duties of game scout most satisfactorily.

Mr Roussel, DC Lou and Mr Bowcock each shot two elephants, in both cases one of them being a very big one. Sayed Buth Diu shot a hippo.

Six giraffe poachers in Bar were sentenced to six months each. There were no other offences against the Game Laws.

Lion, giraffe, elephant, waterbuck, thiang, cob and hippo were plentiful: leopard, roan, antelope and buffalo are reported occasionally.

15. COMMUNICATIONS

Road work was generally good but heavy traffic caused a deterioration of surfaces after February, particularly on the Fangak-Malakal road where a bad job of grading has left a problem in some areas.

Garweir prisoners did splendid work to make a new road, 22 miles in length, from Goat, eight miles north of Fangak, to Gwadhgol on the Zeraf via Wiloni, the new Radh court centre on the Famir. This has opened up a heavily populated area to trade and will greatly facilitate the administration of the tribe.

Dinka prisoners put in some big banks and a number of culverts on the Sobat road.

The ramp east of Ayod was widened and heightened and ramps between Fangak and Fagwir much improved.

The Awoi-Nyaugith road was abandoned since it is little used and the labour this released put on to the Malakal-Bor road.

The radio telephone was satisfactory until the last three months of the year and is still not working properly, but awaits new parts.

16. WATER SUPPLY

The well at Fangak was abandoned in February after six years of effort to find water. This was one of the factors leading to a move of the court centre to Wilomi.

A council well at Ful Lita was almost completed.

Other wells in the district gave water to the satisfaction of the people except Fagwir, which mysteriously dried up.

17. BUILDINGS

District buildings were satisfactorily maintained and were in good repair for the rains.

The following buildings were completed, or almost so, during the year:

Fangak: two offices and store for the ZIRDC; red-brick prison ward; kitchen, bathroom and latrine for the MA; Scale J house (by contract); about 25 sahab frame Article III homes to replace the old round type; two four-seater lavatories; a simple workshop and garage.

Kwemerony: a complete new court centre including rest house.
Wilomi: the same.
Atat: red-brick stockman's house.
Wimalam: R-red-brick dispensary (by contract).

In addition, repairs and improvements were carried out to dispensaries and rest homes at Awoi, Ayod, Atar and Fagwir.

The opening of the brick-making prison camp at the Sobat Ferry has been a great help to the district; it is now both practicable and desirable to construct most buildings in permanent materials.

18. LANDS AND TOWN PLANNING

The D/Gov's inspection in June revealed the need to amend land records in the district.

19. TRADE

There was less money about but Business Property Tax assessments showed a slight rise.

Merchants did admirable work to meet the threat of famine by buying gum and importing about 10,000 sacks of grain. With the permission of the Director of Economics and Trade, a ceiling price of 15 PT per ruba was imposed. This was very welcome: higher prices might have meant serious trouble.

There were three Nuer merchants operating in the district but they will have to make contacts direct with wholesalers in Khartoum before their trading can amount to more than picking up crumbs that fall from the rich man's table.

Appendix 4

ZERAF DISTRICT HANDOVER
NOTES, 1954

INTRODUCTION

These notes are unusually detailed as I was handing over to a northern Sudanese DC who had no southern experience. A glossary of the more common words is provided in the Notes Section. When I was in Khartoum in January 2006, a retired Major General who had been a political prisoner said that he remembered my handover notes as being just what my successor needed to continue running the district as it had been. I thought he referred to Bill Carden's notes, or recently, hearing Philip Roussel's notes praised, perhaps they were his. On reading them again after more than 50 years, however, they do seem quite comprehensive and as helpful as possible. The section on public order, in particular, gives a fair view of how all the three (later four) Nuer districts were governed.

Zeraf Island is the triangle of land having the White Nile to the north and west, forming a near right-angle bend at Lake No and the Zeraf (or Giraffe) River on the hypoteneuse. Fangak (or Fanjak in the Sudanese pronunciation) is on the Zeraf. Some years after independence, the little town was so badly flooded that it was moved to another site.

All Southern administrators were extremely dubious about the future of the South in an independent Sudan. The least that was sought was a federal constitution with a British Lieutenant Governor for the South for 10 years. But the combination of the USA wanting to get a strategic agreement in the Canal Zone, the other Cold War pressures, and Egypt and the northern political parties all insisting on a unitary state, either independent or in union with Egypt, proved too much to resist.

Looking back, one can see that this was an indication in 1953 of how Britain had been weakened by its sacrifices in World War II, which became more obvious in the Suez Canal affair three years later. It also showed how naïve the Americans were. Eisenhower later said that forcing Britain and France to withdraw from Suez, giving Nasser the opportunity to claim victory, was his biggest mistake.

So, with heavy hearts and fear for the future, all we could do was to make the handover as easy as possible for our successors.

(These notes should be read in conjunction with Mr Carden's handover notes, the Annual Report 1953/54, notes upon various files and personality sheets.)

THE DISTRICT

Since the split of the former Cental Nuer District on 11/2/1954, Fangak has become the headquarters of Zeraf District with boundaries as they were before the amalgamation with Lou in 1946. The area of the district is slightly less than 10,000 square miles and the population is estimated at approximately 120,000.

At the time of the division of CND it was thought that the district would be further reduced by joining the Dinka to Malakal. The Governor has decided against this for some time at least: the idea has its attractive aspects, but closer examination of the people and problems involved indicates the necessity for a slow and cautious approach. Among these problems are the diversity of the Dinka tribes involved, the apparent impossibility of finding a uniform code of law, the close relations of Rut and Lak,[1] and above all the difficulty of finding suitable staff to run another, and very difficult, Council.

It should be noted that the district is not co-terminous with the parliamentary constituency. Zeraf Valley constituency comprises only the Nuer areas. The Dinka join with the Lou to form Central Nuer East, which will presumably be renamed.

The district is just manageable with the staff there at present, namely a Sub-Mamur[2] and an Executive Officer. If you lose one of these, you will find yourself overwhelmed as I was before leave. The result will be that some tribal work will be done less thoroughly than it ought to be, and that is a dangerous position. If something has to be neglected through inadequate staff, then neglect Fangak. It is fair to work on the principle that during the dry season, all administrative officials should be on trek for not less than 20 days per month. Leave should be taken from July to October.

STAFF

1. The establishment is:
   District Commissioner
   S/Mamur: Manasseh Eff.[3] Pac
   Executive Officer: Joel Eff. Abbathur
   Book Keeper/Saraf Scale J1: Yoaba Eff. Triay
   Clerk Scale J2: Gabriel Eff. Aluong Kaang (actually not yet J1)
   Storekeeper Art III: William Mabior
   Interpreter and General Assistant Art III: Jok Dong
   Interpreter Class III: Gai Tiriet

2. This is a good staff. Confidential reports are available on all except Yoaba Eff. just arrived.

   It is important that Manasseh Eff. should stay at least until the end of the year so that he can tour the district with you, as I have been unable to do so. He should begin to hand over the ZIRDC[4] so that Joel Eff. has all the threads in his hands by 1/1/55.

3. Jok Dong acts as DC's general assistant and trek secretary. His functions are: (i) English interpreter; (ii) Appeal Court clerk; (iii) Main Court clerk; (iv) Nuer correspondence secretary, i.e. he translates all letters from and to courts and keeps the files or copies; (v) Court commissary, which means noting Court requirements for paper, pencils, warrant forms, ink, foolscap books, court books, galams,[5] laus,[6] sashes and badges and seeing that they are supplied (note – this is for mainland only; EO should deal with Island in respect of all stores except legal forms); And (vi) Supervisor of court clerks' written work, i.e. keeping of books, registers and most important filling in of warrants.

   A good deal of the above work will in fact be done by the DC himself in the course of making court inspections, but even so, it is of the greatest value to have someone to follow up the DC's instructions and to take notes of the numerous petty practical needs which crop up on trek, and then see that they are attended to on return to Fangak. If one is not careful, the innumerable small matters will wear one down in Nuerland and make it impossible to see the wood for the trees.

   Gai Tiriet is invaluable as a walking file. His memory is phenomenal and, what is more, accurate.

4. The post of Sub-Mamur should be upgraded to Mamur. An A/DC would be even better. It so happens that the present holder of the post has had long administrative experience and can act as DC. If the post is left as a Sub-Mamur's, you will be less lucky in future, perhaps having a succession of cadets. It is essential to have a No. 2 who can act for you during leave or sickness.

NATIVE AUTHORITY

Note that practically all of what is said below applies to the Dinka too, though the terminology may be different.

1. The basic Nuer grouping is the family clan, the cieng or gol. At the head of this is the gatwot (pl. gatutni), the son of the stud bull, who is the natural leader of the ordinary Nuer in all the affairs of his life: in migrating to the cattle camps, arranging marriage settlements, holding dances and so forth. The Government has turned the gatwot into a headman and given him a blue sash (bi me car). His duties involve:

    a) collecting the tribute, of which he gets 1/10 remuneration.
    b) keeping up the stretch of road allotted to him for which he is paid £3 per mile, some of which is given to the workers.
    c) helping to carry out all court orders affecting his people, e.g. summoning defendants and carrying out executions of court orders.
    d) arresting wrongdoers from his gol and bringing them to the court.
    e) attending the court whenever required.
    f) maintaining the building for which he had been made responsible.
    g) cutting wood if required.

    For all this, his emoluments are:

    a) 1/10 tribute.
    b) £3 per week road mukafa[7].
    c) 50 PT per tukl[8] maintained.
    d) 1 PT[9] per metre of wood cut.

In practice, he gets a good deal less than this: much of his 1/10 tribute might go to paying for absentees; the road mukafa is cut for bad work and so is the building maintenance payment; the 1PT per metre is lost if the cut is not finished by 28 February.

The result is that the gatwots rightly feel that they do a lot of work and yet get very little pay for it. But the Governments cannot admit the principle of paying headmen. To make things easier for them, Mr Carden, if he had to fine a gatwot, would make sure that another got an equivalent present for good work. I have followed this up by making the sub-chief do more in the way of summoning defendants and carrying out executions. When there is negligence, then the sub-chief bears the greater responsibility, since he is in the senior position and is paid for it. If the job is not done, then the pay can be cut.

A gatwot may have between 30 and 200 tax payers. The ideal number is 60, and no gol should be allowed to split unless both halves have that number. There is a tendency for cousins to try to hive off and become gatwots on their own, and this should normally be resisted. Alternatively the ambitious relative will try to usurp the sash of the holder; this should also be sat upon unless there is convincing proof either that the gatwot does his work badly, or that a large majority of the people no longer support him. The opinion of the court may be taken, but if uncertain, the best rule with both gatwots and chiefs is to back up the man in office. You may well find later that the man is unpopular with his people simply because he is good at his job and makes them work.

In any case, it is necessary to insist that only the DC can sanction changes of gatwots, or he will not know who he is dealing with from one month to the next.

A chief, while actually being gatwot of the gol, may hand the sash to a relative to do the work for him. It saves confusion to treat this man as the gatwot. Some gatwots who are not chiefs appoint assistants, but these are unofficial and should not have sashes, though they will demand them. The rule should be one gol, one sash.

2.   The sub-chief (kwar lamar or wakil) is head of a tribal section. He has both judicial and executive functions since he sits in the court by warrant and is also responsible for supervising the road work, building, executions etc. of his section. There is a tendency for sub-chiefs to sit back, draw their pay and make the gatwots do all the work, blaming them if anything goes wrong.

The theory is that a sub-chief should have at least 400 tax payers. In practice there are many sub-chiefs with less, but at least no more should be created. There are many people demanding a kwar lamar of their own, and they should be squashed.

Previously CPs and ECs have acted as their own sub-chiefs. Provision has been made in the current budget for sub-chiefs to be appointed over their sections, leaving them more time to deal with matters affecting the whole court. I have no doubt that this will improve the quality of their work and also help to make them more impartial, since there will be someone else to argue the particular claims of their sections. As you visit the court centres, therefore, you can go ahead and hold elections for sub-chieftainships to be vacated by the CPs and ECs.

3.   The Executive Chief (EC) wears a broad alama,[10] unfortunately indistinguishable from the Court President (CP). I have always

meant to have initials sewn on so that visitors and newcomers could tell them apart.

The EC's chief duty is public security. He has a force of NA[11] police, organised in posts at strategic points, to help him in this. He must stop, or better, prevent fights, round up malefactors and bring them before the court. He is also responsible for all the executive functions of the court, the wood cut, roads, buildings, execution of court judgements and collections and custody of fines.

In status, the EC is inferior to the CP though he is paid the same. If and when the two rub up against each other, the best thing is to re-emphasise the division of their functions. If the two just cannot manage to work together after that, then one must go, or the court will never be satisfactory.

When sub-chiefs have been appointed to an EC's sections, it will no longer be necessary for the EC to sit in the court. Personally I do not object to him sitting there, as otherwise he may lose touch with what goes on and be reluctant to carry out court judgements which come to him out of the blue, as it were. But he may not vote or take an active part.

4. The Court President's functions are in theory purely judicial. He must hold the court each month at either the new or the full moon. If the chiefs do not attend he should bring them before his court for disciplinary action, and if the offence is repeated he should report them to the DC. He is responsible for ordering defendants to be summoned, but once judgement has been given he should hand over the execution to the EC. In practice he also performs certain police functions since the court is responsible for public security, and if a breach is threatened and the EC is away then the CP must act.

5. Both senior chiefs have a clerk. The court clerk is paid £3 per month: he keeps the court register, issues galams, collects fees, registers appeals and writes out warrants. The executive clerk is paid £2.50 per month: he keeps the fines register and the actual cash of money fines. This is a great temptation and fines should be collected as frequently as possible. The fines register is a foolscap book: this is not strong enough and I have been trying to get something more durable.

The standard of clerks is low in general. They need constant supervision and endless patient instruction. The best way of effecting an improvement is to find money for proficiency pay, to be earned after passing a simple examination.

6. There are two grades of NA police, post and cieng. The post police are higher paid. They are concentrated in police posts with a shawish[12] in charge, and take their orders from the EC.

The cieng police are attached to individual chiefs and are meant to issue summonses and carry out executions within the tribal sections. There is a tendency, which should be corrected, for them to think that their duties are limited to carrying the chief's chair and pipe. For this reason ECs demand personal police too, but this has been refused. Some do have retainers but they must pay for them themselves.

The NA police are very good indeed on the whole. It is their loyalty which makes government possible in Nuer areas. They collect wanted men and, still more difficult, wanted cattle from the most inaccessible places. They do the donkey work, giving effect to every judgement, order or decision, carrying the writ of the government to the individual Nuer. If they did not exist, one would have 10 times the present establishment of government police and they would still not do the job half as well as the NA police do.

Government policeman .... Lathker (askari)
N.A. police .... Bulith

7. Gatwots, sub-chiefs and senior chiefs are all elected in the first place. Gatwots normally emerge by common consent; sub-chiefs are elected by the gatwots of the section; and senior chiefs by all the sub-chiefs and gatwots of the court, though the views of the sub-chiefs should have greater weight than the gatwots. In elections for sub-chiefs and senior chiefs the DC should always be present and confirm the choice, unless he has good reason for refusing the chosen man, in which case he should explain his reason and order another election. However, this should be a rare occurrence.

The whole question of appointments and dismissals the DC should keep in his own hand unless he has an A/DC responsible for part of the district. Nothing is such a frightful cause of fights and disaffection as a dispute over a bi.[13]

COURT WORK

1. Mr Carden's "Brief Notes on how Courts Function in CND" gives most of what it is necessary to know about the machinery. I have made some comments in the Annual Report. In order to assist court clerks and ensure a uniform understanding of the details of procedures, I had intended to circulate simple instructions in English and Nuer to all courts.

2. The main court has only been in existence for a year and its procedure is not yet fully understood. It consists in theory of all the senior chiefs and sub-chiefs of the district, with Kic Wur as President and Mateat Kan as Vice President. In practice

it is an elastic body, and so long as Kic or Mateat is present with more than five chiefs, it may be designated the Main Court. Although the court has powers of only one year more than the Regional Courts, i.e. five years against four, it is invaluable for dealing with the more serious offences, particularly those involving chiefs or tribal disputes or fights. What usually happens is that when something occurs which demands the DC's personal attention, he collects Kic and a sufficient number of representative chiefs to form the main court. They help him to sort things out, then judge the case and pass sentence. All main court sentences should be confirmed by the DC. The register is kept by Jok Dong, and when sentence of imprisonment is passed, he makes out the warrant. When fines are imposed, it should be stated where the fine is to be paid and Jok Sarraf or Ked Diu should be informed with all details, i.e. number and date of case, name of offender and amount of fine.

3. My views on appeal courts are contained in the proposals sent to the Governor in Zeraf District IBI of 18/6/54. This scheme will require some organisation at first, but will pay dividends later in a more smoothly running district and a more satisfactory service to the public. The advantages are set out in detail in the letter. Once this organisation was in being, I had intended to try to get the chiefs' agreement to the following rules:

a) that every appeal must be registered within three months of the original Regional Court judgement, or it would not be considered by the Appeal Court. Registration of an appeal which would cost 25 PT not returnable (financial approval would be required for this) would be made with the Regional Court Clerk.

b) no appeal registered more than a year before would be seen unless appellant could prove that defendant had absconded.

c) the appeal stake to be raised to £1 (financial approval again required) over and above the initial registration fee of 25 PT. If chiefs object to this, they may be reminded that the stake used to be a bull calf and does not a bull calf cost at least £1.25 nowadays?

d) forbid appeals between close relations, i.e. those of such a relationship that a marriage would be incestuous. It is all very well for family disputes to go in a friendly way to the Regional Court but appeals can create bad blood. In END and WND such appeals are forbidden: the chiefs have all agreed that the rule is a good one and I have not come across any injustice resulting from it.

Many people say they have an appeal (take diu) when they are really complaining against the court machinery, usually that the defendant has not been summoned or the execution not carried out. It is as well to sort them out and allot a separate day to investigate their complaints, otherwise a good deal of time can be wasted. Another species of complaint concerns the cow which has died or otherwise met its end between judgement and execution. This should be referred back to the Regional Court to produce a new hukm. There are a number of inveterate litigants who try to take up cases already settled by previous DCs. As soon as this is discovered, the stake becomes forfeit.

I have tried to get Jok Dong to keep the written record of appeals, as is done in other districts. However, the Governor has seen a sample of his work and is not satisfied. Since there is no one better, the DC will have to continue to do the clerking and give Jok more instruction until he can do the job satisfactorily.

4. Mr Carden's notes and Appendix One cover most points concerning Regional Courts. It is worth insisting very strongly on the rule about executions being carried out within two months. From experience in WND I would say that this rule is the best aid one can have in making the courts respected and effective. That is of the first importance, because a large number of fights and homicides are caused by someone becoming fed up with the law's delays and taking the law into his own hands. And one can imagine a Nuer's impatience when, even after obtaining a judgement in his favour, he has to wait still longer for his cow. It is essential for the judgements to be given not in terms of so many cattle but of particular cattle, and the clerk must not write e.g. "Cuol be moi Riak ok dang 3"[14] but "Cuol be moi Riak ok dang 3, yang me jak, kene rwathde me lual kene tut me cotbor."[15] And if they cannot be paid in two months, then the court must say and the clerk write when they are to be paid off, e.g. when Cuol's sister marries or when Ruok is paid for his nephew. When they are paid, the clerk will tick them off. If they are not paid, the judgement debtor and the EC will have to do some explaining. If the explanations are not good, then someone – probably the debtor and perhaps any of the others – will get a month in prison. One or two sentences speed up executions remarkably. The Commissioner of Native Courts thinks that this practice may not be legal and wants such cases treated as debt and passed to the DC for action under the CJO (see correspondence in IBI), but they are in fact treated as contempt not debt: the court orders A to pay to B a particular cow, which is known to be in A's possession, within two months. If A does not pay

and has no good reason for not paying, then the court proceeds against him for contempt. Nuer courts will never ask for a man to be imprisoned if he cannot produce the cattle: creditors are willing to wait years in such circumstances.

With a view to speeding up justice, I was also considering a way of getting defendants to court more quickly and was going to make the sub-chiefs responsible. Perhaps some system could be evolved whereby before the court breaks up, the clerk reads out a list of all defendants against whom cases have been registered who must be brought to the next court meeting. When the court reassembles the next month, the list is read out again. Sub-chiefs must explain absences and be fined if explanations are not satisfactory. But this will take some discussion and thought before it is put over. It is worth emphasising that Nuer are extremely conservative and do not take readily to changes. Further, their minds are not adaptable: they will perform well a routine that they know but will take a long time to learn a new routine.

Relations between courts need watching. Chiefs who refuse to assist in carrying out summonses issued by another court must be dropped on, though it is necessary to make sure first that the summons was a proper one, as many are not legal. Absconding defendants and cattle concealed from execution are the chief causes of friction. So are stolen girls, but it is necessary to insist here that the plaintiff must seek remedy in the defendant's court, as always: if he says the court is biased against him because he is a foreigner, then he can appeal. The Government cannot undertake to return wives and girls who run away. Many disputes between courts turn on which one has jurisdiction over an individual. The deciding factor is what tax list he is on, not where he lives.

5. The Governor has recently ordered that as far as possible, fines should be imposed in terms of money, not cattle. If a man has a cow but no money then he must sell the cow. Chiefs will take advantage of this, as they have in the past, to pay the fine and get a cow on the cheap. But this disadvantage is outweighed by the more equitable nature of a money fine. Cattle fines will have to continue for blood money, and collective fines for fights, which should be used sparingly.

I have not yet had time to put over to all courts this new principle that fines should be in terms of money as far as possible, as it is desirable that changes of this sort should be explained personally by the DC and fully discussed. So the change should be effected in the remaining courts when they are next visited.

I have introduced a new arrangement in the court fines register. The left-hand page is devoted to details which should be recorded as soon as judgement is given. It is ruled in columns as below:

No. of Case	Date of Case	Name	Sub-Chief	Fine Imposed (example) (money or cattle)
Miri 72	27 Jan 1954	Cuol Mut	Rick Muon	1 thak[16] or £3.00

From this one can check with the court register, first that all fines imposed have been entered, and second the fines which are outstanding.

The right-hand page deals with what happens when and after the fine arrives, as in the column below:

Date fine arrived	Description of Disposal or Fine	Initials of Official Accepting	Receipt No.	Accepting Remarks
3 March 1954	(i.e. money or colour of cattle £3.00 or thak me lual)			

The first two columns are for the fines clerk. The third is used to show that the animal is acceptable, as it may well not be. Naturally the Nuer try to get to rid of the old and diseased as fines. The idea of making the clerk write the details of the fine when it is imposed and again when it arrives is so that the actuality can be compared with the sentence. All this detail may seem very elementary, but it is well worthwhile to have a clean and comprehensible system for the fines registers. It saves hours in checking and makes it easy to investigate any charge of cheating fines.

6. It is desirable to have a fixed scale of punishments for certain offences. Then everyone knows where he is. Scales in this district are:

Homicide (fair rights):	4 years + 40 H/C[17] compensation + 10 H/C to Government
Wounding in fight:	9 months + compensation of cattle according to wound

Taking part in fight:	6 months
Brewing araki[18] 1st offence:	6 months
Brewing araki 2nd offence:	12 months
Stealing a girl:	6 months
Singing inflammatory songs:	Usually 6 months

The sentence of nine months for wounding should I think be increased to one year, if the chiefs can be got to agree. The reason is that conditional release reduces the sentence to 6 months 22 days, only 22 days more than the sentence for merely taking part, which is not an adequate differential.

7. No homicide may be seen by a regional court without the sanction of the DC. The procedure is for the court to send in a letter and the DC sends back instructions as to what is to be done, i.e. either await the DC's visit, collect witnesses for a magisterial enquiry, or proceed with the case. This is to ensure that every case which should go to a Major Court will always do so in fact. It is not usually difficult to make a decision. The Nuer themselves distinguish between a homicide which takes place in a fair fight (kur) and between one which involves killing by stealth (biem) or ambush (dhom). However, there is between these a degree of homicide which sometimes causes perplexity, i.e. when a man fights fairly and in the open, but has decided beforehand to fight and kill, rather as in a duel. If there is any evidence of previous intention, then the case should go to a Major Court. The Chief Justice's policy is to extend the sphere of Major Courts, and as far as individual homicides are concerned this is no doubt right, though the DC in a Nuer district has to be careful not to get too far ahead of public opinion or the chiefs might not co-operate in producing accused men. However, Major Courts in large fight cases are a terrifying prospect and it is doubtful whether the justice would be better than at present administered by the Main Court.

PUBLIC SECURITY

1. The peace of the district really depends upon the mutual confidence which exists between chiefs and DC. If that confidence were to a great extent to break down, the results would be horrible to contemplate, perhaps something like the Nuer settlement again. There are four ways by which this confidence is maintained:

   a) by the DC knowing the chiefs and being known by them, as far as possible on terms of personal friendship.

b) by always consulting the chiefs and winning their consent to any new idea.

c) by the DC showing that he really cares for the people and is thus worthy of their respect.

d) by keeping in touch with all courts by constant visits and by runners. If the chiefs are in sympathy with the DC then so will be the native police who do 9/10 of the public security work. To them is due the remarkable fact that there is never any harm done to travellers.

2. Tribal fights are a big problem in Zeraf District, bigger than in any other Nuer district. The best way of preventing them is to keep one's ear very close to the ground, picking up all the local gossip. People composing and singing rude songs about a rival tribal section are often the cause of fights and should be dropped on heavily. Usually a chief or even the whole court are to blame for not taking action which could have averted the fight: e.g. the Radh fight of December 1953 would not have taken place if Garwec Diet and Jal Loh had done their duty in bringing a suspected murderer before the two courts. The Ruweng fight of January 1954 had been preceded by the singing of rude songs by the two sections for 10 months, during which time the court took no action.

When reports of a fight come in the police, either native or Government, may be able to avert it if they move quickly, get between the parties and disarm them. Once battle is joined Government police may attempt to frighten the participants by firing over their heads, but may never shoot to wound or kill unless they themselves are threatened.

After the fight, all those taking part are rounded up and kept in separate camps until the Main Court can see the case. Five H/C (head of cattle) are taken from all escapees and become forfeit if they have not come in before the case is heard. It is essential to make sure that the Main Court goes to the root of the trouble. It usually does but often tries to gloss over the failing of the chiefs.

The best way of using fight prisoners is extra-murally – building banks on the roads in their home areas.

3. Cattle theft can lead to fights and it is essential that courts co-operate in these cases. Theft in the usual sense, i.e. stealing what is unquestionably another's property, is uncommon. Usually a man is merely taking what he considers his own, but without due process of law. There are then two processes to be gone through: first, the conviction of the 'thief' and return of the cow to the possessor, and second, after the sentence has been served, the civil case to determine who really owns the beast.

Difficulties can occur when A of court Y steals the cow of B of court Z. The chiefs of court Y may well consider that A has a good case and that court Z has been uncooperative in bringing B to defend his claim, and therefore they give protection to A and the stolen cow. If they do this they offend, as it is none of their business to judge how other courts work. The point is that A was not given the cow by lawful judgement and must therefore be punished and the cow returned. So one must pay attention when a man complains that his cow has been stolen and taken to the next court area. The best thing is to give him a note telling the next court to hear him and determine whether what he says is true. They will then:

a)   deal with the offender.
b)   return the cow to the original possessor so that case can be dealt with in his court.

4.   The theft of girls and women can also cause trouble, but in such cases I usually tell the complainant to follow the girl and raise a case himself. Intervention is necessary only when the court to which the girl has gone shows itself to be partial to the lover.

5.   It is necessary to insist on the prompt payment of thung[19] cattle, otherwise the family of the dead man might feel obliged to start a feud. On visiting a court the DC should enquire whether any thung cattle are outstanding and record his orders concerning them in the handbook. The EC and sub-chief are the two men responsible: usually one or other is the leopard skin chief who performs the purification and peacemaking ceremonies, receiving the customary payments. Sometimes chiefs have used their position to try to establish a monopoly over leopard skin functions. I have resisted this, saying that a man may go to the kwar muon he wishes.

A thung case to watch is that of Gany Nual, a Bar man who killed a Nyang. He is half Dinka and the thung is to be 25 H/C from the Dinka (Rut). At the moment there are 8 H/C outstanding from Bar (sub-chief Buth Yint) and 18 (I think) from Rut (Deng Pakak.)

In Bar there are one or two old thung payments still not completed and a systematic enquiry is desirable. Cuol Kur needs prodding when it comes to screwing cattle out of people.

6.   Kujurs[20] or gwan kwoth[21] have to be watched closely as they can easily emerge as the real leaders of the Nuer in the event of any disaster. They were the people who were found in charge when government was first brought to the Nuer; the structure of chiefs is almost entirely artificial. If the gwan kwoths were to

recover their positions the chiefs would be without a following and administration would collapse.

All gwan kwoths know the policy: that they may practise their spiritual functions unhindered so long as they do not attempt to interfere in administrative matters or speak or act against the government. All information about them can be found in the Kujur file and the personality sheets. The big men are, in order: Dwal Diu, Gatbuch Yol (Kerbiel), Macar Teny and Riak Lunyjok. The first three are all Bar. Dwal lives on the Duk ridge, Macar and Kerbiel in the southern part of the Island. Ruot Yuot has been told that he is responsible for reporting anything odd to the DC when he is next in the area, but Kerbiel might be excused, so long as the reports are favourable, as he is not really fit to walk. Dwal Diu can easily be seen as his luak of stupendous dimensions is beside the road. Riak Lunyjok lives at Fagwir and often comes begging in Fangak.

7. There is no formal defence scheme for Fangak. I was awaiting a chance to get the views of the Chief of Police but will now prepare a draft which will be attached as Appendix III (to be sent from Kosti.)

8. In December 1953 there was a theft of about £200, some of it government fines, from the shop of Mubarak Yusif in Falagh. Two fights prevented an immediate full investigation, and in May I pended the case for lack of evidence, telling the chiefs to look out for anyone with money to burn. Garwec Diet has just told me he has arrested a man called Dol Les, sub-chief Catluck Banyjang, Bar, who has confessed. All proceedings to date are in the office.

POLICE

The police establishment is quite inadequate, comprising only 23. The reason for its being so low is that most police work is done by the Native Authority. However, NA police are not disciplined and could not be relied on in the event of trouble, i.e. they would certainly not take action against their own people. In February the Chief of Police asked DCs' views about the mounted police, and my reply embodies my views on district police needs in general, i.e. a 50 per cent increase in foot police and a mobile half section with a vehicle and bicycles.

The establishment of other police posts would depend on where trouble was expected. Kwemerony, Atar and Wilori are obvious places, but generally I am against posts unless absolutely necessary. Their administration takes a lot of time and it is difficult to maintain the morale of the men. However, Ayod post is certainly necessary. Mr Carden thought it should be moved to Wau, 10 miles north on the Nyang/Bar frontier, but I have preferred to leave it at Ayod, which is a crossroads and within a day's walk of both Awoi and the Bar boundary. It is also near to Dwal Diu.

When the roads open, an effort should be made to work a plan whereby the police can benefit from the co-op of which they have become shareholders. There is some correspondence about this.

Police personality sheets are up to date.

PRISON

The prison is too small and is insecure. Please see Mr Moon's report on an inspection made in March, and my comments on it, containing my proposals in some detail.

Replacement of the wire fence is the most urgent matter. If prisoners show signs of trying to escape it is necessary to mount a guard of two patrolling sentries along the wire, which wears out the police in a very short time. Perhaps a supplementary grant could be got on grounds of immediate public security needs.

I have started to improve latrine accommodation which is at present inadequate and insanitary.

Rations are rather a headache. An attempt to draw up a contract with adequate penalty clauses has failed and probably no merchant in Fangak is reliable enough to do the job. Perhaps it is best to purchase in bulk in Malakal through the Mudiria.

Prisoners' documentation requires constant supervision. The district has not had an effective police clerk since February; PC Jal Maka should be able to make an improvement. The valuable check is the Monday morning inspection when every new prisoner has to be brought before the DC to check his warrant and entry in the register. If both of these are signed or initialled mistakes should be avoided.

Prisoners' appeals will be much easier to arrange when the new appeal system is in being.

It is necessary to keep hammering away at the two orders: (a) every prisoner must have a warrant in the correct form; and (b) not more than one name on a warrant.

LOCAL GOVERNMENT

1. My views sent to the Governor in June still hold. Stripped of elaboration, they are:

   i)   extend the council area to the whole district as in Bor.
   ii) emphasise the legislative functions of the council, especially through control of the budget, at the expense of executive activities.

2. Elections should be held in November and December so that new councillors can be in place to debate the budget in January. For the purpose of explaining the budget, there is a tally board in the rakuba near the Sub-Mamur's house. The electoral college consists of gatwots and above.

3. The council needs to get more money for services to the public if it is to become popular. This is difficult in the small area, but the possibility of obtaining a royalty from firewood might be investigated. Also I think that ZIRDC is hard-hit in having to maintain all its roads without a grant. You will know how to put this up to the Ministry.

MISCELLANEOUS TRIBAL NOTES

1. The court handbooks are useful and well worth keeping up. However, for greater flexibility I think that each court should have a file too. In this would go copies of the personality sheets, tribute lists and a cross reference of any correspondence affecting the court or area.

2. The amalgamation of the Radh Courts should go ahead as soon as possible. The idea is extremely popular with chiefs and people, and there are buildings ready at Wilori. The appointments I would have preferred would have been: CP[22] Gatcang Jal, sitting at Wilori; EC for Mainland Garwec Diet in charge of police post at Falagh; and EC for Island Euot Yuot in charge of police post ar Nyod. Jal Loh will thus be demoted to sub-chief, and about time too. The court should take No. 4 galam so that galam No. 7 will go out of use. A ferry at Gwadhgol, for which a canoe has arrived from Nasir, should be instituted as soon as possible to improve communication across the river, hitherto one of the main obstacles to amalgamation. A disadvantage of the new set-up will be that the Duk Ridge Nyang will be even further away from the court centre and will have to be watched for separatist tendencies.

   Last March Philip Redh Kwer accused Garwec Diet of stealing £16 from his shop. The case came to me on appeal and I held that there was no evidence to show either theft or, if there was theft, that Garwec was responsible. Garwec feels strongly about this accusation and he and Philip have been told that the case will be cleared (in Nuer eyes) by swearing on the leopard skin. It is essential to do this as soon as possible.

3. One lesson of the Ruweng Dinka fight of January 1954 was that the court could not control properly the whole of that large and heterogeneous area. The Governor agreed that the best solution was to set up a sub-court for the Luaic at Wunangap and all the

chiefs are most anxious that this should be done. Powers should probably be three months or £10 fine or three head of cattle, with an appeal to the court at Atar. This court would be an extension of the Atar court and under its jurisdiction: therefore it would presumably not need a warrant. The President obviously would be Awer Agwer and the members sub-chief Non de Kat and the gatwots. It will probably be best to give Awer's section a sub-chief, but I cannot see the man at present. There is a gatwot called Wio Lam who was sacked for taking his people over to the Ngok last year. He now wants his lama back, but as he has been replaced by Nom Kat, who has done no harm, he has been refused.

The question of the CP at Atar is a difficult one. Gajang Mareang wants it desperately, of course, but I would only agree to his appointment were it absolutely necessary, i.e. if it became obvious that no one else would obtain obedience. I would like to see Deng Patak as CP and perhaps Dwal Deng, old as he is, as EC.

4. These are the following matters left over from the Dinka fight:

    i)   when convenient, 50 men of s/c Gajang Mareang and 50 men of s/c Macar Baduct will work for another 40 days on the roads in their tribal areas. They are men released last June to cultivate.

    ii)   There are 16 H/C seized from escaped prisoners awaiting disposal.

    iii)   Deng Patak has caught one escaped prisoner and will bring him when the road dries.

    iv)   There are a few escaped men still in other districts who will have to be followed up.

5. In Bar there will have to be an election to replace s/c Mut Gien. I have heard gossip from various quarters that EC Cuol Kur is not as co-operative as I have always thought him, so he had better be watched.

6. At Kwemerony EC Oth Deng has quarrelled again with the Nuer merchant Peter Wual Tuong.

7. The gatwots of s/c Kolang Nyxon (Fagwir court) are in rebellion saying that he is idle. I have said it is for the DC to judge this, and that he is ever-watchful.

AGRICULTURE AND FORESTS

1. Agriculture is a gamble. There is either too much water or too little, and then there are bugs and birds and budda.[23] Perhaps the best approach is threefold:

   a) banking and drainage.
   b) diversification of crops, e.g. lubia, groundnuts and rice.
   c) find an answer to the budda. If the last five years' experiments have shown anything it is that there is no quick way of increasing crop production in UNP.

2. Forests are a different matter. Once trees are got going they do well, as can be seen in various parts of the district. The best lines are neem, sunt and bamboo. There are doms west of Let, but they are inaccessible and perhaps they would grow round Fagwir as the soil is dry and sandy. Mahogany are dubious. The Forest Reserve items can be used to extend the plantations each rains.

3. The wood cut is well organised and notes on file should be a sufficient guide. Kuol Juic has at last got the increase of pay he deserves. Two of the forest staff are on district budget and four on Forest Department (including Kuol).

EDUCATION

1. Wanglel does not take up much time, but a close interest is appreciated. My views on the school committee, which would be a good thing, I think, are on the file.

2. Doleib Hill wants to open a day school at Atar. This should be encouraged as it might bring the Ruweng on a bit: at the moment they are more backward than the Nuer in spite of being more accessible. But these bush schools do have to be watched; if the teachers lose their morale they can do more harm than good.

3. The district needs a Government school which should be at Fangak, perhaps at Noni Mac. This year for the first time there has been a greater demand for education than Wanglel can fulfil. Previously Wanglel had been filled up with Lou boys who should now be discouraged.

VETERINARY

1. Cattle production is the most promising line of development. The Nuer love cattle and know about them. There is lavish

grazing and if the cattle population were doubled it would probably still be enough.

2. The best lines of development are two-fold:

    i) prophylactics and cures for disease. The attenuated goat virus produces almost complete immunisation against rinderpest and it is essential to keep it up each year if the ground gained is not to be lost. Dimidium bromide is a cure for trypanosomiasis but the vaccine for CBPP is not very good. What is needed, as SVI[24] knows, is more of these medicines and a more regular supply.

    > (Rinderpest – Nyapec
    > Tryps – Lod or Like
    > CBPP – Dop
    > Haemorrhagic septicaemia – Malpedh)

    ii) propaganda which means that the stockman must always be out in the luaks or cattle camps, talking to the people about the management of their cattle, demonstrating methods that are better and treating cattle whenever required.

3. All this requires a stockman of a higher standard and greater devotion to duty than at present. The Veterinary School should gradually improve matters, but at the moment the SVS staff spends much time in Fangak and requires constant prodding. The district really requires a classified official in charge who may be expected to have a greater sense of responsibility.

4. Better methods of hide preparation can be pushed when the new legislation is in being. There are two posts in the budget for men to do this. Better hides and better prices for them could be worth thousands of pounds to the Nuer, but if any campaign is started it is essential to see that there are good facilities for selling and the merchants will have to be watched.

5. I put in for a Vet post at Let and probably it will be approved. It should now be moved to Wilori which is ideally situated near the cattle camps on the Famyr. The building arrangements will be simpler if both vet dispensary and medical dispensary go up at the same place at the same time.

MEDICAL

1. The medical side is the one on which I have been most keen to see expansion. The dispensaries are few and far between and even then are not really well patronised. There are many difficulties in

the way of bringing medical attention to the Nuer, such as the scattered nature of their habitations, the annual migration to the cattle camps and the short period during which the roads are open, with consequent hindrances to supervision and supply. The people themselves are often apathetic and uncertain of the value of European medicine. The dresser may be unable to put propaganda over since often enough he does not speak Nuer.

Nevertheless the work of the dispensaries is of indubitable value: one has only to read descriptions of the condition of the Nuer before the Government came to realise how much has been done. Yaws, for instance (Nuer – top), which formerly affected about 80 per cent of the people, is now rarely seen in an advanced stage. Many of the more intelligent chiefs appreciate the dispensaries and give all assistance.

2. The present organisation in the district is as follows:

> Fangak Dispensary: MA[25] Joshua Eff. Nyal
> Dresser: Golong Kwith
> Wathkec Dispensary: Dresser Yowin
> Let dressing post: Dresser Ojwok
> Awoi dressing possible: Dresser Stanislaus Ammum
> Wunalam (K Felus) Dispensary: Dresser Obadiah Deng

Each dispensary or dressing post has attached to it a farrash[26] paid on SMS budget, an eye-dresser (PLA) and a runner (PLA).

There is also a well-equipped mission hospital at Wanglel. Unfortunately the doctor has been transferred to Nasir and there is only a dresser in charge. I have been trying to persuade the AUPM to send a doctor if only for two months in the year. At least he could do minor operations which could wait for him, e.g. trachiasis, and save sending people into Malakal hospital.

3. Personnel – The MA and all dressers outside do good work and it would be as well if none were transferred for a while. Golong Kwith in Fangak needs more training and discipline and should go into Malakal.

Eye-dressers need a good deal of supervision. The dressers should be more strict with them and the chiefs encouraged to report on their activity. It is a good idea to make them take a piece of grass for each patient treated and bring the bundle back to the dresser to record the total number. Obviously an eye dresser can make a fictitious bundle if he wishes to deceive, but it is a check of sorts. Eye-dressers should not hang about the dispensaries and suqs but spend their time in the villages and cattle camps, attending particularly to the children. Nuer women neglect their children's eyes in a shocking manner; they see no connection between dirt, flies and disease.

The farrash acts as cleaner and general assistant. He should be able to take charge of the dispensary when the dresser attends to cases in the villages. For this reason it has been my policy to employ ex-schoolboys who can read labels and keep the grain account.

The runner keeps the patients in order, takes messages and comes into Fangak monthly to collect the pay.

4. Administration – The grain is drawn daily from a selected local merchant. At the end of the month the dresser sends in the merchant's bill with the runner, together with his list of in-patients and daily issues to tally. Sometimes the merchant runs out and it is necessary to supply direct from the merkaz store. During hungry months it will be found that the number of in-patients grows enormously. The patients really do need attention; the trouble is that they will not bother to come in when there is grain at home. To keep down the number of passengers I have ruled that only passengers accompanying child patients under 15 may be fed, and then only one passenger per family. PMI[27] has agreed to this.

The supply of drugs and bandages has to be watched as delays can easily occur, either because the dresser does not send in his requisition box or because it does not return from Malakal for some reason. In April, six months' supplies are sent to last the rains. It is as well to make sure of getting the boxes to Fangak by the end of April or they may have to be portered, which can mean breakages.

5. Epidemics – Nuer are so scattered that epidemics do not trouble them much. But CSM[28] must be expected from February to May in the Dinka area. Two or three extra dressers are supplied from Malakal to staff quarantines at Atar court, Lam and possibly the Zeraf mouth. Propaganda is put out among the chiefs to get the people to bring in the sick. If they arrive in time they will be cured. It is well to help the good work by attaching two NA police to each quarantine to see that the patients do not run away before they are cured.

Last year I obtained from the Government an order forbidding movement of cattle camps across the Zeraf; it might have done some good. The PMI and PHI give every assistance and the S/O should be of help this year. With the first rains, the disease disappears.

6. Public Health – The first sanitary overseer, Ramadam Eff. Daw el Beit, was appointed to Fangak only last March. He is keen and should be given more scope. He might be able to take charge of

the organisation and training of the eye-dressers, as suggested by the PMI. The sanitary proposals for Fangak are on the file and are I think comprehensive. They were too late for the current year and the Governor said he would re-submit for 1955/56.

It is most important that PMI builds a house for the S/O during the current year. It was made clear when Ramada Eff. came that the district could only house him temporarily.

Every effort should be made to finish off as soon as possible the two latrines awaiting more bricks.

7. Programme for 1954/55 – First priority will be the building of the new dispensary at Wilori, if PMI agree to the site. It should be of red brick and if possible CI^{29} roofing. Materials can be taken by steamer to Gwadhgol to reduce haulage costs. Dispensary should be on Fangak plan, and should dresser have red-brick house with 4 x 4 room and 4 x 3 verandah with separate tukl for kitchen. Funds will probably not stretch to red-brick wards but it may be possible to build two 6m x 1m wards of large mud brick with grass roof held up by girders.

It is to be hoped also that there will be funds to improve Fangak dispensary which cannot cope with numbers during the dry season. If money can be found the following work has been planned:

a) complete third red-brick ward of which the foundations are already in. General ward 8 x 4 and isolation ward 4 x 4.

b) complete building next to MA's house of which foundations are in. To contain three 4 x 4 rooms, namely S/O's office and store, clinic for midwife and ward for patients of rather higher standards, e.g. chiefs, policemen.

c) wire-in present verandah of dispensary to make fly-proof treatment room and extend building to make a waiting verandah 4 x 4.

d) build 8-seater latrine for patients.

e) build Art. III house for midwife who will probably be here in December.

f) complete extra buildings for MA and build also asmalia and store.

It will be necessary to give considerable assistance to the midwife, who is called Nyankin Lum, if she is to have any success among the Nuer. It appears that she is doing well in her course and she should be helped by being a relative of Sayed Buth Diu. It is work which is worth every encouragement as Nuer methods of midwifery are extremely primitive, and infant mortality is at a very high rate. The best way to launch the work is to start an ante-natal clinic to be held on two mornings a week. The days of the clinic must be published as widely and continuously as possible. If the midwife can get in touch with the pregnant women she should be able to know when the births are to take place. The MA should help in the organisation and keep the records as the midwife is illiterate.

8. Future Medical Development – I think that the next place to have a dispensary should be the Duk ridge, as people from there must walk to either Wilori or Awoi. It would be as well first to find out exactly how many people live there. The site should be either Ayod or Wau. Ayod is easier administratively but Wau is more central. DC Lou might be asked his views as quite a number of Lou would be served by the dispensary.

Fagwir dressing post, to be maintained by the ZIRDC, has already been agreed on in principle, and provision will have to go into the 1955/56 budget.

Wathkec has few patients during the rains and should move with the people to Kwemerony. A dispensary building and a dresser's house will be required.

If the Fagwir post is a success, and more money can be found, the ZIRDC should think of building a similar post at Mareang. In which case it might (I only say might) be desirable to move Let dispensary to Nyod, specifically for the Island Radh.

The Dinka are a problem medically as they are so scattered. The Lusic now have Wunalam and the Ruweng will be more ready to go to Atar School dispensary when the causeway has been built. However, the great area between Atar, Fangak and the Zeraf Mouth is not covered and there are people scattered all over it. No one site could serve more than a fraction of these Dinka: perhaps the best place would be the Zeraf Mouth, which would be accessible to local Nuer and Shilluk too. But this must be some years ahead.

It is worth persisting with the scheme of eye-dressers. The idea is not fully understood at the moment and the eye-dressers need constant supervision, but eye diseases among the Nuer are appalling, and if the dresser can save one person from blindness he has justified his existence.

Midwifery, as I have said, deserves all help that can be given. But above all the district needs constant propaganda to get people to make use of the dispensaries, and once there, to stay until the treatment is finished. The Nuer are shockingly selfish in refusing to carry in people who are seriously ill; in parts of Western Nuer the chiefs agreed to make this an offence against tribal law and punishable as such. I think that more persuasion will be needed before this is acceptable here.

One way to get propaganda over is for the medical staff to trek more. I should like to see Wilori eventually with an MA to supervise Let and Awoi dispensaries, i.e. with responsibility for medical work in Garweir and Thiang. MA Fangak could then take charge of the Lak and Dinka areas.

ROADS

System of Maintenance

Each gatwot is given a stretch of road in proportion to the number of his people. He is responsible for its upkeep which consists of hishing (nger), re-surfacing (nyaiyo) and repair of the ramps (lat dier: dir = ramp). For satisfactory work, he is paid £3 per mile.

Sub-chiefs and gatwots can be fined administratively by the DC for not doing road work. Sub-chiefs are inclined to say the work is the responsibility of gatwots alone: this is not right as sub-chiefs are paid a salary. Since gatwots are not paid, it is advisable that a fine taken off one should be given as a present to another who has done good work.

Allotment

When the roads are altered or tribute lists change appreciably, it is necessary to re-allocate the work on the road. For this one needs a lorry marked with 1/10 of a mile on the HM. The Commers we have are not so fitted so we have to ask the Governor to lend one. Last year the SDIT lent us a vehicle.

There will have to be a good deal of re-allocation this year and I suggest a suitable vehicle is forwarded for about a fortnight in February. You will need it not only to re-allocate for 1955/56, but also to determine how much certain gatwots have done this year in the places where new roads have just been opened, i.e. Kwemerony, Berboi and Wilori. I say February, because it is necessary to make road payments before tribute is collected.

The best method of re-allocation is as follows:

1. get a list of the gatwots with numbers of taxpayers and check that it is complete, i.e. no gatwot left out.
2. run the vehicle over the stretch of road and see what the distance is. Do not take a distance from the file as it will have been read from another vehicle and will probably be different. If you are to be fair, you cannot afford to be more than 100 yards out.
3. take the total number of tax payers for whole road; divide into length of road and find distance which one man must do, e.g.

39.5 miles divided by 2106 taxpayers – 0.0187 miles per taxpayer.

4. from this, find distance which each gatwot has to do – e.g. a gatwot with 74 taxpayers will have to have 1.4 miles (ie. 0.0187 x 74 to nearest decimal point).
5. arrange list of gatwots in the order which is most convenient to them from the point of view of distance from their homes.
6. go to the start of the road and take the reading of the milometer. Then before you get out, work out in the list in front of you what the milometer should read when each gatwot's stretch is reached, e.g. the milometer reads 143.2 – gatwot A has to do 1.4 miles: therefore his stretch will run from 143.2 to 144.6. Gatwot B who has 2.3 miles to do will run from 144.6 to 146.9, and so on. Subtract the initial reading from the final reading reached on your list to check that the distance is the same as in the first run over. If it is not, then either a gatwot has been left out or a calculation is wrong.
7. then motor along the road with the gatwots and road foreman, stopping to mark the limit of each gatwot's stretch by stakes as his reading comes up on the milometer.

I have described this system in such detail as it is essential to be accurate. Very hard feelings can result if, when you come to the end of the road, you find that you have to give to the last gatwot twice as much as he ought to do because a mistake has been made. Nuer dislike road work and a genuine grievance could lead to an outright refusal to do it.

Roads to be re-allocated this year are:

1. All Kwemerony roads in view of: (a) closing road to Berkony; (b) opening a new one to Berboi; (c) making a new road through Kwemerony leaving Jwaibor to the west.
2. All Nyang roads in view of: (a) amalgamation of court; (b) opening of Goat-Gwadhgol road; (c) closing of 4 miles south of Aard. This will relieve the Mainland Radh who have hitherto had the heaviest road work while the Island Radh have had the lightest.
3. All Dinka roads, both Fangak-Sobat and Sobat-Waat. The first because the tax list was inaccurate when the road was re-allocated last year, the second because the allocation is out of date and unfair and I promised that it should be done this year. The side roads to Atar Court and School must not be forgotten when the Fangak-Sobat road is done. It should be noted that much of the K. Fallus road, at the Sobat end and at the Lam end, is done by Ngok of Malakal district with the Luaic

sandwiched between. All know where the Ngok-Luaic boundaries are, i.e. at Maling and Wanador.

It should also be noted that the arrangement for Dinka and Nyand yomis on the Bor-Malakal road is separate from the allocation to gatwots.

Fagwir and Thiang allocations are satifactory and need not be changed, but the tax list might show that the Awoi-Lou border is unfairly allocated.

General Notes

Reports show that road work this year is going on satisfactorily although impeded by heavy floods. It does not appear that any roads beyond Fagwir will open before 15 November. The exception to the good reports is Bar, where I hear that only Po Gau is at work. There is no excuse for this as they have less road work than anyone else, and this year less water. There is a note in the Bar handbook that I said in April that the Ayod-Awoi road must be well nyaiyoed this year – otherwise fines.

At the road making time, there are two extra road foremen employed at yomia rate. One, Gai Dong, is in Bar and the other, Ruot Jwai, in Radh (Nyang). One of these will have to replace Tut Deang if he does not return from Lou where he is now very ill.

Details of all road payments for 1954/55 will be found in road file and personal file.

It is advisable to re-issue the closure of roads order before May each year.

Improvements: 1954/55

The following balances are in hand for expenditure during the current year:

Serial	Page in Grant Book	Title of Project	Balance on 10/10/54
1	17	6m. culverts	£241
2	14	Sobat-Fanjak road	£252
3	14	Sobat-Fanjak road (approved March 54)	£2,183
4	16	Bridge at Nyinyar	£370
5	17	Banking of Nyinyar	£130
			£3,176

I have asked also for £200 for banking the Goat-Gwadhgol road and the Governor has added a proposal for culverts there, so probably more than £200 will be available for this road during the coming year. However, say a grand total of £3376.

Note that this is on the assumption that items 1, 2, 4 and 5 have not lapsed. I can find no mention of revotes so presumably they have not.

Out of this sum, the following bills will have to be met:

43 culverts 24" p 557 of 58 A	£903
20 culverts 36/ p 567 of 58A	£540
1 PWD bridge p 574 of 58A	£500
	£1943
Balance for use in current season:	£1433

Note 1: Of the 43 24" culverts noted above, about half have arrived but I cannot say exactly how many because there were no waybills and I am still awaiting a reply to a query from PWD.

Note 2: The funds approved for a bridge and banking at Nyinyar, serials 4 & 5 above, should be used for a bridge at Langtam if Governor approves the switch. See P 574 of 58A and preceding correspondence.

The £1433 left I suggest be used as follows:

1. £200 for Goat-Gwadhgol road plus any money granted for culverts. At 5 PT per day, which is a fair rate for road labourers working in their own home area, this will allow the employment of 50 men for 80 days which should be enough to make the banks and instal the culverts you need.
2. £1000 to be spent on extending banks on the Sobat-Fangak road. A great deal has already been done by the prisoners. Many parts have been heavily flooded this year and it will be best to concentrate on them. Jal Biar knows them. Over many stretches of road there will be no drinking water for the labourers after mid February, so such work should start on these stretches as soon as possible, i.e. as soon as the road opens to Atar to make arrangements and carry equipment. £1000 will provide for 100 men to work for 200 days. i.e. from approximately the beginning of December to end of June. It is best to have two gangs of 50, each with its road foreman. If rations have to be provided, as they probably will, pay must be reduced accordingly.
3. Finally, there will be £233 still left. I suggest you get Governor's approval to switch this to banking the road between Fangak and Tongwan which is still under water on 12/10/54. It may be

311

argued in support that the Dinka prisoners did a good deal of work on the Fangak-Sobat road last year which was not charged to the grant, and that therefore there is an economy which can best be used on the Fagwir road. There is the further point that road work will act as famine relief this year and that the benefits should be spread to the Lak who will be most hungry.

4. The bridge at Langtam, costing £500 including installation. PWD should be asked to put this in as soon as possible as we do not want to be committed to big repairs of the present unsatisfactory bridge if it is to be removed very soon.

5. There is usually a balance to spare from the annual grant for Upkeep of Communications. This can be used to add where desirable to work the suggested in paras (1), (2) and (3).

NB Last year prisoners built a ramp across a khor near Atat Court as a shortcut for people approaching from the west. Much has been carried away during the rains and it is not worth persevering with the project as it is not essential.

Methods

It is always best to put roadworkers on to piece-work. Divide them into gangs of 10 or 20 and lay out each gang's stint with ropes and stakes of the required height at the beginning of each day. As a guide, one man should be able to do 1.5 cu.m. of ramping in one day. 20 prisoners therefore can do:

7m long x 7m wide x 60cm high in one day
Or 8½m x 6m x 60cm
Or 10m x 6m x 50cm
Or 12m x 5m x 50cm
Or 15m x 5m x 40cm
and so on

The stint may have to be varied because of the texture of the soil. The aim should be that a good gang working really hard should finish in six hours. The rest will then do it in about eight hours.

Hishing figures: 1 man can hish 250 sq. yds in one day.

Working on the Bor road which is hished to a width of 8m for the grader, one man should therefore do 31 yds. (Actually he can probably do 40 as the soil is mostly sandy.) Working in hard soil with high grass, the figure could drop to 23 yds.

I recommend that banks built in future on main roads are made 7 m wide like the Bor district main road. It is much safer for traffic and saves work in the end.

A good supply of tools is important, and one must accept a considerable wastage as they do break in the hard ground. The store is well stocked now; only baskets are missing and these have been ordered from Bor. If they cannot be got, the soil can be carried in boarded sacks.

Future Development

There are some ideas on file, but in general it would be best to concentrate on improving existing roads, i.e. by banking, culverts and bridges, so that they can be used (with discretion) until 30 June, and will normally open by 1 November.

Any new roads later should I think be made in Garweir. There is a vast gap between Falagh and Awoi in which most of the people live. Awoi itself is in an uninhabited area. A start has been made during the rains by putting some prisoners on clearing a trace to Turkec – some 15 miles NNW where there are many people and usually a lot of grain, though not this year, I am told. The possibility should be investigated of linking the Bar to a meshra, e.g. Rupkwac. At the moment it is impossible to get grain to them after 15 May. But nothing should be done without careful survey on foot during the rains. It is very easy to waste great sums of money on ill-considered road projects in Nuer districts.

The Governor is not happy about the closing of the road to Berhony opposite Tonga. Experience may prove that it is desirable to re-open it.

MAIL SERVICES

The division of CND gave Lou 10 mail runners and Zeraf district 5. This number is only just adequate during the dry season and not at all during the rains. As from the closing of the roads, a pair of runners should go into Malakal every 10 days until the road opens again. This interval enables the mail to be collected from Malakal and dealt with in Fangak before the next pair of runners leaves with the replies.

There is no item in the distribution of the Approved Budget for mail services, but Mr Roussel told me that the district may use £94 of the Province items. It would be well to check on this. This will allow you to take on, say, one extra runner at MUNP basic rate all the year round, and another four at yomia rate during the rains. It is no economy to keep the number of runners too low. A frequent mail service to all courts is the best way of keeping in touch with everything that is going on. A chief will send back a useful routine report with a returning DC's runner when he would not send one of his own police especially.

The despatch system to courts is rather haphazard and I had intended to put Gabriel in charge of it and have pigeonholes constructed in his office for each court. Non-urgent letters could then accumulate in the pigeonholes and be sent out at regular intervals, say once a fortnight. This would help in particular the NA and private correspondents.

Runners get 10 PT each when they go into Malakal but do not receive TA or any other emoluments.

The corps of runners is the best mode of entry into the police force and a police candidate should, if possible, serve an apprenticeship as runner.

AYOD LANDING GROUND

It is officially referred to as Ayod, so that it will not be confused with Wau BGP, but it is actually at Wau, Zeraf District, about 10 miles north of Ayod and 1 mile off the Malakal-Bor road. Measurements are 1,200 yds x 100 yds.

It is the district's responsibility to keep the landing ground hished and the markers painted and in position. For this there is a grant from Civil Aviation of £100 per year. The work is done half by Radh and half by Bar in October with the respective EC's responsible. Omb Ruot Ler supervises the job and knows all about it. Yomia lists are kept and £45 paid in all to each court. Rate per man-day is worked out within this limit. Thus £10 is kept aside for upkeep or markers and second clearing, which may or may not be necessary in March.

It is worrying that the landing ground is probably unusable during July, August and September owing to the high grass. The funds will not run to keeping it permanently hished throughout those months. Yet if an aeroplane had to land and broke up, the DC would have some explanations to make. The best solution is to grow groundnuts for which the soil is suitable. For this, it will be necessary to find out what area a man can keep planted and hished if he works full time during the rains. Then work out the number of men required and the cost of their wages. The seed groundnuts could be charged to prison rations suspense a/c, and the a/c cleared when the crop comes in. To make labourers work better, it would be well to give them a portion of the crop. When detailed figures are ready, the necessary extra money can be asked for. If it is refused, then the DC can make clear that he is unable to keep the ground hished during July to September. The scheme would require a part-time clerk and a reliable gang of workmen in charge of one of the Ayod askaris, and would have the advantage of:

a) ensuring that the vegetation was always kept down.
b) relieving the NA of a tiresome job which it should not really have to do.
c) producing groundnuts.
d) encouraging the growing of groundnuts on the Duk ridge, much of which is ideal for the crop.

BUILDING

1. Maintenance – I mention maintenance first because one of the biggest problems is to find enough money for it. I estimate that mud buildings on district charge may be valued as follows:

Fangak – 80 sahab[30] framed Art III houses @ £20	£1,600
Court centres –100 NA tukls @ £3	£300
Awoi – 1 mud dispensary	£70
Fangak – Dairy	£140
Fangak – Scale K house	£150
5 sahab framed rest houses	£200
	£2,460

Maintenance costs on mud buildings in this province cannot be less than 20 per cent which means an annual upkeep of £492. With the use of prison labour the present grant of £290 would probably suffice.

But what does not seem to have been generally realised is that in UNP the PWD does less than half of the permanent buildings. Each year the district has to put up more permanent buildings, yet no provision is made for their maintenance. At the moment the district (not the council) has the following permanent and semi-permanent buildings on charge:

Prison	£400
K. Fellus dispensary	£450
Fangak dispensary and buildings	£800
3 brick rest houses	£800
Scale J house	£400
	£2,850

At 5 per cent, maintenance of these buildings costs £142 p.a., and 5 per cent is a very low assessment as all have grass roofs which need to be completely renewed every three years.

The result is that you will go into the red unless either (a) mud buildings grant is increased, or (b) districts are given funds for the maintenance of their permanent buildings as distinct from mud buildings, or (c) there happens to be lashings of prison labour.

2. Maintenance Methods – There are three categories of buildings to be maintained:

    i)   Native mud buildings outside Fangak. These are maintained by the gatwots and paid for on the scale to be found in the court handbooks. Sahad frames, namalia, doors and windows, if present, have to be maintained by special arrangements by DC, gatwots in such cases being responsible for mudding and thatch.

    ii)   Mud buildings in Fangak. Repairs are assessed in November and a programme prepared. Most labour is done by prisoners. Thatching is done by a gang of Shilluk but I see no reason why some Ruweng should not do it. They thatch quite as well if not better than Shilluk; payment is on a piece-work basis.

    iii)   Permanent buildings. Repaired as necessary by special arrangement by DC.

3. Materials – Cement and namalia[31] now in fairly good supply. Bricks can be got from the prison camp but see there are plenty: at least 150,000 will be required this year. Timber is a problem. Bamboos and sahab can be got from Shambe merchants and paid for via A/DC Yirol. Sahab can also be got from WND. Mahogany is coming from Nyinakok, about £70 worth. White wood is the most difficult: PWD have very little and Malakal merchants not much more. Perhaps it is best to order direct from Buildmore in Khartoum. Use CI[32] when possible: it costs a lot but cheaper than thatch in the long run. Bor district supplies ropes, which we need in large amounts.

4. Accounting – It is always necessary to stock up for the coming year: if current grants will not allow, then one may stockpile with the permission of the Governor.

5. I cannot give a building programme for the current year as approvals are not yet in, but I have taken care to keep the building file well supplied with notes on future plans and materials required.

WELLS

In pursuance of para 30 of Mr Carden's handover notes, the following has been done:

i)   A successful well completed at Ful-Lita.

ii)   Grant for wells at Kandag and Cuilbuong surrendered.

iii)   Proposals put in for wells at Kwemerony, Mereang and Margug (on the Duk ridge – the place to which the police post should move from Cieth).

Assuming that money will be available, since more was surrendered than asked for, work has started at Kwemerony and Mareang.

TRADE

Merchants should bring all applications concerning trade to the BPT[33] assessment meeting on 1 January every year, and such applications are not generally considered at any other time.

The policy, and I am sure it is a right one, is to concentrate shops, as a rule, in suqs[34] of not less than three which must be on the roads. Single bush shops are normally only allowed where there are police posts, but not enough people for a proper suq. There should not be need for any more single bush shops except possibly at Pabil, a newly made police post north of Awoi.

The idea of having suqs is that it induces competition and discourages exploitation of the Nuer. The insistence that shops be on roads is to facilitate supervision by the DC. Nuer will often plead to have a shop next door but the isolated bush shop, though convenient to them, is not really in their interest.

Wilori should be able to support a suq of four shops and anyone who wishes to move from Fangak should have first choice, though at least one shop should stay at Falagh to serve the police post there, which will remain, but reduced in numbers. I have more or less promised Tayib Osman, a merchant of Malakal, that if he brings a lorry to the district he can have a shop at Wilori. This could also be a starting place for Abdalla Abden Sallam if he wishes to extend to the district.

There was a move to start a suq in Longtam on the border between Thiang and Lak. The Fagwir and Mareang merchants objected that it would take away their custom. But it is a popular area and has a police post: it might well support three shops.

If it proves possible to open a road from Awoi to Turkec, all the merchants will want to move there. But the chiefs loathe them all except old Yusif, and want other merchants brought from outside. Bar is the last place in which one wants gellaba trouble and it would be well to consider the chiefs' views carefully.

The only other place where a new shop might be opened is at Atar where Beshir Abdel Rahman has a monopoly. Jadalla Nafi has been given the chance but should get on with the building, as the Dinka are pressing for some competition.

Otherwise, I do not think any more shops are required, for some time at least, unless you get a good Nuer applicant or the chance of a really go-ahead merchant coming to Fangak. For a district HQ, the suq is a disgrace.

Since the new road to Kwemerony has left Jwaibor, any merchants who wish to move from there to Kwemerony should probably be allowed to do so, but there is no need to insist on their moving as Jwaibor is well populated and lorries do not need a made road to get there during the dry season.

There are only two Nuer merchants and the policy is to encourage more by giving a free licence for two years so long as the applicant can read and write, and has a capital of £50. The two Nuer merchants are Peter Wual Tuong at Kwemerony and Philip Readh Kwer at Falagh. They take up far too much time as they are always in trouble with the chiefs. I think the fault in the first place is with the chiefs who resent the independent position of the Nuer traders and try to bully them; the traders reply by bringing complaints against the chiefs to the DC. Philip Readh has had a bitter feud for two years with Garwec Diet. Oth Deng was jugged for four months in April for beating Peter Wual and there is more trouble between them which will have to be settled on the next visit to Kwemerony.

In this coming year of famine it may be well to extend the system of supervised cattle auctions to Mereang, Ful Lita, Kwemerony and Wathkec. I started auctions in Fangak and Fagwir in June and the price of cattle shot up almost 100 per cent. There is an auction register which is kept by the court clerk (in Fangak by Ked Diu). The regulations are in the file and posted in auction registers. The area of applicability can be extended by adding a schedule.

The DC now has powers to fix the price of grain. However, if in a period of shortage, cattle prices fall and grain prices rise excessively, there may well be serious trouble. The solution is to ask the Governor to ask the Director of Economics and Trade to fix a ceiling price. At present it is 15 PT per ruba.

Chiefs and merchants sometimes make unofficial agreements for the sale and re-sale of Nuer grain. Usual prices are: Nuer grower to merchant – 5PT per ruba (ket); merchant to Nuer buyer – 6½ PT. On whatever the price to the Nuer grower, add on 1½ PT for the merchant's trouble and profit. These agreements have no legal sanction but they save trouble all round and merchants usually realise that it is not in their interest to evade them.

The supply of consumer goods in the shops is not nearly good enough. There is an only partly fulfilled demand for chairs, tables, groundsheets, good clothes, good cooking utensils etc. However, on the whole the merchants do a fairly good job; it is unfortunate that a minority do not realise that their existence depends on the goodwill of the Nuer. Abdel Magid Abdel Rahman understands the facts of life and is most public spirited in keeping prices reasonable and relations between Nuer and merchants fairly happy.

There is a regulation that all shops must display a price list and it is desirable to insist on this, as it is a protection for the simple Nuer.

The list must be in either English or Nuer as well as Arabic so that local literate Nuer can interpret it to the illiterate.

FINANCE

1. The main problem is to keep the tribute lists complete and up to date. To help with this I have tried to obtain strongly bound cieng books[35] but they have not yet arrived. The idea is that the executive clerk keeps the book continuously up to date, making alterations as and when they are reported to him. Then during the rains the tribute clerk amends the office copies from the cieng book with each gatwot present before him. He also sorts out with the court any transfers which are applied for. I have brought the rules for transfer up to date and they are on file. I think a copy of the tribute list should be in the tribal file so that they can be referred to on trek: quite a number of awkward little questions turn up on whose list a certain man is on. My rulings lay down a £1 fine for any chief or gatwot who conceals names and this is worth sticking to. When in a cattle camp, it is a good idea to collect a number of young men and check their names on the lists. When a man becomes very old or otherwise unable to cultivate, he may be struck off.
2. Next year mainland tributes should go up to 40 PT unless it comes under the council.
3. No poll tax is collected. I think that if one looked around there would be over 50 people liable, and it would be worth doing. I am sure that many merchants' poor relations pay nothing in the North and are probably liable to pay poll tax.
4. It is well worth making the Sarraf[36] stick to Mr Carden's accounting routines. I have found them invaluable.

P.P. Bowcock
District Commissioner
Zeraf District
9 November 1954

Appendix 5

THE SUDAN REVISITED,
JANUARY 2006

From Sudan Studies *No. 36, November 2007.*

The Sudan became an independent republic on 1 January, 1956. Because of the complications caused by condominium status there was none of the ceremonial attending the moment of independence which was later arranged for former British colonies and protectorates, including the attendance of a member of the royal family. Most British officials had already left. It seemed more like a divorce than a coming of age. There was already a mutiny in Equatoria and 50 years of tribulation followed.

It was particularly welcome therefore to British servants of the Sudan under the condominium to receive an invitation to revisit the country on the fiftieth anniversary of independence. The invitation came from the Sudanese Association for Archiving Knowledge, which has much wider cultural objectives than its reference to archives would suggest. The chairman is Sayyid Ibrahim Moneim Mansur, a former Minister of Finance and Economic Planning and currently the chairman of the Fiscal and Financial Allocation Commission, set up under section 198 of the Interim Constitution following the Comprehensive Peace Agreement, now universally referred to as the CPA. His son, Mohammed, was to be a most beguiling host and guide throughout our visit.

The invitation generously extended to sons and daughters, since most pensioners would by now be over 80. In the end only one genuine pensioner was able to go, Sir Donald Hawley, who was the leader of what the Sudanese called the "delegation". There were however four other former Sudan Political Service members who were appointed after recruitment on pensionable terms ceased.

(British officials were more percipient as to what the future might hold than Martin Daly gives them credit for in his fascinating book, produced with Jane Hogan, Keeper of the Sudan Archive in Durham, "Images of Empires, Photographic sources for the British in the Sudan", Brill, 2005.) KDD (Bill) Henderson, one of the founders of the Archive, and Glencairn Balfour Paul, who had just published his entertaining memoirs "Bagpipes in Babylon", were represented by descendants. Among others of our band of 20 were Professor Peter Woodward, Peter Evrington, who had taught in secondary schools after independence, their wives, and Mrs Jane Hogan.

The letter of invitation given to Sir Donald Hawley as Chairman of the Sudan Government British Pensioners Association said that "SUDAAK and many other Sudanese across the country appreciate the British staff who served in the political and civil service of the Sudan and contributed much to the shaping of contemporary history and development of the country". Their invitation had the support of the Vice President, HE Ali Osman Taha, who would be patron of the visit.

It became clear that Sudanese hospitality was to be the keynote when the Ambassador came to see us off and we were flown in business class. It was wonderful to arrive, after half a century, in Khartoum in the middle of the velvety night to be greeted by smiling, courteous gentlemen in immas and jallabiyas, and ladies too, the executive committee of SUDAAK. We were given refreshment in the VIP lounge, while the entry formalities were conducted elsewhere on our behalf. We were then taken with a motor cycle escort, which stayed with us during our weeklong stay at the Hilton Hotel.

It was very moving, the following morning, to raise the blinds and see the meeting of the White and Blue Niles with Tutti Island's neat cultivations right opposite. In the Mohsen gardens below, the mudiria clerks had entertained me to dinner before my transfer to Upper Nile. My future wife used to ride with me before work in the Sunt Forest to the west. The public rooms had their Christmas decorations still on display, an augury of the tolerant atmosphere we were to find everywhere.

We had arrived not knowing what to expect and found an excellent programme arranged for us. An early visit was to the former Anglican Cathedral, a red sandstone building by an Italian architect, and it was reassuring that there was none of the desecration one might have feared. It is well maintained as a museum, its memorials in place, with an exhibition for the meeting of the African Union the following week. Sadly the handsome clock tower has been removed as it was said to have been used by rebels to threaten the Republican Palace in President Nimeiri's time. We went on to the Republican Palace and signed the book for the President, as for the Governor General in former times. We also visited the National Museum with artefacts rescued from the land covered by the waters of the Higher Aswan dam. Later on in our stay we went to the replacement Episcopal cathedral where on Sundays there are seven services in different languages to cater for the refugees from the south.

We visited three universities, Ahfad, Ahlia and Khartoum. At Ahfad, one of the staff told me how much he owed to "Dougie" Udal, the Principal of Gordon College. I was able to introduce him forthwith to Dougie's son John and his granddaughter Joanna – a remarkable record of three generations of service to the Sudan. Rev. Joanna Udal is assistant to the Episcopal Archbishop. She joined our party and was obviously welcome wherever we went. Ahfad University is for women, carrying on the Bedri tradition of education for women. Students come from as far away as Tanzania and converse easily with charm and humour. Ahlia is a brave enterprise, being the people's university independent of government. Khartoum University is of course the flagship, having developed from Gordon College. It was there that we went to an excellent lecture by a lady, Dr Mahasin Abdul Gadir Haj el Safi, on "The Sudan and the Commonwealth" based on her research in the UK as well as the Sudan. There was a view in the hall that joining the Commonwealth could be beneficial in a number of ways, and if Mozambique can join, why not Sudan? But this would have to await the outcome of the CPA on completion of the transitional period.

There were two visits outside Khartoum, south to the impressive Kenana Sugar Company in Kosti and north to the pyramids at Bijarawiyah, each with what appears to be a chapel on its east face. There are fascinating Meroitic reliefs and inscriptions dating from between 200 BC and AD 300. It is tantalising that the script has not yet been deciphered, although one scholar is said to have been close to it before his death. Two very pleasurable outings were a cruise on the Blue Nile and a delightful lunch under the trees at the farm of Kemal and Taj Mohamed Osman Salih. The expansion of Khartoum and the desire for a higher standard of life have led to enormous demand for garden flowers and shrubs.

In the evenings there were receptions by SUDAAK, the Sudanese British Friendship Society, Mr Anis Hajar and the British Ambassador, all most enjoyable with an opportunity to talk to a wide variety of people. There was also a cultural show in Omdurman. On Friday afternoon, not part of the official programme, most of us attended a Gadiriya Sufi Zikr in Omdurman, where we were warmly received and reassured that the generous openness of Islam in the Sudan still persisted.

Another unscheduled visit was to a refugee camp west of Omdurman. It is a difficult life and many have at last hopes of returning to their homes. Others will probably stay; many of the jobs as porters, ghaffirs and the like are now done by southerners. Though my Nuer is even poorer than my Arabic now, just a few words brought a delighted response.

We visited two of Harry's Homes in Khartoum, one for boy orphans and the other for girls. They live in normal, simple houses in a street, each with a house mother and supervision by Social Services. The children attend school and church or mosque and most have some members of their extended family in the vicinity. They are delightful; polite, cheerful and obedient, turning off the children's cartoons on the television as soon as they were asked. It is hoped that foundling babies will be cared for in the future. The Harry whose name is used died as a boy in a traffic accident and his family, the Hendersons, were part of the visitors' group.

The fine mahogany trees along the Blue Nile waterfront are still there and the Ministry of Energy and Mining has been built beyond the trees over the water. There we enjoyed a memorable last evening, appreciating the fine collection of condominium scientific and literary publications and learning about the vast differences to the life of the people the oil has made and will continue to make. It was evident also that it had brought numbers of Chinese and Malaysians to the country. Another sign is the huge expansion of Khartoum and the occasional new mansion sitting out in the desert on its plot waiting for the town to catch up. Yet as the Eid approached the flocks of sheep waited patiently to take their part in the feast, as they always have done.

What conclusions? The country appeared relaxed and peaceful with no traffic jams and no sign of security forces. The Government of National Unity is still in place and so is the Government of the Southern Sudan in Juba. The Evringtons went on to join in the first year celebrations of the CPA there. Darfur is still a huge problem: the difficulty appears to be in getting the factions of the rebel movement to agree. The greatest change which we old Sudanis noticed was in the position of women, attending the receptions and moving among guests with assurance and charm, no longer dressing in the old black or indigo blue tobs but in bright colourful prints. We were accompanied and organised in most visits by the Hon. Secretary of SUDAAK, Fawzia Yousif Galaladdin, a journalist. For me it was like an old love affair, forgotten and renewed after many years.

Appendix 6

RETURN TO ZAMBIA:
THIRTY-FIVE YEARS ON

Record of a visit to Zambia in 2000, with Matthew and Oliver.

Inspired by Colin Rawlins in 1998 and Paul Bourne, I visited Zambia
for two and a half weeks in June and July 2000 with my son Matthew
(born in Kabwe in 1956) and Oliver (born in Kasama in 1961).
Stella (born in Kabwe in 1955), with four children aged between 1
and 13, was not a candidate for the expedition.

We aimed to see again where we had lived and worked and where
the children were born and baptised, as well as enjoying a holiday.
The planning was done with the help of Chris McIntyre's invaluable
book *Zambia: The Bradt Travel Guide*, £12.95. Chris works for
Sunvil Discovery, part of Discovery World Wide Limited. Details of
addresses and books are at the end. He and his colleague, Robert
McDowell, both visit Zambia regularly. They turned our wishes into
a practical itinerary and booked accommodation, transport and
activities. Local organisation was by Zambia Safaris of Lusaka.

The flight from Gatwick by BA took about nine hours. Because of
Zimbabwe's troubles the air crew were over-nighting in Lusaka, so
we did not have to go via Harare. There are four flights a week. We
arrived to a rather cold overcast day, the only one of our visit. For
the rest of the trip we had the well-remembered bright, clear days of
the Zambian winter, with a fire being welcome in the evening. Our
driver Rodrick Mwiila met us with his own Mitsubishi Pajero,
bought, we later discovered, with his savings from UN peace-
keeping duties with the Zambian Army. He turned out to be an
excellent driver and an agreeable and informative travelling
companion, never daunted by the worst of roads. He is a Bemba
from Luapula Province. The President, Frederick Chiluba, a Lunda,

is also from Luapula, but his opponents say he was born in the Congo so he is not eligible to be President, like Kenneth Kaunda. The litigation grinds on.

An early call was to the Standard Bank to get kwacha. The tourist industry operates on US dollars but sterling can be exchanged in the banks. There is no exchange control now, which means that anything can be obtained if one can pay the price. There are 4300 kwacha to £1. When one considers that at independence there were over K2 to the £1, which itself has been devalued to about one tenth of its 1964 value, it will readily be seen what suffering inflation must have caused. In Lusaka and Livingstone, Switch and Connect cards will produce fat wads of kwacha from holes in the wall, but elsewhere one has to go inside to the bank counter or deal with a private trader, who may pass forged notes. Another early task was to get Matthew's mobile phone to work. In Zambia mobile phones are widely advertised and used, though there are many areas without transmission masts. From the towns there was no problem in speaking clearly to the UK. The banks, mobile phone operators, tourist offices and the like are staffed by smart and courteous young Zambians, men and women, but we were told that the employers have great problems because so many, when trained, then fall ill with AIDS. Others refuse promotion when it means having a health check. At least the Government acknowledges the problem and there are many warning posters. The other official messages are "No Sweat, no Sweet" and "Compete to Survive".

The Government Offices were little changed from what I remembered, though lacking maintenance and the gardens looked worn and tired. The Anglican Cathedral was open, clean and apparently active, with two European names among the clergy and office holders. The flags of the Northern Rhodesia Regiment and the shields of various British Forces units were still in their chapel. We had a warm welcome wherever we went. Cairo Road is full of activity and the market is enormous. A new market has not displaced the old, which still remains, though very dilapidated. There was no hassling and everyone was polite. Privatisation has meant that many people have lost jobs and have to trade to make a living. There are strong resemblances to Russia after the fall of Communism. Lusaka has grown greatly but looks generally run down. This is recognised by a sign announcing Stage 1 of Lusaka Refurbishment, but residents are sceptical as to whether anything will happen.

We stayed at Lilayi Lodge which has comfortable rondavels in a park with a game farm, which we toured by bicycle. It was great to make contact with the bush again and see zebra, hartebeest and bush buck. John and Gretta Hudson came to dinner and gave us an invaluable background briefing and introduction for our coming journey. As John was for nine years Executive Director of the National Farmers' Union and is a Trustee of the Belt Trust and representative of British Executive Service Overseas, he is in touch with much that is happening in Zambia. Gretta told of the consequences of AIDS: for the first time there are street children because sometimes the extended family cannot cope or are all dead.

Lilayi Police Training School still exists. The police seem on the whole to be valued and are polite at the frequent road checks.

The next day we travelled to Choma. The tar road to Livingstone is good for the most part with occasional pot-holed stretches. Sugar is big in Mazabuka. The court has been moved from the Boma building (still so called) to two rather unimpressive buildings. Choma is rather squalid. We found our old house with difficulty, occupied by a retired driver from Lundazi who could not afford to maintain it properly. Nearly all Government housing seems to have been sold. The Beit School where Matthew and Stella went to school, now called Adastra, is in a bad way, with little money for maintenance and having to cope with three shifts a day. There is a fine museum of Tonga life in the old Beit boarding house with a well tended garden. It was given by the Dutch and is an example of how aid should be given with provision for future maintenance, just as the National Trust here will not accept a property without an endowment. All over Zambia one sees aid wasted for lack of maintenance. Beside the short road up to Mpika Boma on its hill, we counted seven broken-down vehicles or major pieces of machinery.

I called on the Resident Magistrate Mr E. Musona, who was most welcoming. Fortunately his female deputy was sitting in Court so he was free to talk and explain how the complete separation of judiciary from executive now works. Chiefs or local courts deal only with customary personal Law. I remember being shouted down at a conference at London University with Roland Hill in 1962 when I suggested that while the separation of judiciary and executive was correct in theory, it would in practice in rural areas lead to great delay and insupportable expense. So it has proved. Later we learnt that if a poacher is caught in the South Luangwa National Park he has to be sent for trial in Mpika via Chipata (Fort Jameson) and Lusaka. So offenders often get off. It was eerie being in the chambers, just the same except that the picture of the young Queen Elizabeth, which I now have, was replaced by President Chiluba, and the windows were covered with cloth. Most of the books were the same, including, for example, Woodfall on Landlord and Tenant, which has gone through several editions since. Mr Musona said the absence of up to date books made his work much more difficult since the High Court, which has the books, sometimes overruled him, basing its decision on a later precedent. The cause list, posted outside, still referred to a court being "holden".

Jill Beckett invited us to dinner but Mike was away at the tobacco auction in Lusaka (prices poor). We met their son Nick and his wife Rebecca, from England but living in Zambia. They produce milk, tobacco and beef. Life is not easy but a lot better than when the "stasi", as they called them, operated under the previous regime. The Southern Africa rural craze is now for polo cross, a poor man's polo played on horses with lacrosse sticks instead of mallets.

Their neighbor, Ian Bruce-Miller, farms game and runs trophy shoots for the very wealthy. They arrive from Lusaka by train in a luxury carriage and return the same way with expensive trophies.

We stayed in traditional rondavels at Joe Brooks's farm, saw his crocodiles and heard lots of good stories.

The Falls are still virtually unspoilt, unaffected by the Western compulsion to put barriers everywhere. There is bungee jumping from the frontier in the middle of the bridge. We watched a blond Texan woman jump off in tandem with her son aged 10. It looked just as terrifying from the boiling pot below. There were very few tourists about because the Zimbabwe trade had dried up on account of Mugabe's atrocities. New hotels are being built but should not spoil the Falls. There are a number of luxury camps about 15 miles west of Livingstone. We stayed at Tongabezi, which is superb, in thatched houses quite open to a great bend in the Zambezi, the height of eco-chic and expensive to match.

We had to get to Sesheke and back in a day, because there is nowhere to stay. The road to Kazungula is good, to cope with big lorries bringing imports through or from Botswana. At some time a huge sum has been spent on a raised tarmac road to Sesheke. It seems never to have been maintained and, as Rodrick said, we spent most of the day "jumping into potholes". It was often better driving in the sand alongside the tarmac, and the locals have reverted to their sledges. Electricity lines ran alongside the road.

We called into Mwandi and found it all set up for the agricultural show, awaiting formal opening by the District Administrator. There were stalls for the agricultural, veterinary and medical departments, all very forthcoming about what was going on, which was uncannily similar to 40 years before. The Paris Mission has become part of the United Church of Zambia. The hospital has greatly expanded and is supported by churches in the USA, including an annual eye team visit. The chief was away but his residence where I used to call on Chief Lubinda seemed little changed. As the Barotse have been largely stripped of their powers in what is now Western Province, the titles have become grander. Letters are headed "Barotse Royal Establishment Mwandi; Office of the Liashimba", and the chief lives in a "palace".

Sesheke is much larger, with a secondary school, police station, hospital and big market, but rather sad and uncared for. River transport to Kazungula is no more, and there are no scheduled air services, but the Katima Mulilo pontoon was working and lots of people were using it. The road to Senanga and Mongu was said to be passable. Mulobezi Sawmills were nationalised and so became bankrupt: two possible private buyers are engaged in litigation. Everything is against poor Sesheke, but we found our house with two bougainvillea and a frangipani surviving, while Matthew located his path down to the river where he used to catch tiddlers at the age of six. (Did we not worry about crocs?) Unfortunately the DA was going to Mwandi, so we missed him and got back to Tongabezi very tired.

On to Kafue South National Park with Chundukwa Safaris run by Doug and Dee Evans (her father having been chief mechanic for Wenala at Katima Mulilo). They are currently the sole concessionaires and have a beautiful little bush camp overlooking a lagoon on the Nanzhila plains. There is plenty to see both on foot and from a vehicle, in daylight and at night. Ben Powell, a young South African, was a great guide, and George, a tiny Ila, was superb at spotting game as well as producing masses of food.

Further north, the Ngoma elephants are still present but the big camp built in PWD style in the old days is derelict and awaits an offer to privatise. The Itezhi-Tezhi dam on the Kafue, planned before independence but built after, makes a fine lake, where we spotted a considerate sign: "Beware of crocodiles by order of management". An ambitious hotel was built, now run down and stranded in the 1970s. Apparently it catered for Lusaka weekenders, but the condition of the road connecting with the good Lusaka-Mongu road now puts them off. As evening fell a rather stroppy elephant appeared beside the swimming pool. After much shouting a spotlight was brought, and he trundled off into the night.

Mumbwa is much enlarged, like all the bomas. It boasts an enormous, beautifully maintained mosque. I never found out why or how it got there. Opposite was a café with the sign: "The Mosque Cafe, God is Great. Relax and have a drink". Lucky for Zambia that it has no ayatollahs.

Soon back on to a ghastly earth road to Landless Corner, still so called with a Landless still in residence, and plastic tunnels for UK supermarket vegetables. I wanted to see how the agriculture had developed from Keembe Peasant Farms. There is now a Farm Institute, presented in 1966 by Sir Harold Samuel, running courses for local farmers. The farm manager claimed to be greatly encouraged by the results. A lot of cotton seems to be produced here as well as in Mumbwa and Kalomo, brought into the corrugated iron sheds one sees at intervals. Another cash crop, rather surprisingly, is dried peppers. Nearby is a boarding school provided by Danish donors, training children orphaned by AIDS in a trade. There are still European-owned farms round Kabwe (Broken Hill). The town has grown though the mine employs only a small number exploiting the old spoil heaps. Mukobeko African Township, which I had a part in laying out in 1955, is now well populated though untidy, and the town plan is still identifiable. We found the hospital where Stella and Matthew had been born. Like the Town Hall it shows the confidence of the early years of the Federation, so soon cast down. The Elephant's Head Hotel is now called Tuskers and has been well refurbished at some expense by a local farmer called Paddy Doyle. The bar is the local meeting place and the tragic murder of John Roberts is a big topic, thought not to have been politically inspired.

The District Administrator was not in the urban Boma when we called, but he heard about us and came from the Council Office where he was lodging while the old office block is being renovated. He explained that he wanted the place to give a good impression – very different from most offices. We had a good talk, chiefly about his gratitude for the toughness of the Truancy Officer on the Copperbelt who had kept him at his studies, without which he would not be DA today. He gave us a female messenger to lead us to St George's Church where John Munday had been priest in our time. There it still is, now in the middle of a market, and we even found the picture that we gave to the church when we left in 1958. In the church hall two nice women were running a play school for about 20 cheerful infants.

We found our first house in Marshall Avenue. The occupants were friendly, but that was universal so I will not repeat it. This was an AK3 house and the best maintained of our old houses. Next door, outside the house of the RM, Geoffrey Scarr, is a neat sign saying: "Welcome to Aunt Maggie's Hair Salon: Specialist in all styles with affordable charges". The composition and painting of signs seems to be a growth industry. On one particularly bouncy road we followed a lorry enjoining us to "Be still and know that I am God".

The Old Boma which was so beautiful is now known as Mutwe Wa Nsofu. It is approached through what remains of the mine and is depressing. It is dominated by a spoil heap; the cricket ground and tennis court have gone, and the old houses have been sold to people who cannot afford to maintain them. But on the mine sports ground we saw the Kabwe Lions rugby team training – 13 black players and 2 white. The old DC's office is roofless but the DO's, in the same block, is occupied by the Education Department. Surprisingly the mud and thatch guest rondavel of our house just survives.

There is a large Chinese textile factory on the north exit from Kabwe, providing some of the employment lost from the mine. The town of Kapiri Mposhi is 10 times as beastly as it ever was and there was a fuel scam in operation. A rumour that the price was about to go up resulted in claims that the pumps were dry, so we had to pay well over the odds from a youth who was probably selling what was in the tank of his employer's lorry. This was the only apparent dishonesty encountered on the whole holiday.

Mkushi and Serenje, like all the bomas, have grown greatly with bank, fuel station, small supermarket and lots of small traders. We got diesel at Mkushi without trouble and cracked on at a good pace on the excellent tarmac road recently remade by the Danes. I hope they have left something in a trust fund for maintenance. There is little traffic but a small market of local produce, bananas, peanuts etc. at each turn-off. The Tanzan railway, now working, accompanies the Great North road until Mpika where it diverts to Kasama.

North of Serenje the Chinese road, also tarmac and in good condition, goes to Mansa (Fort Roseberry). It cuts out the journey through the Congo pedicle, but is much longer of course if you are travelling from the Copperbelt. After about 18 miles one comes to the Kasanka National Park, David Lloyd's remarkable and praiseworthy effort to preserve and increase the fauna of the area and particularly the rare sitatunga. The dawn viewing over a swamp from a hide 60 feet up in a colossal mululu tree is a great experience. There is much to see and commend at Kasanka – conservation projects, camp accommodation, catering, welcoming staff and company. As we left David was out with his staff early burning the grass (the controversy about whether this is the right thing to do still rages).

Mpika's boma is still impressive on its little hill and the very scattered township shows considerable development. The last 20 miles or so into Kasama is bad but the contract for renewal has been signed. Ewart and Hazel Powell at the Thorn Tree Guest House made us welcome and comfortable. As Ewart had been headmaster at Mungwi Secondary School, we had much to talk about. Because of his success in promoting agriculture at the school, the Bemba chiefs had offered him a farm between Mungwi and Malole on land selected by him. We went to see it: citrus, cattle, poultry providing the eggs for Kasama and above all coffee irrigated by a dam and furrow. There are great hopes for Zambian coffee, which seems to enjoy a good reputation and price.

Mungwi has developed greatly and is to have its own District Administrator shortly. Perhaps he will smarten it up. But most of the development seems to be fuelled by government departments or overseas aid and not by local wealth creation as had been hoped. The farms have mostly reverted to subsistence. We found our house rented by Mr Chileshe, the Education Officer. He is retiring to a farm in

Mungwi on which he is building a house, not to his home district of Mporokoso. The garden of our house consists of sweet potato ridges.

We found the weir, still providing the water supply and looking just the same. The pump attendant, when told I was the first DO there, asked incredulously "Are you Beecock? You will have known my father. He was the UNIP Chairman". Not bad to have got so close to my name after 40 years. I showed pictures of Barnabas Mwamba and other old friends as we travelled, but never managed to make a contact.

The Powells had told us that the community church, where Oliver had been baptised by Canon Hewitt, had been burnt down by a lunatic and was abandoned, but when we went, we found not only an Anglican congregation but much singing and dancing with robed womens' choirs, because of the visit by the bishop from Ndola for confirmation. We were invited to stay and did so. The Bemba came back with the loan of a service book in English and Bemba. Father Cornelius, the local priest, took us to the cemetery which is sadly neglected. With the help of the Powells, it is hoped we can do something about it.[1] We found the old European Hospital where Oliver had been born in 1961, now occupied by a woman school teacher who is negotiating to buy it.

We were in Kasama over the old Rhodes and Founders holiday, now called something else but still in the same slot, so I was not able to call on the District Administrator or Deputy Minister. We said good-bye to Rodrick at Kasama airport, which is very quiet now that there are no longer any scheduled air services. We were told that Ministers treated the planes as private air taxis and bumped the paying air passengers. Bankruptcy inevitably followed. Reliance has to be placed on private charters, which are efficient, with prices coming down. The pilot of our Cessna flying us to the South Luangwa had been a marketing manager in South London; our later pilot for the return to Lusaka was a New Zealander. Although chitemene (slash and burn) cultivation is supposed to have been forbidden there were as many circles as ever until we passed over the Muchinga escarpment, after which there were no signs of human activity until the Bisa villages on the east bank of the Luangwa.

Tafika camp has its own airstrip, some distance away. The site is superb, on a bend in the Luangwa with magnificent trees and grass obligingly mown each night by the hippos, their munching being heard through the grass walls of the guest suites. The accommodation, catering, activities, guiding and general care by John and Carol Coppinger are all first class. The usual routine, after breakfast as the sun comes up, is to cross the river and walk in the park with a guide and a man with a rifle in front – necessary because the day before they had disturbed a sleeping elephant. Then at a lake there is a brew-up and a demonstration of how to start a fire without matches (dried hippo dung is the best tinder) before returning to lunch and rest. In the evening there is a drive in a four-wheel-drive vehicle with a drink as the sun goes down, after which one returns in the dark with a spotlight picking up the nocturnal creatures.

John Coppinger has a microlight aircraft and the flight in the early morning was a great thrill, with many animals seen. Poaching is being contained but is still a problem, not helped by the rigidity of the legal system mentioned earlier. The rhino have been completely liquidated but by a happy irony the elephant have been reduced from the dangerously excessive number of 60,000 to the optimum 10,000.

So south by Land Rover with more to see on the way to Mfuwe, an international airport. The charter plane which connects with BA flights took us to Lusaka, passing over the Mulungushi dam on the way. Then, in 10 hours, we were being met at Gatwick.

SOME REFLECTIONS

Zambia has maintained reasonable peace within its borders and violent crime does not appear to be a major problem outside the large towns. Of its seven neighbours, all except two have been unstable and Angola and the Congo are still. It may be significant that the two more or less stable neighbours, Tanzania and Malawi, along with Zambia itself, were governed and handed over to an elected successor government by the Colonial Service. The contrast with the other territory where I served, the Sudan, could not be greater. There we allowed ourselves to be pushed out by the pressures of the Cold War and the Co-Dominus, Egypt, before we were able to establish a constitution and leadership to protect the South, resulting in a ghastly civil war which still continues.

By good fortune, on the first day at Lilayi Lodge I found a book by John M. Mwanakatwe called *End of Kaunda Era*. I knew him as Education Officer Kasama in 1960. He became a Minister in Kaunda's first government, and after retirement from politics in 1978 he became Chairman of the Zambia Privatisation Agency and is now Chancellor of the University of Zambia. As we travelled I read the book and filled in the events of the last 35 years, as seen on the spot.

Mwanakatwe distinguishes three periods since independence:

The First Republic 1964–72: Kaunda inherited a full treasury, a fair copper price, a functioning civil service and vast goodwill overseas, resulting in generous aid. There was a great expansion of education and other services. Opposition was weak, but existed.

The Second Republic: The One Party State 1972–91: Mainza Chona headed a commission which produced the required recommendation that Zambia should become a One Party Participating Democracy". At the same time the programme of nationalisation was stepped up with almost every enterprise worth pillaging, including the copper mines, taken into public ownership. By 1982 the income per head had dropped to $US390, about half its 1970 level. In 1989 Zambia's debt was $1 billion, meaning that every man, woman and child owed about $1000 to the international community. Looking at it another way, in 1964 the gross domestic product per person was twice that in South Korea; in 1999 South Korea was 27 times that in Zambia. This economic misery was compounded by the personal oppression usual in one-party states. It is referred to now as the period of the Stasi.

The Third Republic: The Movement for Multi-Party Democracy 1991 to date: Opposition to UNIP rule grew among the professional class and the churches, but it required the muscle of the trade unions to convert the opposition into a mass movement. The Movement for Multi-Party Democracy (MMD) was headed first by Arthur Wina and he was succeeded by Frederick Chiluba, a trade union leader. Under pressure from both inside and outside Zambia, Kaunda agreed to free elections in October 1991, believing the courtiers who said that he would win.

After the mediation of the churches a new constitution on democratic lines accepting the rule of law was introduced in September 1991. The elections the following month were generally held to have been free and fair: the result was a landslide for the MMD and Chiluba with 76 per cent of the votes; UNIP and Kaunda won only 24 per cent. The belief is that it was President Jimmy Carter who persuaded Kaunda to accept the result and preserve some reputation.

It is an irony that most of us in the field considered that the Labour Party's sponsorship of trade unions in the colonies in the 1940s was just inviting trouble, which it did in the short run: in the long run, however, the unions in Zambia, and it seems in Zimbabwe, have also been able to mobilise opposition to oppression.

I detect four main influences upon the development of Zambia since independence:

1. The centuries-old structure of tribe, clan and family, still powerful but affected by many new developments such as compulsory service in the army, the proclamation of English as the sole official language, television, the limitation of chiefs' power to personal matters etc. This structure still provides the social security of mutual family support, but by the same token

family obligations take precedence over duty to the state or employer, accounting for some of the "corruption' that outsiders complain of.

2. The churches. Church buildings are as numerous as in the southern USA and are often the best maintained buildings around. The mainstream churches have spawned a multiplicity of sects, but are still influential.

3. The Civil Service and Judiciary. The structures set up before independence appear largely to have survived with the exception of the provincial administration. The system of UNIP district secretaries and district governors proved disastrous. Quite apart from the iniquities of one-party rule, there was no one with the authority and impartiality to co-ordinate government activities and the many overseas aid projects. In 1995 a Constitutional Review Commission to consider structures following the one-party era recommended the restoration of non-political provincial and district commissioners in response to an overwhelming response to public consultation. Instead there is now the district administrator who does have some political functions, one told me – seemingly a halfway house. In provincial headquarters and district bomas all the old departments appeared to be represented, though activity seems somewhat lethargic.

4. The fourth influence came from the vociferous proponents of independence as soon as possible, the one-party state and widespread nationalisation, who might be described as the Hampstead Thinkers. Their policies have been disastrous and are being reversed by the MMD. It has been truly observed that it was a tragedy for Africa that the attainment of independence coincided with the Cold War and the high water mark of extreme left-wing ideas, which many African leaders had imbibed while still engaged in the struggle for independence. The human tendency in politics to disparage one's predecessors was exacerbated by distortion by British academics: e.g. Tordoff and Molteno's judgement that "the rural sector off the line of rail was badly neglected". If one of the many hard-working and devoted AOs or ASs wants to put him right, I know Bill Tordoff and have his address. Success may have been limited, but that is not the same as neglect.

Conclusion

I feel proud to have had a small part in the constructive phase of Zambia's history and in a tradition of honest, sensible and diligent service to its people. The country is working its way back and this is the time to visit, while the going is good. There are fears for what might follow President Frederick Chiluba.

BOOKS AND ADDRESSES

Chris McIntyre – *Zambia: The Bradt Travel Guide*.
Bradt Travel Guides, UK.

Lucy Farmer – *A Visitors Guide to the Kasanka National Park*.
Kasanka Trust, Zambia.

John M Mwanakatwe – *End of Kaunda Era*.
Published by Multimedia Publications.

John Hudson – *A Time to Mourn*.
A personal account of the 1964 Lumpa Church Revolt in Zambia with extracts from the 1995 Report of the Constitutional Review Commission, set up following the restoration of multi-party democracy. ISBN 9982-24-012-9, Bookworld Publications, Zambia.

Appendix 7

ZIMBABWE ELECTION
SUPERVISORS' REPORT

*This is a transcript of a joint report by the two election supervisors for
Victoria Province, John Barratt and myself, to the Governor, Sir
Christopher Soames. A similar report was submitted by each Province.*

VICTORIA PROVINCE – MARCH 1980

Area of Responsibility: Its Characteristics and Problems

Geographically Victoria Province falls into two parts, the high veld,
comprising Gutu, Bireita, Ndenza, Victoria and Chibwe Districts,
averaging 1000 metres above sea level, and the low veld with the
two huge districts of Chiredzi and Nuanetsi, having an average
altitude of 400 metres. Statistics on the districts with names of
Election Supervisors are at Appendix 1.

Cattle are reared and prized throughout the province, both by
Europeans and Africans, but there have been appalling losses from
stock theft which still continue. Maize and ground nuts are the
principal crops and at Chiredzi there are the hugely successful
irrigated Triangle and Hippo Valley Estates comprising 100,000
acres of sugar cane, cotton and wheat. There is the potential to
increase the irrigated area of excellent land six-fold.

The rainfall is not everywhere adequate and the increase of
population in the Tribal Trust Lands (TTLs) has resulted in
overstocking and over-cultivation, though fortunately the land has
been well controlled on the whole.

There are a number of mines throughout the province of which
the most important are the asbestos mines at Mashaba, about 20
miles west of Fort Victoria. All of the larger mines as well as the

Chiredzi estates have managed to carry on during the war, but most of the agriculture in the province has been severely damaged.

The main road from Salisbury to Beit Bridge runs from north to south through the province. The southern part carries the railway lines to Beit Bridge and Maputo. The former has continued to run, guarded by some 700 Guard Force and a small army detachment. A few acts of minor sabotage occurred after the cease fire.

Administrative Arrangements made for the Election

Although the arrangements remained under the overall supervision of the Provincial Commissioner, Mr R. Menzies, he was assisted by Mr J.E. Whenman, District Commissioner in the Ministry of Home Affairs who was seconded to the province for election duties. He arrived in the province at the same time as we did and during our first week we visited all districts with him.

He discussed such matters as the proposed number and location of polling stations, the availability of suitable personnel to act as presiding officers and polling staff and requirements for stores. We were, therefore, in at the beginning of the planning process and continued throughout our time in the province to be in close and friendly touch with Messrs. Menzies and Whenman.

On 30 January, District Supervisors went to their districts after two days' briefing at Fort Victoria. They continued to work with District Commissioners in detailed planning, and cooperation everywhere was very good.

After careful consideration and discussion it was settled that there would be a total of 73 polling stations in the province. A map showing the actual location of the 26 static stations and the approximate area of operations of the 47 mobile stations (green) is at Appendix 2.[1]

While it would obviously have been more convenient to a number of voters to have a greater number of polling stations, we accept that factors of transport, security and staff made this impracticable. A number of changes were made as a result of representations by political parties. We are satisfied that there was adequate coverage, having regard to all the circumstances, and that no party more than another was disadvantaged by the distribution of polling stations except insofar as the support for ZANU (PF) was probably greatest in the Tribal Trust Lands (TTLs).

The recruitment of polling staff caused a number of problems, particularly with regard to otherwise suitable black civil servants whose political views were well known. Their presence as presiding officers might have caused fear or mistrust. Arrangements were made for such officers to be exchanged between districts.

337

Transport and security arrangements were under the control of the Joint Operations Committee run by the Army (TOC) who received two visits from the NED during the election period.

The Security Situation and the General Environment in which the Election was Conducted

The security situation dominated the whole campaign. Apart from a small area in the east of Maranke TTL in Nuaneti District the province was a ZANLA area of operation. The population were in protected villages with their own locally recruited auxiliaries. The major problems arose from men filtering out of the Assembly Points.

In Gutu the ZANLA elements operated in larger groups than elsewhere, sometimes over 50, often carried their weapons and were more aggressive. An analysis of incidents relevant to the election campaign was made from JOC Sitreps for the period of 20 days from 31 Jan – 19 Feb, and this is at App 3. It will be seen that the number of clashes in Gutu were more than the rest of the province put together. This continued right up to the election. The only polling station to be threatened with attack by armed ZANLA men was at Mawera in Chilewanda TTL. Incidentally, the supervisors' helicopter may well have saved lives here since it was able to visit the station which was out of communication by road or radio and report back so that a relief convoy was arranged forthwith.

There were undoubtedly a massive number of arms in the TTLs and the villagers were aware of this. A number of caches were revealed by captured men, particularly in Chibwe district. Photographs of arms captured between the end of the cease fire on 4 Jan – 22 Jan are at Appendix 4. Those are only a small proportion of the arms in ZANLA control in the province.

During the war, ZANLA had created a tight and disciplined organisation with its commissions and "courts" to control the population, ousting the traditional structure of head man and chief. The loosely linked military and political control continued to be exercised by ZANLA right up to the time of voting.

There were numerous acts of violence throughout the election period. An attempt was made to blow up Mugabe on his way back to Fort Victoria Airport from a meeting. Two Roman Catholic priests, one white and one black, were killed in Chibwe and Victoria District respectively. Deaths in clashes between ZANLA and security forces and by mines, some laid after the cease fire, were common. Firearms were everywhere.

The Conduct of the Administration –
and the Performance of Their Duties

The administration had been living a beleaguered and dangerous life for some years. They had conducted a successful election against armed opposition in April 1979 and could have been forgiven for being unenthusiastic about repeating the exercise, particularly under the supervision and observation of so many outsiders. Yet they carried out their duties on the whole with efficiency and integrity. In spite of all the difficulties caused by the rains and the security situation, every stage of the election process was well handled and there was satisfactory improvisation wherever it became necessary, as it inevitably did.

Salient Elements of the Campaign Conducted by the Parties

NDU Did not campaign but polled 2448 votes.

NF2 This party suffered a blow early in the campaign by the defection of its leader Mr Michael Mowena to the UANC. It continued to campaign under Mr Peter Mandaza, without meetings but with extensive posters and newspaper advertisements. Its appeal was to Karanga pride primarily. The Karanga, one of the Shona group of peoples, comprise 22 per cent of the population and Victoria Province is their main area of settlement, although they spread into Buhera District in Mawialand to the east and into Midlands Province to the west. The party polled 2070 votes and Mr Mandaza told us that he would be staking a claim for the next election when a sense of tribal identity would be stronger.

PF At our first meeting with PF officials they told us that they were afraid to go into the TTLs but would try. When they did so a candidate was abducted and his car disappeared. His body was later found showing marks of torture. Two companions escaped and said that they had been told that since ZIPRA had not fought in that area, Mashalea TTL in Chibwe District, they had no right to campaign there. There was one well-conducted meeting of about 3000 people for Mr Nkomo in Victoria, at which he spoke in a statesmanlike way of reconciliation, and another in Chiredzi. The party officials said that they were afraid to do much else. The party polled 6107 votes of which a substantial number probably came from the Amandabele in the western part of Nuenetri District.

UANC This party was led in the province by two able former ministers, Messrs Zindoga and Zinutu. It held quite a number of meetings and put up many posters. It complained, with reason, that it was unable to campaign in the TTLs. A lorry returning from a meeting was ambushed, a bus of supporters had a grenade thrown into it, killing a woman, a girl party worker was abducted and badly beaten, and various supporters were threatened or disappeared. Eventually the party decided that it was unfair to its supporters to expose them to risk by holding meetings anywhere except in the main centres. Although expected to maintain a presence of at least one seat the UANC managed to gain only 14,615 votes out of 326,711 – under 4.5 per cent.

ZANU This party held few meetings but its posters were widespread. It hoped to boost its support by recruiting two of the Mozambique preachers who came from Victoria province, Messrs Madyividza and Hamadyipiri. They presented themselves as belonging to the Christian and democratic wing of the ZANU movement who had been ousted by Mugabe, supported by Machel, the Mozambique President. They wanted the elections postponed so that they could get their message across. The party polled 8938 votes.

ZANU (PF) This party was led by a number of well educated and articulate men. It clearly had a large measure of support in all classes of black society. Its meetings were not so numerous as expected and there was less enthusiasm at Mr Mugabe's big meeting in Fort Victoria than we had foreseen. There were comparatively few posters, most with the cock[2] and a cross to push the message of how to vote. Much of the energy of party officials appeared to be engaged in bringing allegations of unjustified arrests by the police and army, beatings and killings by the auxiliaries in order to create an impression of officially inspired intimidation against their party in the minds of observers and journalists. Much of the time of supervisors, police advisors and army monitors was taken up in investigating their allegations, most of which turned out to have been complete fabrications or at best grossly exaggerated. Meanwhile the real campaigning was taking place in unlawful meetings, often at night, called pungwes, where the people were instructed that all must turn out and vote for the jongwe (the cock) or be killed. The results were seen in the vote of 285,277 or 87.317 per cent of the whole. We suspect that in most TTLs the turn out and the votes approached 100 per cent.

ZDP This party had an office which was rarely manned but put up plenty of posters. It did not hold meetings but claimed to be in touch with the spirits, which might account for the vote of 7256, a little more than PF, a little less than ZANU and half of the UANC vote.

Party votes and percentages are as follows:

Party	Total Valid Votes	Percentage
NDU	2,448	0.75
NFZ	2,070	0.63
PF	6,107	1.87
UANC	14,615	4.47
ZANU	8,938	2.74
ZANU (PF)	28,5277	87.32
ZDP	7,256	2.22
TOTAL	326,711	100

Special Factors with Potential Influence on the Electorate

Security Force Bases Owing to the number of Zanla men who did not go into the assembly places the security forces deployed in strength immediately after the cease fire. We kept in close daily touch with the British monitoring forces and accept that most army activity was proper and necessary, although there were some units who were too ready to shoot at anyone who did not stop immediately on challenge. There were surprisingly few complaints about the security forces and in spite of dire warnings by ZANU (PF) there was no sign at the polls that the people were afraid to approach.

Patriotic Front Assembly Points AP Hotel is at Chipenda Pools in Chivedzi District and AP Golf just outside the province at Mutandawe. They hold about 1000 and 1200 men and women respectively. For most of the time there was a responsible Patriotic Front Liaison Officer. Mr Agnew Cambiu in Fort Victoria and Lt. Col. Stuart Green, Royal Anglian Regiment, maintained a difficult relationship with great diplomatic skill. There was some spillage from the APs into surrounding areas and this probably had an effect on the protected villages and the Chiredzi estates, but less than JOC believed. Arrangements for the poll went very smoothly.

The Security Force Auxiliaries It soon became apparent that the Auxiliaries would become a major political issue and the only one on which all parties except the UANC agreed. Accordingly we asked the British Monitoring Force to direct a substantial proportion of their effort to monitoring the Auxiliaries, and this was done. The responsible officers, Lr. Col. Sugden and Capt. D. Clements, reported subsequently that the Auxiliaries were very variable, ranging from the valuably constructive to an undisciplined rabble. The number actually deployed was about 3000 and there were probably fewer real problems (as distinct from loose allegations) in Victoria than elsewhere because of the policy of concentrating them in "green areas". We believe that complaints against the Auxiliaries were planned and organised by ZANU (PF) as a smokescreen to try to hide the activities of ZANLA and to induce weak-minded observers and journalists to conclude that the intimidation by both sides cancelled out. There was no doubt that in spite of instructions to be neutral the Auxiliaries were partial to UANC, and so some people fell into the trap of thinking that this equalled ZANLA pressure. Our assessment is that the undue influence of the Auxiliaries probably did not amount to one tenth of that of ZANLA.

The Mujibas Although there were a few signs before the election that the Mujiba system was breaking down in Victoria District because of parental revolt, this did not become general, as the election showed. There were widespread reports of Mujibas rounding up people and accompanying them to pungwes and subsequently to the polls. They remained a most effective feature of the ZANLA/ZANU (PF) organisation, acting as messengers, scouts, stewards, thugs and bully boys.

Effectiveness of the Cease Fire The cease fire was only partially effective because of the failure of a proportion of the ZANLA forces to withdraw to the APs. The war therefore continued, though at a much lower level than before. However, since it was ZANU (PF) policy to get as many votes as possible there was no actual interference with the election arrangements.

Protected Villages The only protected villages are in the TTLs on the south-western border of Chiredzi district. The Shangaan PVs in the Sengwe TTL are protected by their own auxiliaries known as the Shangaan Army. Most problems in the Matebi 2 and Sangwe TTL PVs arose from the proximity of the APs Hotel and Golf.

Intimidation This was a dominating factor in the election and will be dealt with in the final chapter containing the overall assessment.

Incidents The most important was the attack on Mr Mugabe's life already referred to, the origin of which is still a mystery.

The Information Campaign and Confidence in the Secrecy of the Ballot Roads in the TTLs were only gradually being opened up as the campaign proceeded and we were concerned that the useful leaflets distributed by the Information Dept. might not reach many areas. The various channels of distribution were investigated and it seemed that the only way of reaching many people was through army patrols. The JOC cooperated in this by giving the information distribution high priority, but stipulated that anti-Marxism/

Socialism material, which the Governor had forbidden, should not be mixed with the National Election Directorate material. However, this was not everywhere complied with, we suspect. At first there was almost an iron curtain round the TTLs so the radio was important. Inquiries as to the number of radios working in the TTLs showed that the distribution was patchy. Where the buses had begun to run people were replacing batteries but there were, we believe, a number of areas where the only information came in spite of all official efforts from ZANU (PF).

On the whole people understood and valued the secrecy of the vote, certainly in the areas outside the TTLs. However, within the TTLs we think that the intimidation and other pressures operating in some cases right up to the moment of entry into the polling station were such that the concept of secrecy must have become rather theoretical to many simple people. They had been told that the party had means of knowing how they had voted by a magic black box, through a satellite, through the spirits, by checking on the number of ballot papers, or because the planes with the ballot papers were going to Mozambique. Steps were taken to counter these allegations, but our impression is that many simple people must have felt that it was not worth taking the risk of not voting for the Jongwe, even if they had wanted to vote for another party.

The Poll

The Atmosphere The crowds at the polling stations were on the whole cheerful and good tempered in spite of the vast numbers who got out of control on the first day. In some places, however, there were reports of quiet apprehension and a number of people remarked on the absence of the carnival atmosphere which prevailed in the 1979 elections.

The Attitude of the Electorate It may be that people were reflecting that in the last election they had been promised and had expected the end of the war, which had not happened. Now it could only be brought to an end by voting for the cock. The anti-Marxist campaign led by official bodies in the UANC might have raised certain long-term fears, but the immediate need was to vote for the party which had power to stop the war and had said that it would continue the war if not elected.

The Turnout Most stations were quite overwhelmed by the numbers of people waiting to vote on the first day. In some places queues stretched for over four kilometres in all and occasionally the queuing system broke down. Security staff had problems of crowd control in which they had not been trained. To save lives in the crush they had to abandon their proper role of ensuring that all people could vote in a free and orderly manner. At Chibwe, two babies were suffocated in the crush and there were several cases of old people who had collapsed being rescued from being trampled underfoot. It appeared that in many cases people had been ordered to vote early and to vote at particular stations. From Chibwe, Ndanga and Gutu there were reports of people bypassing a nearby polling station and walking an extra 20 km to go to the chosen one. Nor was this due to a preference for static stations over mobile, because in one case the three-day station at Chacumba in Ndanga District was ignored in favour of the one-day mobile at St Anthony's mission. People were clearly most anxious to cast their vote on the first day and the only incident of deliberate unruliness was the stoning of some polling stations when they had to close at night, leaving some people to return on the second day. On the second and third days there were far fewer voters at the static stations and the three days provided adequate time for the very high turnout.

Conduct of Polling Station and Security Staff In most cases the conduct of polling station staff was exemplary, even in the most difficult conditions caused particularly by the weather and the crowds. Their instructions had been varied from time to time, particularly over the rights of the polling agents and of certain categories of persona to enter the polling stations, and this caused some understandable confusion, but with only minor consequences. In some places the number of assisted persona was as high as 30 per cent and it was impossible for the Presiding Officer to keep the required record. We are satisfied that the only failures by polling staff were due to absolute necessity.

The security staff were caught unprepared for the crowds on the first day and so had not organised protective fences and gangways. There were one or two places where firearms were rather unnecessarily in evidence, but it certainly did not seem to deter voters. ZANU (PF) had warned us beforehand that many people would be prevented by the security forces from coming to vote, particularly from villages known to support their party, but in the event there were virtually no complaints and certainly none that were justified. We find that both police and army, regulars and reservists alike, performed their duties fairly and efficiently, although occasionally a caution might have been sufficient instead of an arrest.

The British Police were universally welcomed and praised both by white Rhodesians and the black political parties.

Adherence to Election Plans and Procedures There were very few failures to follow the procedures correctly. At one station in Zaba the Presiding Officer had thought that because the perforating machine did not obliterate the number the rubber stamp must be substituted, but this was because of an ambiguity in the instructions. Records could not always be kept of assisted voters because of the large numbers in some places, which was perhaps an insurance policy by them as the number was often shouted out. In the press on the first day some under-age voters probably got through the net and not all men in uniform were scrutinised for age. Attempts at double voting were, we think, usually detected.

The weather disrupted plans for the deployment of polling stations in a number of areas, particularly Gutu. This had been foreseen and a plane arranged so that people were informed of the change of any plan. The Supervisor at Gutu estimated that a maximum of 5000 voters could have been disenfranchised but certainly a number went to Bireita polling stations and it is believed that the ZANU (PF) organisation was so efficient and effective that in the end very few were unable to cast their votes.

Conduct of Party Agents and Supporters There was some confusion over the timing and method of appointment of party agents, but as events turned out UANC and PF had fairly widespread representation and ZANU (PF) apparently universal. There was one incident in Bireita when a ZANU (PF) agent came into the polling station and looked at the marked papers of two voters before they put them in the ballot box. He was arrested. Generally, however, supervisors considered that party agents performed a useful function during polling and their rights to inspect, seal and sign ballot boxes were essential to allay the deep suspicions expressed to us beforehand. Except for the incidents of intimidation referred to in Chapter 12, party supporters behaved well.

Incidents Apart from incidents referred to elsewhere in this report the only other one of note was at Chibwe when a polling clerk was arrested for passing the numbers of papers to a ZANU (PF) supporter. The numbers were then used to try to persuade people in the queue that the party would know how they voted.

Overall Assessment of the Elections

It has to be remembered that few people taking part in the elections had experience of a free election between competing parties on equal terms. There was a great deal of naivety and misunderstanding.

ZANU (PF) could not appreciate the distinction between seizing control of territory by force and peaceful persuasion of the people living there. UANC went in for some blatant bribery, with free beer provided by the party and free fertiliser by the government. The Rhodesian authorities found it difficult to withdraw from the fray and adopt a detached and neutral position.

In most of the TTLs the parties other than ZANU (PF) did not have a fair opportunity to campaign freely, for the reasons given earlier. However, it has to be recognised that, except possibly in Gutu, the reception for these other parties would in any case have been hostile. Over the previous three years complete ZANLA control had been established, backed by murder and torture, but even without these methods there would have been wide support for what was seen as the genuine nationalist party. A collective will in favour of ZANU (PF) had been established in all sections of the black community. This was not understood by the Rhodesians, who could not accept that such support could be due to anything other than intimidation.

In light of this it is even more unfortunate that the ZANU (PF) campaign was marred by the violence already recounted. During the period before the election there was some reduction, but there were widespread reports of a recrudescence before and during the election. People were herded to the polls under threat of death, the ZANLA men and their mujibas staying with them right up to the entrance to the polling stations, particularly in Gutu District. Agents and supporters of other parties were threatened with beatings if they did not vote for the cock. The elderly and infirm were turned out and some were even seen running with desperation to vote. Mujibas crowed or moved their arms like a cock's wings and positioned themselves like platoon commanders in the queues to keep up the pressure. Sometimes ZANU (PF) officials purported to make lists of names or numbers; the threat did not need to be spoken.

We do not think that all this made much difference to the decision of the majority of voters. We suspect, however, that it did have an effect in two ways: firstly, people who might have preferred to abstain were not allowed to do so; and secondly, some voters who really supported other parties were frightened out of their allegiance and few were brave enough to report accordingly. It is in the nature of terror that few are prepared to report it, and it is possible that the reports received were the tip of the iceberg. This makes the final assessment extraordinarily difficult. Our conclusion is that the result in Victoria Province broadly reflected the wishes of the people but that the background of war and the unacceptable degree of intimidation which occurred produced some distortion in the poll to the disadvantage of parties other than ZANU (PF).

The majority of the people wanted two things – an African government and an end to the war. They believed that they could only achieve the latter by voting for ZANU (PF) which had said repeatedly, if not officially, that if it did not obtain power the war would go on. It was the inevitable effect of having an election immediately after the end of a war that the major issue of peace would obscure all other factors. In this sense, the party with the power to stop or continue with the war as it chose had an overriding intimidatory influence, against which the secrecy of the ballot was irrelevant.

One final point – all of the parties seemed to have unlimited money. Even the smaller parties were able to take numerous full-page advertisements in the Herald at $800 a time. The bills for printing posters must have been huge. The larger parties spent lavishly on buses, cars, hotels and subsistence for people attending rallies. The ZANU (PF) subsistence rate was $2 per head, we were informed, and the UANC spent blatantly on beer and other handouts – where did it all come from?

J.A. Barratt
P.P. Bowcock

Notes

CHAPTER 6

1. Peter Lumsden had a long life and, remarkably, celebrated two silver wedding anniversaries.

CHAPTER 7

1. Bryan died a few years ago, but I remained in touch with Michael and Ralph. On a visit to Oman in February 2001 I met Ralph and Elizabeth, whom he married quite late in life. He had been Adviser in Conservation to the Sultan for many years and did not retire until April 2001 at the age of about 77, probably the last of the British Arabian adventurers. Even after retirement he and Elizabeth spend six months of the year in Muscat. He had the principal part in successfully re-establishing the white Arabian oryx in its homeland in the Empty Quarter after all had been shot out there. He died in about 2007 and Elizabeth still lives in Oman. Michael had a long and happy spell as Secretary at the Royal College of Surgeons, which occupies a modern building in Regent's Park. His last district in the Sudan included the Abyei area with the richest oilfields. He has been very active in helping the Dinka there to obtain the implementation of the Common Peace Agreement of 2005.
2. We must never forget that the Jewish Old Testament, the Christian New Testament and the Holy Koran are closely linked. Muslims acknowledge the adherents of the three faiths as being together the "ahl al kitab – the people of the book". They do not have, or should

not have, any problem in celebrating Christmas as the birthday of Jesus, who in the Koran is Issa, the last of the prophets before Mohammed. His mother Mary or Miriam is likewise respected.

CHAPTER 8

1. Daoud Abdul Latif's later career was far from smooth. He was appointed Governor of Bar el Ghezal Province after independence but was forced to flee back north in one of the early southern uprisings.
2. I see that Carlton Ware china, the manufacturer of which is long defunct, is now being sold as antiques in Otford, my local village.
3. It has to be acknowledged, though, that in some countries after independence the trade unions were virtually the only organisations of civil society. In both Zambia and Zimbabwe they have been the principal effective opposition to oppressive and corrupt dictatorship. To this extent we can be grateful for the policies of encouraging trade unions.
4. After Sudan's independence Arthur (or Charlie) became Speaker of the new Legislative Assembly in Aden. Tragically, shortly after being knighted he was assassinated after his regular tennis game with three Arab friends at their club. Terrorists aim at those who build bridges, not those who remain on the other side.

CHAPTER 9

1. There is a wider issue here. Nationalist politicians and some academics have so disparaged the work of the "colonialists" that the present generation could be unaware of the work that was done. In this way, valuable information could be lost.
2. *Sudan Studies*, No.43, January 2011.

CHAPTER 10

1. Later note: Last heard of in about 2009 at Cornell University, New York State.
2. Later Note: Jack Wilson was A/DC of Western Nuer. The spear was said to have passed right through his body. It was cut off at the back and Wilson was carried on a native bed some 50 miles to Lake No. Fortunately, he was picked up by the province's hospital ship, the

Lake Baker. In 1948 he and a colleague, Roan Laurie (father of Hugh the actor), won an Olympic Gold medal for the double sculls.

CHAPTER 11

1. The Lou Nuer tradition of raiding the neighbour's territory has continued and worsened. During the civil war they raided the Bor Dinka and in 2012 there were reports of a revenge attack upon the Murle of Pibor District in which they killed hundreds.
2. For these songs the men would gather round in a semicircle with one man in front. He would begin with one line in falsetto, almost a screech, and the chorus would respond rhythmically in a lower register. I have a tape from a disc obtained by another DC, Beadon Dening, in Easter Nuer.

CHAPTER 13

1. Broken Hill Man has gone up in the anthropological world. On 23 February 2013 an article in *The Times* stated: "The latest research on the skull not yet published dates it to between 200,000 and 300,000 years old, which would place it just after the estimate for when the primitive human species *Homo heidelbergensis* diverged into modern humans (*Homo sapiens*) and Neanderthal man."
2. On retirement F.M. Thomas lived in the house in Somerset which now belongs to my son-in-law's (Stella's husband, Charles') sister Deborah and her husband, Christopher Wolverson.

CHAPTER 14

1. I noticed no reluctance to use the word for "tribe" – mtundu. It was the same in the Sudan in 2006, yet the British Museum uses "people" which is not nearly so precise. Another example of quite unnecessary political correctness causing obfuscation.
2. At the ferry across the Zambesi from Sesheke to Katimo Mulilo some years later, the Head Messenger said to me, "See those children playing round the ferry in the water? One day a croc will eat one of them. Then they will not play in the water for a few weeks, but after that they will forget and return." Sure enough, only a few days later a child was taken.

3. Recently a man came to fit some new cushion covers in my cottage in Otford, in Kent. Noticing some of Brenda's African portraits he asked where I had been. It turned out that in the 1970s he had been the engineer in charge of the mine's electricity, including the Mulungushi hydro-electric scheme.

CHAPTER 17

1. Cooperation was as close as between neighbouring districts in Northern Rhodesia. There was no sign of the harshness of the apartheid system seen elsewhere. It was a shock to read a few years later of gunfire being exchanged across the Zambezi between Katima Mulilo and Sesheke.
2. The Caprivi strip resulted from the negotiations at the Congress of Berlin in 1878 where the Germans insisted upon having an outlet to the Zambezi river. It was named after Count Caprivi, the German Foreign Minister who negotiated it. The objective was misconceived since the Zambezi has too many waterfalls and cataracts to be a useful channel of communication over long distances.

CHAPTER 22

1. Quasi-Autonomous Non-Governmental Organisations.
2. Reflections on the Revolution in France, 1790.

APPENDIX 4

1. Nuer tribes.
2. Mamur: administrative assistant.
3. Abbreviation for effendi, a Turkish term for an educated man.
4. Zeraf Island Rural District Council.
5. Court Order.
6. A cloth, knotted over one shoulder.
7. A fine.
8. A small thatched round hut for women and children.
9. PT: a piastre, or one pence.
10. A chief's sash of authority. Sometimes also called a lama.
11. Native Authority.
12. A sergeant.
13. Bi is Nuer for a cloth and was used for the sashes of office for head chief, sub chief and clan head.

14. "Cuol will deliver to Riak three head of cattle."
15. "Cuol will deliver to Riak three head of cattle with the sex, age and colour specified."
16. A bull.
17. Head of cattle.
18. Home distilled spirit.
19. Compensation.
20. Holy man or witch doctor.
21. Servant of God.
22. Court President.
23. Or buda, a parasitic weed, "striga hermonthica".
24. Senior Veterinary Inspector.
25. Medical Assistant.
26. A rest-house keeper.
27. Provincial Medical Inspector.
28. Cerebro-spinal meningitis.
29. Corrugated iron.
30. A type of timber.
31. Mosquito gauze.
32. Corrugated iron.
33. Business Property Tax.
34. Markets.
35. Books in which were recorded details of each cieng, or extended family group.
36. Accountant/cashier.

APPENDIX 6

1. We were able to do something. The cemetery was designated a Pioneer Graveyard, cleaned up and walled with contributions in particular from John Dean and Cyril Greenall, whose infant daughters are buried there.

APPENDIX 7

1. Not attached here.
2. The cock was the symbol of ZANU (PF).

Index

Note: PB = Philip Bowcock (the author)